REMEMBERING
MR. MAUGHAM

BOOKS BY GARSON KANIN

NONFICTION

Remembering Mr. Maugham   1966

NOVELS

The Rat Race   1960
Blow Up a Storm   1959
Do Re Mi   1955

PLAYS

Come On Strong   1964
A Gift of Time (adaptation)   1962
Do Re Mi (adaptation)   1961
Fledermaus (libretto)   1951
The Rat Race   1950
The Live Wire   1950
The Smile of the World   1949
Born Yesterday   1946

REMEMBERING
MR. MAUGHAM

By Garson Kanin

With a Foreword by Noël Coward

Atheneum   *New York*   *1966*

Foreword by Noël Coward

There has been much written about the late W. Somerset Maugham recently, and I expect that, during the next few years, there will be a great deal more. Then perhaps the bandwagon will lurch to a halt and a decade or two will elapse before some new young writer, untinted by the dangerous colors of personal reminiscence, will read afresh his plays, books, short stories and autobiographies and give a detached and unprejudiced account of him.

There is little doubt, I think, that his immense readability, the diversity of his subject matter and, above all, the lucidity and economy with which he employed the English language will ensure his literary posterity. Whether or not his novels, plays and essays achieve as equal a level of professional perfection as his short stories is a debatable point. Personally, I plump for the short stories as being the most dazzling jewels in his crown, but I cannot say that there are any of his published works (with the exception of his very late efforts) that I have not read and reread with whole-hearted attention, enjoyment and a definite gratitude for his superb craftsmanship.

In this personally reminiscent book, Garson Kanin remembers Mr. Maugham with affection, kindness, admiration and a deep respect for his talent. Also, having a perceptive mind *and* the common sense to keep a diary, he remembers him with considerable accuracy. He has permitted himself only the most casual comments on Maugham's private life, unhappy marriage and sexual inclinations, realizing, with innate discretion and taste, that these aspects are to a large extent irrelevant and of little importance measured against his brilliant contribution to the literature of his age.

Nevertheless, the old truism that a writer's character is usually reflected in his work is particularly applicable when discussing Willie Maugham. He was a complex man and his view of his fellow creatures was jaundiced, to say the least. He of course had his friends and his loves, and I myself am indebted to him for nearly fifty years of kindness and hospitality, but I cannot truthfully say that I really knew him intimately. He believed—rather proudly, I think—that he had no illusions about people, but in fact he had one major one and that was that they were no good. With all his brilliance and verbal clarity, he rarely drew a sympathetic character—probably, I suspect, because he quite genuinely believed that no such phenomenon existed. Even Rosie in CAKES AND ALE, obviously one of his most loved creations, he demolishes at the end of the book by transforming her into a vulgar, elderly, bridge-playing bore. Willie had little faith in the human heart, perhaps because, having started his career as a medical student, he was unable to regard it as anything but a functional organ.

It is not my intention, however, in this brief Foreword to attempt to analyze the complex and intricate causes of Maugham's disenchantment with the human animal. He was a man of almost painful sensitivity and was a great deal more shy and vulnerable than he would have us believe. He knew Garson Kanin and his wife, Ruth Gordon, in the last twenty years of his long life, and the genuineness of his feeling for them was beyond question, as, indeed, was theirs for him, and it is the warm glow of that mutual affection that illuminates this observant and loving memory of him.

REMEMBERING
MR. MAUGHAM

15 December 1965. Beverly Hills.

Somerset Maugham is dead. A few minutes ago, at the beginning of the eleven-o'clock news on CBS, the announcer speaks "the teaser":

"Life in the sky and death on earth," he says. "These stories and others, after this message."

A commercial, during which I say to Ruth [*my wife, Ruth Gordon*], "I'm afraid he's gone. It has that sound."

"Yes," she says.

The announcer returns with the news we have been half expecting, half dreading for the past five days.

It is over, then. Our good friend is no more.

An era ends. A most civilized and articulate link with a gentler time is broken.

As with the death of all great men, his is only partial. His ravaged body will soon be ash; his brain is blacked out; his spirit, extinguished—but the best of him, his work, remains. In addition, those of us who were fortunate enough to know him have a legacy of rich remembrance.

He lived for ninety-one years, ten months and fifteen days.

[Did anyone ever cleave to life more tenaciously than he in his final years? We are all, if sane, expected to do so. Breaking the law of self-preservation carries the death penalty even in those states and countries which have abolished it.

Yet Somerset Maugham astonished all who knew him with the power of his penultimate struggle. His enemies called it stubborn, his friends thought it valiant. Why were we surprised? Simply because throughout the long course

3

of his life, and especially during the last two-thirds of it, he seemed to regard existence, with a cynical eye, as a cosmic practical joke. Only fools took it seriously, he observed.

There are those who say he was inspired by the example of his brother Frederick, Lord Maugham, who lived to be ninety-one; others claim he was arbitrarily aiming for one hundred; he is said to have said it would amuse him to outdo Bernard Shaw; and one waggish chum suggested that Maugham could not bear the idea of a span shorter than that of his difficult mother-in-law, Mrs. Barnardo, who died at one hundred and two.

In the winter of 1954 he was spending a few months in London at the Dorchester. My wife and I called on him and were delighted to find him in great form.

When we arrived, we found him sitting in front of the television set watching an inane quiz program. He motioned us to chairs.

"It will end . . . shortly," he said, keeping his eyes on the set. "Sit down. Get them a . . . drink, Alan." [Alan Searle, Maugham's secretary-companion from 1945 until the end.]

Ten minutes later the program ended. He jumped up— I mean jumped—moved with great rapidity to the set and struck it dumb. The picture, however, was left on and continued to flash, squirm, bounce and jerk for the next hour and a half in frustrated silence.

"You don't mind that, do you, my dear?" he asked my wife as he kissed her. "We keep it on all day long—and all . . . night as well, so far as I know."

"Why?" I asked.

He regarded me coolly as we shook hands.

"Because," he said carefully. "It is an . . . innovation."

We sat down to talk, to catch up with one another after almost a year.

4

"*Well,*" *I began heartily,* "*have you had any adventures since we saw you last?*"

"*Yes,*" *he said.* "*I . . . dddied.*"

The final word was slightly delayed and partially stammered, adding to the shock effect.

He looked us over, unabashedly pleased with the bull's-eye dramatic effect of his revelation. Had it come later in the visit, I might have handled it easily, since we were old friends and conversed on an anything-goes level, in a bantering key.

My voice was unsteady as I broke the long silence.

"*Is that the end?*"

"*Come now. You—you of all people should recognize a splendid . . . dramatic opening. The rest of the story is this.*" *He lit a cigarette in slow, deliberate motion before continuing.* "*I felt ill and was taken to hospital in Lausanne —excellent—where all sorts of things I did not want done to me were . . . done to me. I grew weaker by the hour and was drugged a good deal of the time. Surgery of some sort was performed, and after a few days the doctors . . . conveyed to me the intelligence that I was better than ever. I am a doctor myself and so I did not . . . believe them. A young American intern said something about 'out of the woods'—whatever that may mean—and actually clapped me on the shoulder. But no one knows more about a . . . patient than the patient and I knew that I was not functioning as I should—as I had been for eighty years. There was no point in telling them so. They had done—good chaps— all they could. That night I refused the sedation—I felt it might do me in and rob me of the resources I needed. I began to sink. The doctors returned. I felt needles in my arm and in my . . . bum. Time ended. It might have been an hour or a century. The light began to change. To my surprise, it did not grow darker—but lighter! It became iri-*

5

*descent, blinding. I could sense my pulse . . . fading and
my heartbeat slowing and still the light increased in in-
tensity—and then, and then the most exquisite sense of
release* [or did he say "relief"?] *set in and continued. Very
like a . . . prolonged orgasm, if you please, but not merely
of the genitals—a great final orgasm, a giving up of the
whole being—body, spirit, all. I knew that the end had
come and I remember being grateful to . . . nature for making it so exceedingly pleasant. I don't mind that at all, I
thought. Half an hour in a . . . dentist's chair is far worse.
Oh, well, I mused, as the last of life left me—I've had a
good enough time, and all in all it's been a most . . . grati-
fying experience. Then something told me to let go and I
smiled and I let go and . . . dddied."* At this point he lit
another cigarette from the burning end of the butt in his
hand. He continued. "Imagine my consternation when I
was awakened by a . . . cold thermometer being pressed
into my anus. I moved away and shouted something . . .
vile and stayed cross all the day. It was not until teatime
that I realized my good fortune. Now that I knew what . . .
death was like, I need no longer fear it. I can describe it
accurately—natural death, I mean. I know nothing of violent death. Natural death is the . . . final relaxation, nothing
more. Give them another . . . drink, Alan."*

Thus, Somerset Maugham in 1954 at the age of eighty.

*Almost everyone around when I was around called him
"Willie." It was something I could never bring myself to
do, and even now I do not know why. Reporting on him to
mutual friends—it was the same. He was never "Willie" to
me. For one thing, I was awed by his great age. (He was
nearly forty years my senior.) For another, it was not a
name which, in my opinion, suited him. I cannot think of
Henny Ibsen or Gus Strindberg or Tony Chekhov or*

Charlie Dickens or, it follows, Willie Maugham.

*What, indeed, to call him became a problem. "Mr.
Maugham" sufficed for a year or two, then became affected.
Writing to him, it was easier. There was "WSM," "Dear
Boy," "Young Man," or "W." But these appellations
hardly fell trippingly from the tongue.*

*One day I tried "WS," sounding like a pushy account ex-
ecutive, and abandoned it forever.*

*One evening, at his home in France in the summer of
1953, I took his hand and greeted him with "And how are
you tonight, Somerset?"*

*He dropped my hand as though it were aflame and
turned from me angrily.*

*"That is ... not my ... name, sir!" he said. "I am
'Willie' to my friends."*

*Even after that I could not call him "Willie," but you
may be assured that I never used "Somerset" again.*

*I have tried, many times since, to solve the mystery of
the offense I gave him that evening. What hidden pain,
what hurtful secret did that middle name hold? Still, he
preserved it and dropped the William and even the W. in
later years. I surmise that he was Somerset to someone,
somewhere in his life, and that the experience was not a
happy one. But this is hardly a satisfactory solution.*

*I may be giving the impression that he was a cranky
man, at least with me. If so, I am reporting badly. It is true
that he liked my wife better than he liked me, but that is
neither here nor there. In the main, he was a warm and
generous friend who helped and encouraged and advised
unstintingly.*

*The notes which follow and his already quoted verbatim
Lausanne report need, perhaps, a word of explanation.*

Blundering through the vagaries of self-education, one

is forced to devise a methodology. In my case, it has been to write things down. Questions, answers, and unanswered questions. Notes, impressions, opinions, and opinions of opinions. Vows and recantations. Plans and, later, reasons for their abandonment. Above all, words of wisdom—which are usually exact words. I have found that if I begin to set down a conversation on the same day on which it took place, I can report large portions of it accurately. If sleep intervenes, the work becomes more difficult, often impossible. Oddly, what is hard to recall, at any time, is my own part of the conversation. But this, in most cases, interests me less than what has been elicited.

Imagine the good fortune of meeting and coming to know W. Somerset Maugham, the more so if you happen to be an aspiring writer or dramatist or both. Imagine further that he proves willing, at any mutually convenient time, to tell what he knows of life and of work, freely and frankly. His manner was always that of a seasoned traveler who has been there and is anxious to make your journey more pleasant by giving you the benefit of his experience. Of course, the matter of individual taste comes up—what worked for him might not do for you. He was well aware of this, and gave his counsel with the built-in admonition that the old clothes he was giving you might have to be retailored for size or for fashion.

In a long life of journalizing (eventually refined and influenced by a study of A WRITER'S NOTEBOOK by W. Somerset Maugham) I have failed many entries. A number of reports which would doubtless have been of value to myself and others were postponed into oblivion, or simply forgotten, half remembered, or mis-recalled.

Fortunately for me, this never happened in the case of Maugham. Meetings with him were always events and

I took care to prepare for them. If a meal was involved, I repeated to myself Benjamin Franklin's useful maxim: Eat not to dullness; drink not to elevation.

I have been drunk my share of times, but only once with Maugham. Leaving him, I always went directly to the paper. That night at the Dorchester when he told of dying, I did not even risk leaving the hotel, but set down his words in the writing room off the lobby as soon as I reached it.

On other occasions I have given copies to others who were present, for correction or elucidation.

Now I have been asked to share some of these notes with the reading public, and I do so gladly.

From the great spill for which he was responsible, I have selected those passages which in my judgment are of general interest, omitting material which I deem too personal or technical or indiscreet.

When he published A WRITER'S NOTEBOOK, *he gave me a copy, saying, "Read it carelessly."*

"Yes," I said. "What?"

"Jottings," he said, "nothing more. Grand for the . . . W.C. At any rate, dip into it now and again. You may find it of passing interest. Don't, for Heaven's sake, read it chronologically as though it were a . . . narrative. It is not. I am a novelist, but it is not a novel. Invent your own order and it will be the . . . right one for you."

In a sense, this is what I have done with the WSM sections of my own jottings. They are arranged, not by date, but in my own order.

Without apology, but merely by way of further explanation, I would remind the reader that what follows was not written to be read, but only to be remembered. Therefore, the style often lacks aim and address. A man is talking to himself—if you care to listen, you may do so.]

1942. New York.

Mr. Maugham has an idea firmly fixed in his head: that I am a financial wizard. I cannot imagine where he picked up this cockeyed notion, but he looks upon my disclaimers as covering modesty. He asks Ruth to bring me over to the Ritz, where he is living at present. No food, no drink—just a long, serious money talk sitting in a corner of the quiet lobby. He tells us that his financial position is good.

"I can continue to live as I now live for . . . twenty years more—but of course I have no intention of doing so." [*A Maugham miscalculation.*] "What concerns me is those for whom I am—or have become—responsible." (He does not name them. Liza, I guess [*Maugham's only child—then Liza Maugham Paravicini; later Lady John Hope; now, since her husband's elevation, Lady Glendevon*]; and her children by Paravicini [*Vincent Paravicini, Liza's first husband*]; and Haxton [*Gerald Haxton, Maugham's secretary-companion from 1914 until his death in 1944*]; and ?) "I want to transfer certain of my copyrights—they have great value, some of them—to these . . . persons. Am I allowed to do so? I used to know a good deal about . . . matters of copyright, but I have not kept up with the changes. I am told that I may not give these things freely and that they must be . . . considered as currency. But who sets the value?"

"I don't know, Mr. Maugham, but I can find out. I know an expert."

"No, no," he says impatiently. "I don't . . . want an expert. I want you. Experts never speak to me in a language I can understand. And several of my literary agents have recently . . . fleeced me. I much prefer the assistance of friends."

[*As it happened, I was unable to be of use to him on that occasion, since it was wartime and he was not in a position to convey the complete and necessary information. I understand, however, that he did eventually succeed in transferring a number of his copyrights to his daughter. This proved to be a wise move because, in 1947–1948, one of the first of the so-called television "omnibus series" was* THE SOMERSET MAUGHAM THEATRE, *generating a large, unexpected income from a number of his short stories. Each program was introduced by him in shots made at his home in St. Jean–Cap Ferrat. I doubt that he ever needed financial advice from friends or experts. His own good cold hard sense of practicality became sensitive business acumen.*]

April 1949. New York.

Somerset Maugham is a stammerer. He does not stutter. He stammers. That is to say, he does not repeat a consonant over and over again before completing a word, as *n-n-n-n*-night. Rather, his organs of speech seem blocked, stuck—making the sound more like nnn*night*. I had always thought that "stutter" and "stammer" were synonymous until one night in London at Claridge's he explained the difference in great detail. Obviously, he has given much time and thought to the subject, although he discusses it rarely. In his many autobiographical works—THE SUMMING UP, POINTS OF VIEW, STRICTLY PERSONAL, A WRITER'S NOTEBOOK and so on—he scarcely mentions it.

[*In 1933 WSM wrote an introduction to a new, special edition of Arnold Bennett's* THE OLD WIVES' TALE. *In these pages he discusses not only the novel but the novelist. I always found him to be somewhat patronizing toward Bennett. He was fond of telling teasing stories about Bennett's gaucheries and pretensions and stinginess—as when AB once set up a mistress but offered to share her with WSM for the purposes of economy.*

Yet, there was always a soft spot somewhere in his feeling for AB, a sense of compassion. I wonder now if it did not have something to do with the fact that AB, too, stammered. Consider this passage from WSM's essay on AB: "Arnold was afflicted with a very bad stammer; it was painful to watch the struggle he had sometimes to get the words out. It was torture to him. Few realized the exhaustion it caused him to speak. What to most men was as easy as breathing, to him was a constant strain. It tore his nerves to pieces. Few knew the humiliation it exposed him to, the ridicule it excited in many, the impatience it aroused." (What a use of words!—"the ridicule it excited"; "the impatience it aroused." Only deep feeling brings forth such writing.) "The minor exasperation of thinking of a good, amusing, or apt remark and not venturing to say it in case the stammer ruined it. Few knew the distressing sense it gave rise to of a bar to complete contact with other men. It may be that except for the stammer which forced him to introspection, Arnold would never have become a writer."

I wonder if WSM here is not talking as much about himself as he is about Arnold Bennett. He finds a graceful, objective, selfless way to express his feelings on the subject; to convey to us something of the agony of his own affliction.]

His stammer is without doubt the scar of a childhood nervous disorder and all attempts to eradicate it have proved fruitless. It gives him considerable difficulty. The strength of the stammer varies from time to time, depending, I suppose, upon his emotional state, his fatigue, his passion, or upon the surrounding company. (I have known him to go through a long evening without stammering once.) Sometimes, in an effort to release the consonant, he snaps his fingers, hard. At other times he punches his right fist into his left palm, violently. Often he clutches the edge of a chair or a table. Always he suffers. One can see the physical strain. Now and then he will surrender and switch to a different word. This, I judge, must be the result of teaching or advice. Although he is now resigned to the condition, there was a time when he hoped to cure it. (The stammer is said to be represented by Philip Carey's clubfoot in OF HUMAN BONDAGE.)

[*In regard to the above, an interesting and exciting development once took place in Maugham's life. He heard of a speech therapist who had helped King George VI, similarly afflicted. (This was an elderly Australian named Dr. Lionel Logue. He was not a medical man, but an effective healer and apparently hypnotic coach. He first began to work with King George in 1926 and from that time on rehearsed him for every important address, including the accession, the Empire Day speech in 1940, the opening of Parliament in 1943, and the D-Day speech in 1944.) Maugham lost no time in seeking out Dr. Logue and began a series of treatments or, as he put it, "lessons."*

The results were not spectacular, but they were significant, and WSM began to feel more at ease in interviews and less fearful about public appearances.

In 1950 Goddard Lieberson, the brilliant and imaginative president of Columbia Records, conceived the idea of recording a group of outstanding writers in readings from their work. The result was the monumental Columbia Literary Series. Fittingly, WSM was the first to record. As we discussed the project, he voiced some misgivings about his ability to carry it off, despite his great progress with the new teacher.

I explained to him that the recording would probably be done on tape and that any slips or errors could be easily erased and corrected. He was at once fascinated by the technical aspects and giggled like a child when I told him of opera singers beginning a session (while fresh) with the most difficult passages, and of the famous diva who sang more than twenty high A's before the recording supervisor got one he considered good enough.

"I shan't provide more than three of my high A's no ... matter what they say!" said Maugham.

*On October 24, 1950, WSM recorded (easily) seven of his stories, of which two—*THE THREE FAT WOMEN OF ANTIBES *and* GIGOLO AND GIGOLETTE*—are included in the album.*

According to Goddard Lieberson, a minimum of retakes was required, no more than usual. It would seem that because WSM knew that correction was possible, he was relieved of some of the strain and tension. Without the net below, he might have fallen. With its reassuring presence, he triumphed.

He told me once of a previous recording experience. He had been invited to read selections from OF HUMAN BONDAGE *for a recording for the blind. He began well enough, but, as he got into it, was more and more overcome by emotion. Somewhere in the first chapter he found himself unable to speak and a few minutes later broke down completely.*

14

"I suppose," he said, "the damned thing was more . . . autobiographical than I'd ever been willing to admit."

In writing about Maugham, there is a great temptation to attempt to reproduce his stammer upon the printed page. Oddly enough, it gave him added color and personality. Further, it brought added dimension to his oral storytelling style, giving it an odd beat which it might not have enjoyed had his delivery been fluid. There were times when he seemed to be using it for effect—the final word of a joke held back a breath or two, making the ending just that much more explosive. It caused the suspense to build, and made his listeners hang on eagerly, impatiently. It gave him a sort of progressive-jazz rhythm—absolutely unique and strangely exciting.

In preparing this material for publication, I first attempted to reproduce the effect in type. After much experimentation, I decided to rely largely upon the reader's imagination. I have indicated the pauses, as best as I can remember them. Otherwise, the reader is asked to keep in mind that much of what is quoted of Maugham was originally expressed not with ease, not mellifluously, but with great effort.

The achievement of the Columbia recording is the more impressive when one considers how late in life it came. This old dog learned some new tricks, all right. He was able, after all, to give many talks and to make a number of important addresses. It is true that in most cases they were carefully prepared beforehand, written out and painstakingly rehearsed, with special emphasis on those words and phrases and liaisons which might have given him trouble. There was the celebrated lecture before the Royal Society of Literature on November 12, 1947: THE SHORT STORY.

15

And there was the gala event at the Garrick Club so vividly reported to us by Alexander S. Frere, then chairman of Walter Heinemann, Ltd., Maugham's publishers. WSM was being honored by the Garrick Club as part of his eightieth-birthday celebration. Only three other men had been so feted: Charles Dickens, William Makepeace Thackeray, and Anthony Trollope. WSM must have had deep feelings of time and tide when he recalled that it was his father, Robert Maugham, who had proposed Thackeray for membership in the Garrick Club.

Frere tells us that the occasion was stately and moving, but that it began in a disquieting, nerve-testing way. Maugham was introduced, took a standing ovation and, when the guests had regained their seats, began his address. He spoke the customary salutations, paused for a moment and said, "There are many . . . virtues in . . . growing old." He paused, he swallowed, he wet his lips, he looked about. The pause stretched out, he looked dumbstruck. The pause became too long—far too long. He looked down, studying the tabletop. A terrible tremor of nervousness went through the room. Was he ill? Would he ever be able to get on with it? Finally he looked up and said, "I'm just . . . trying . . . to think what they are!"

The house, as can be imagined, came down.]

1962. New York.

Dinner with George C. [*George Cukor, film director*], who is here for a few days on his way back to California.

He spent some time in Venice with WSM and Alan. His report is a worrying one. The old boy is, according to

Alan, behaving oddly. He has somehow got himself switched about so that he is drowsy all day and wide awake all night. (I have heard of this symptom several times recently. Is it common to aging? Ask Gus [*my friend Dr. Gustav Eckstein, physiologist and author*].) Alan reports that WSM often wakes at 2:00 or 3:00 A.M., comes into his room, and paces about, smoking and talking until morning. The talk is full of wild, impractical schemes and plans: writing projects; legal devices to protect elements of his estate; money-making ideas; and vindictive, vengeful pranks.

It is not at all like him, and Alan is concerned.

From his own experience, George reports a single unsettling happening: They were staying, all three, at the Gritti Palace. During lunch one afternoon WSM began to improvise an imaginary account based upon the possible relationship between two strangers—an elderly couple—sitting across the room. Meanwhile, a funeral passed on the Grand Canal—always a bizarre sight, the black gondola followed by the mourners in gondolas—and the attention of George and Alan was drawn, briefly, to the sight.

WSM threw down his fork and shouted, "You're not listening! Are you? Here I am—giving you gratis—a fine short story and you're not listening!"

With this, he got up and stalked out of the dining room.

When they all met later in the day, he behaved as though nothing untoward had happened earlier.

1953. St. Jean—Cap Ferrat.

WSM speaks often (too often) of death. Whistling in the light?

Today he says: "I suppose when people one day hear

of my death, many of them will say, 'Good Lord! I thought he died years ago.' "

It cues me into a George S. Kaufman remembrance and I tell it.

George, who had not seen Peg Pulitzer for a long time, met her at a party and said, "My God! I thought we were both dead!"

WSM laughs until he coughs.

1951. St. Jean–Cap Ferrat.

Mr. Maugham is a fast eater. I am a slow eater, especially when the food is superior, as it is here.

These two facts have been causing twice-a-day friction.

To add to the complication, Maugham is always served first. It is the way he runs his house. Is it the French way? Or simply his way? The host is served first, before the service moves counterclockwise around the table. Thus, the person sitting on his left is the last to be served. I have noticed that when there are six or more, Maugham has literally finished every morsel on his plate by the time the guest on his left is being served. He then puts down his utensils, lights a cigarette, and smokes it impatiently, looking about at everyone's plate.

I think he eats too fast. But who am I to say?

At the first luncheon, I admit I was perhaps *too* slow, because I made the mistake of trying to talk. Everyone had finished, and I was still at it.

He looked across the table and asked, "Don't you like your food?"

"Why, yes, I do."

"Why don't you eat it, then?"

"I am."

"Oh."

But I took the hint and wolfed what remained. On the next course, I erred again. I thought it best, instead of letting the situation fester, to talk about it. With the help of Ruth, it became a sort of joke.

Later, when we moved out onto the terrace, I said to him, "Do you agree that most of the human friction in the world is caused by variations in rhythm?"

"Of course," he says. "I can imagine a sharp little story about a man and woman . . . deeply in love who come to a bitter end of their relationship because she eats . . . swiftly and he eats . . . slowly."

"I'd like to read it. Why don't you write it?"

"I no longer write . . . short stories," he replies. "I am now the . . . well-known essayist."

"How about an essay, then, on the subject?"

He brightens. "One could do a good one, you know. The various rhythms in which people . . . behave most certainly affect compatibility. Nothing is more irritating than someone at your side walking either too swiftly or too slowly, as the . . . case may be. And the differences in the rhythm of card playing may be the worst of all. All of us who play have been . . . maddened sometimes by slow players. I, for my part, refuse to take part in games with slowpokes. And when it comes to the rhythm of physical . . . contact or of love-making, I suppose an adjustment of the rhythm makes for successful relationships and a . . . failure to adjust makes for unsuccessful ones." He goes on for some time on this subject, warming to it. "Rhythm, I suppose, is the . . . major element in the organization of the universe. Think of the rhythm of the . . . seasons, of one's heartbeat. Consider that almost every object is rhythmic in the sense

19

that it is a repetition of a. . . pattern. Your face, for example. If I put a line down the . . . middle of it, I have a
half which is then . . . repeated for the other half. Most
beautiful trees are . . . symmetrical. And flowers. And animals. And art objects. The heartbeat, rhythmic. And I . . .
gather it's what makes poetry so . . . passionate and music
so moving. From this, it's only a short . . . bridge to form.
One might say that a non-rhythmic thing is lacking in form.
All the words surrounding this idea . . . mean the same
thing in the end, don't they? Rhythm. Form. Tempo. Pace.
Organization. Balance. Form. That, I suppose, has been
the major preoccupation of my life. Form."

[*Looking at the above material, I find it easy to understand what many have wondered about. Why did WSM
wish to be buried in the graveyard of Canterbury Cathedral? It was because he went to the King's School, which
is attached to Canterbury Cathedral. Since he had no close
family ties, his sense of home was the King's School. Just
as he wanted to die at home, at the Villa Mauresque, and,
in fact, did so, he wanted to have his ashes returned to his
other home, his original home, the King's School. A sense
of form which he maintained to the very last.*]

January 1965. Beverly Hills.

Dinner-table discussion at George's last night
brings on an interesting quarrel. Perhaps quarrel is the
wrong description—heated discussion might be better, or
simply debate. It begins by George referring to someone
as a genius and my asking what he means by the word.
George is not certain, but chooses to say that it means some-

20

one who does what he or she does superbly, supremely, and way ahead of anyone else in the field. There is much disagreement with this definition, and in time everyone agrees that it means one who is able to do instinctively something which a normal person cannot do without training, study, practice and experience. Even a normal *talented* person. Some people can play the piano, or paint, or draw, or write verse without knowing how or even why they do it.

I venture the opinion that although genius is something to be held in awe, there is nothing necessarily admirable about its possessor. If the gift is enormous and requires no particular effort or work or discipline, you might as well admire someone for being redheaded or tall or beautiful. Genius is rare and something to be grateful for, but respected? Admired? Then, although I know it is going to cause disagreement and lose Ruth for me in the discussion, I say that in my vocabulary the word "professional" is the highest praise. I point out that I have known a great many talented people and a few geniuses, but damned few professionals. Ruth, as expected, disagrees. The table splits and the discussion takes place.

George tries to pin me down, wants to know if I consider myself a professional. My answer is that I try to be, but that I do not claim to have succeeded except sporadically and periodically. There have been times when as a director in films or in the theatre, or as a writer, I have lived and worked as a professional for a certain length of time. Alas, I have not succeeded in establishing a continuing discipline. I tell him, to his surprise, that I consider *him* a professional. Margot Fonteyn is, too; and Artur Rubinstein and Ruth; Kate [*Katharine Hepburn*] and Spencer [*Tracy*], both consummate professionals; Fred Astaire,

Cole Porter, Picasso—who happens to be a genius *and* a professional. What a combination!

This leads us to talk of Maugham, one of the purest professionals I have ever encountered. He is not what is called "a born writer." He had to work at it, and in so doing, went on and on improving and perfecting a style; finding a self and expressing that self. Think of him as the medical student who vaguely feels he has something to impart, to convey, to say. He begins to write in what is a popular genre of the time and achieves a social-realist novel called LIZA OF LAMBETH which even now, by any standards, is damned good. It goes well enough to encourage him to continue. He moves ahead, doggedly. I greatly admire the discipline with which he works and studies and experiments. There are so few men of letters in the true meaning of the phrase. He has written criticism and essays in addition to his fiction and plays. He has done editorial work. He has concerned himself with radio as a medium of literary communication, and with television, and films. I grant that it is not remarkable to deal in diverse fields, but it is remarkable to have succeeded in all of them. He has been an important influence, and a help, artistically and materially, in continuing the great line of literary effort. All this stems from his being a professional and putting his work first; respecting his craft to the point where very late in his life he was not only willing but eager to turn a whole manuscript over to Edward Marsh [*British civil servant and literary expert; secretary to Winston Churchill*] for comment and correction. By this time Maugham was a figure, an author whose writings had sold millions of copies everywhere in the world. Yet when Marsh went over his manuscript, compiling page upon page of hard criticism and correction, switching sentences about, suggesting substitute words, objecting to punctuation, Maugham sat and considered it all in good part because—I must use the word again—he was a professional. What else is meant by the word? One who faces up to his responsibilities as a craftsman. I cannot imagine a professional throwing his manuscript at a publisher to do whatever about cutting or trimming or producing the book. Every professional I have ever known or known about gave the closest attention to the matter. I think of Shaw going to the printing house of THE SATURDAY REVIEW, when he was its drama critic, and waiting for the first set-up in type so that he could check punctuation and spelling. This seems the exact sort of work, the infinite capacity for taking pains, which has been erroneously called genius. As I see it, a genius does not *need* to take infinite pains. A professional has to and does.

It is interesting to note that there are certain people—artists, and mutual acquaintances—who are invariably discussed; others are not. The former are the big ones, the giants. How often we talk of Maugham, sometimes critically—but no matter. What he does and says and writes and thinks and feels is important to all of us who know him. I cannot imagine anyone coming into close contact with WSM and not benefiting by it.

I think of that list of writers Henry James prepared fifty years ago and wonder to what extent they will remain in the stream of English-speaking culture. H. G. Wells himself pronounced most of his work "dead as mutton" toward the end of his life. He usually dealt with burning issues which, in the course of progress, disappeared. John Galsworthy is hardly read or performed. Arnold Bennett? D. H. Lawrence, I imagine, has a public still. What happened to the others?

I surmise that Maugham will have the ups and downs

of literary celebrity, but that in the end an important part of his work will fall indisputably into the standard stream: of the novels, OF HUMAN BONDAGE, CAKES AND ALE, THE MOON AND SIXPENCE, THE RAZOR'S EDGE; of the plays, THE CIRCLE, OUR BETTERS, THE LETTER; much of the essay work; and almost all the short stories. No one in this century achieved a higher standard in the delicate, difficult field of the short story.

Maugham understands this form as well as anyone. He had a certain advantage in the formulation of his style. Maupassant was an early influence on WSM (who was partly French by culture), as were other writers during the Parisian vogue for short fiction. Maugham was able to take the form thus acquired and add the content of his own experience and observation.

His wide study and erudition gave him a healthy respect for Chekhov as well. Out of Chekhov and Maupassant he forged a way of his own in English. Perhaps if his influences had been English writers, his style would have evolved into something imitative or echoing or carbon-copy-like. The fact that Chekhov was Russian and Maupassant French made it possible for Maugham to come under their thrall without showing it obviously in his work.

I have given his short stories, one at a time, to young people—readers of fourteen, fifteen, and sixteen. They have invariably become interested and asked for more. In some cases they have then gone right through the short-story collections. I know older people familiar with the stories who reread them often and are willing to argue strenuously about their favorites, discovering new, hidden meanings.

For myself, I find Maugham not only a storyteller, which is what he dubs himself, but a spellbinder. I have scarcely ever begun a story of his which I have not finished at the same sitting. There is something hypnotic about his narrative magic, his hints, his characterizations, his developments, his surprises. He has never been known as a particularly sexy writer, but his short story THE TREASURE is about as erotic as it is possible to get on the printed page, and he does it all in cool, precise English, without the use of a single word which could not be printed in THE TIMES.

July 1953. St. Jean–Cap Ferrat.

That darling Claudette Colbert decided to give a party last night (Saturday). She has rented the Villa Fiorentina from Lady Kenmare and has been a bright ornament of the community for weeks. She is, as always, as everywhere, enormously popular, and last night she chose to return the hospitality which has been shown her here.

She first mentioned it to me about two weeks ago.

"I'm going to give a party," she said, "in a couple of Saturdays."

"Great."

"What would you think of a luau?"

"A *what?*"

"A Hawaiian luau," she said calmly.

"Here?"

"Why not? I can't do a French dinner anything like as well as some, and American's been done, and so has Italian —yes, I think a luau is just the thing."

"But where will you get the stuff?"

"I'll get it."

"And who'll prepare it?"

"My bunch. I'll show them how."

"They'll love that."

"The terrace is absolutely ideal. I've been studying it. I'll put down four big mats—twenty at each mat."

"You're going to have *eighty?*" I asked.

"At least." She frowned. "There's only *one* problem," she said. "The girls'll have to wear something they can sit on the ground in—but not slacks."

"Sarongs? I doubt there are forty sarongs in St. Jean. I doubt there are *four*."

"No, no," she said. "Not sarongs. Evening dresses— this is black tie—but something to sit on the ground in."

"Well, I'm all set," I said. "I can sit on the ground in my black tie—but thanks for telling me in advance. I'm going to start practicing. By the way, am I invited?"

"Yes," she said. "As a matter of fact, I was hoping you'd help with the drinks. Find out about rum punch."

I thought that as time went by and difficulties mounted she would give up the formidable undertaking. But no. Time went by and difficulties mounted, but served only to power Claudette's resolve. She has many talents and not the least of them is her creativity and efficiency as a hostess.

So last night—a luau on the terrace of the Villa Fiorentina. A great success in every way. How she managed to provide that food, I do not know. It was first-rate and plentiful.

There was an orchestra of Hawaiian guitars. Don't ask me. How do I know?

I had, naturally, forgotten to find out about rum punch, but that did not deter me. Remembering old Beachcomber days in Hollywood, I simply kept pouring and mixing and tasting until something interesting turned up. It went well and Claudette thanked me and everyone was going on about how good it was until Maugham arrived. He was dressed in his white dinner jacket with a dark-red boutonnière, looked dapper, carried a sofa cushion, and was clearly ready for a good time. I handed him a cup of my rum punch.

"Thank you," he said. He took a sip, said, "Filthy!" and handed it back to me. "Martini, please," he ordered. "Very cold and dry."

He is a true no-nonsense man, and did not propose to put that concoction of mine into himself just to be polite.

When the time came to sit down to dinner, I had a sudden concern. How was the Old Party going to manage? At almost eighty, sitting on the ground and getting up again pose problems. I need not have worried. He took it all in stride and behaved as though he attended luaus regularly. To begin with, he stepped out of his pumps and put them to one side. All at once, everyone else was doing the same. He dropped his cushion, lowered himself to it, and sat, comfortably cross-legged. He began to study the feast. He fell to it at once and everyone else at his mat watched him so as to know what to do. There was one fine moment when, having finished eating the meat from a chicken bone, Maugham nonchalantly threw it over his shoulder into the bushes. All the others followed suit, which was all right, except that half of them, who were seated *facing* the bushes, tossed their bones over their shoulders and onto the next group of guests.

The South Seas atmosphere mellowed Maugham and he talked of Tahiti and his travels in that part of the world.

"I don't enjoy . . . travel," he said. "I find it interesting but not enjoyable."

"Why do you do so much of it, then?" someone asked.

"I don't, any longer," he said. (I know that he has been, in the past year, to London, Paris, Vienna, Madrid, Zurich,

Venice and Abano. But I suppose he does not call this traveling in the way he used to.) "But when I did, it was to find . . . material. Do you imagine I would have written THE MOON AND SIXPENCE had I not gone to Tahiti? Some think I went there . . . because of the book. It was, actually, the other way about. I did the book . . . because I went there."

The party got going for fair shortly after dinner. We had all become accustomed to the restful posture and were reluctant to leave the ground. So there was a lot of crawling about and lolling—at one time Claudette was the only one on her feet, seeing to things.

Lady Kenmare and her group had decided to come as for a fancy dress. She, an elderly British beauty, had blacked up from head to toe and wore a grass skirt. Her group ranged from tribal chieftains through British sailors to beachcombers. David Herbert was one of the latter and, at one point in the evening, was prevailed upon to do his dance. It is apparently a party stunt for which he is renowned. He looked about, considered the guests and demurred at first—but the hour and the temperature of the proceedings were such that finally he let go. It is a long, outrageous, erotic fandango. The fact that it is performed by the son of the Earl of Pembroke is what gives it, I suppose, its kick.

Shortly after he had begun, and when the tone of the performance had been made clear, I looked about to see how the audience was taking it, individually and en masse.

My eyes hit Maugham, who sat there, clearly bored, smoking a cigar. He beckoned to me. I went to him at once.

"Sit down," he ordered. "Here."

I sat down beside him. The music was blaring, the dance

continuing, the audience responding vociferously—some egging the dancer on, others screaming with embarrassment.

"I would like," said Maugham calmly, "to have some . . . intellectual conversation with you."

He puffed his cigar, holding both my eyes with both of his and somehow removing us from the time and place.

"Very well," I said. "Do you think there is a God?"

(We had discussed the subject at length four or five years ago, in New York, but I was eager to know whether or not the passage of time had caused a change in his feelings on the subject. Many embrace some sort of faith in old age.)

"I don't know," he said. "I do know that you've chosen a . . . question which I've pondered a good deal. As you can see, I am a very old man and I have . . . lived a full life in many parts of the world. I've known many thousands, encountered hundreds of thousands, and seen . . . millions. I've talked and listened and read—I suppose it would be . . . accurate to say that I've tried to find an answer to that question in one way or another all my . . . life. Now here I am, nearing the end, and the best I can offer in answer is to say: I don't know. Not very satisfactory, is it?"

"No," I said. "The agnostic view seems to be a cop-out. I'd rather have someone hold a strong opinion than try for the middle. Don't you agree that in these matters—hope, faith, belief—a positive wrong is better than a negative right?"

"I wouldn't know about . . . that—but did you say 'cop-out'?"

"Yes."

"What does it mean?"

"It means to make an excuse for not acting. They used to say cop a plea—now it's cop-out."

"It is underworld in origin?"

"Probably."

"The American language," he said. "I admire it, but I can't . . . write it."

We were being offered brandy. He took some. I declined.

"Well," I persisted. "What about God?"

"I hesitate to . . . cop-out," he said, "but the best I can give you is this: Whether He exists or no, I cannot tell for certain but I am . . . willing to say that I think it . . . mm*most* unlikely."

The dance ended as Maugham spoke these words. He joined in the applause, got to his feet, picked up his cushion, turned away and went looking for Claudette. I saw him say goodnight to her. I watched him go down the long stone steps to his waiting Rolls.

Ruth, who knows the trick of leaving while she is still enjoying herself, soon suggested that we go, too, and so we did.

July 1951. Villa Mauresque.

I have been reading Henry Miller for a week. My reaction to the stuff changes from page to page. I ask Maugham about it tonight.

"Henry Miller?" he muses. "Yes. When he is . . . pornographic I find him most amusing, and when he is . . . philosophic I find him dull. But I don't want to talk about . . . literature tonight."

1951. St. Jean–Cap Ferrat.

We are staying here at the Villa Mauresque as weekend guests of WSM. We drove over this morning from the Hotel Aioli in St. Tropez.

I have never been here before and although I have heard about it and read about it and seen pictures of it, I am bowled over by the actuality. Too many aspects come at you at once and the effect is like that produced by mixing wines. I feel absolutely cockeyed and we have been here only a few hours and nothing, of course, to drink.

A job finding the place. We had careful instructions and even a map, but the map was made some time ago and does not take into account many of the new roads and landmarks which now exist, or the disappearance of some of the others. We reach St. Jean–Cap Ferrat and the right part of it, but cannot seem to find the road or the gate. Ruth keeps thinking she remembers, but it has been some time since she was last here and her memory betrays her.

We ask for help, but get none. Some of those questioned do not know, others are not disposed to help people in a great big American Ford station wagon.

"Pardon, m'sieu," I say to an old man sitting in a doorway. "Où est la Villa Mauresque?"

He looks at me.

I try again, slowly. "Vil-la Maur-esque."

He shakes his head.

Famous the world over, I gather, but unknown in the town.

I plow on. "C'est la résidence de M'sieu Maugham. Somerset Maugham? Le grand écrivain anglais?"

"Sais pas."

We ask two others, no luck. Look for a phone, no. Finally we overtake a corduroy-clad little man who is walking up the road. We stop and ask him. He takes off his beret and frowns.

"Mawm?" he repeats. "Mawm? Non."

Now he lets loose what sounds to me like a single, exceptionally long word.

"What'd he say?"

Ruth translates. "He says there's no one by that name in this vicinity and he'd know because he's with the post office, and he asks do we know that there are other St. Jeans which are *not* Cap Ferrat."

"Of course we know. Tell him to buzz off. We're in the right town—we're just in the wrong world."

Ruth, with a sudden inspiration, decides to spell it. To spell it in French.

"Maugham," she says. "Em-ah-oo-zhay-ahsh-ah-em."

The succession of sounds makes me laugh, but all at once our friend says, "Ah! Maw-*gum*. Vous cherchez M'sieu Maw-*gum!*"

"Yes!" I shout. "Oui. *Maw*-gum, Maw-*gum!*"

He asks, "L'écrivain anglais?"

"Oui!" I yell. "Yes."

He begins to talk and to point graphically. His hands and arms move up, down, right, left—at one point his hand appears to do a loop-the-loop, and at another we are plainly being advised to go in two directions at once.

"Comprenez?" he asks, ending his display.

"No!" I say.

He shrugs, indicating that I am hopeless, puts on his beret, opens the door and shoves in beside Ruth.

"Allons-y!" he says, pointing straight ahead.

In five minutes we are there. I recognize the celebrated

exotic device on the garden wall beside the gate. I realize that we have been circling the place for an hour. Our guide gets out of the car. I thank him and offer him a tip. He refuses. I insist. He takes it. We drive up the steep driveway and enter the private heaven of M'sieu Maw*gum*.

The spot itself is the first wonder. Even if no great house stood here, even without its gardens and terraces and pool—if you camped here in a trailer for a night or two, you would never forget it. The top of a ridge (the highest point on the peninsula?), the lovely Mediterranean, the stately curve of Nice and its Promenade des Anglais, and what surely must be a private sky.

As to the house, it obviously has had the benefit of artful, cherishing attention for a long span of years. It has the stamp of great good sense coupled with exquisite taste.

The famous pictures reflect knowledgeability and sound historic judgment and love of art. (A bizarre experience in the hallway upon arriving: Maugham, wearing silk Japanese pajamas and kimono, comes padding out to greet us—he is a symbol of hospitality, all welcoming, smiling, and making us feel at home. As we stand in the spacious foyer, chatting, there looms up behind him on the wall the cold, forbidding image which is the Graham Sutherland portrait of WSM. Which is the real Maugham?)

The house runs—rather, *is* run—and it all works and you are aware neither of the strings nor of the machinery. He comes up with us to our rooms—yes, *rooms*. There are two bedrooms, separated by a small sitting room. There are books and desks (such as the perfect one I am writing at now) and fruit and mineral waters and in a moment two attendants, a maid and a valet.

He presents them casually and says to me of the man,

"He speaks beautiful English. I've heard your . . . French. I shall be on the terrace at . . . quarter of one if you care to join me. I'm delighted to have you here."

And he is gone. It is almost a quarter of one now and I had better stop and change. I care to join him.

. . . Later. Lunch was sort of unbelievable. A clear white tomato broth, native seafood, salad, and at the end—avocado ice cream.

"The sort you have in America," he says.

"Where in America?" I ask. "I've never even heard of it."

"Oh," he says archly, "haven't you?"

On to other things.

He talks about his house. "This place is my second child. When I bought it, it was as ugly as a . . . newborn baby, but, as you can see, it's quite grown-up now and has been greatly . . . refined. So many people dislike it. Some of them come to . . . stay with me and exclaim about its beauties and then go back to London and make . . . sport of it. I don't mind, really. I've prepared it for my way of living and . . . comfort and it suits me down to the ground."

He looks up. "It had an enormous cupola up there and all sorts of other . . . baroque horrors, but I had the local architects and carpenters and plasterers and . . . painters in and told them exactly what I wanted done. No one ever made a suggestion which I was willing to accept or even . . . discuss. I suppose that's why I like it so much. It is . . . precisely what I want. As you can see, it is . . . simple; and, as I know, it is . . . functional.

"It was a ruin when I came . . . back to it after the war. It had been . . . looted by the French and occupied by the Italians, then commandeered by the Germans and shelled by the . . . British. I couldn't . . . bear the sight of it and thought there was . . . nothing to do but dispose of it. The

34

agents pointed out that a . . . shambles would be difficult to sell, so I went to a hotel in Nice—the Negresco—arranged for the . . . place to be put back in order, and went off to London. When I returned, I fell in . . . love with it all over again and . . . decided not to sell it, and indeed I never shall. Never."

He grows corn here in the kitchen garden. He learned to like it when he lived in California. In France corn is fed to livestock and is not considered human food.

"I tried some of it," says Maugham, "and they are . . . perfectly correct. It is not. I imported these seeds from California. It grows very well here although the . . . gardeners resent it. What makes the French so difficult," he goes on, "is that they are certain they can do everything better than anyone. Cook, paint . . . farm, love, govern. The fact that they are . . . quite right about this most of the time is not a . . . mitigating factor."

I tell him that I find the Villa Mauresque overwhelmingly attractive.

"I'm going to . . . tell you what I paid for it in the first instance," he says. "Shall I tell you why?"

"Please."

"Because you haven't asked me. So many . . . people do and I always pretend not to have heard the . . . question. After all, I don't see that it's anyone's . . . business but my own. I paid about $35,000 for it. Of course, a dollar was worth far more in 1928."

"What's the property worth now?" I ask indiscreetly. "Do you have any idea?"

"To me or to you?" he parries.

"To a rich American millionaire, say," I suggest.

"Oh, I should think it might be worth . . . two of his millions."

"That much?"

"If less, not . . . *much* less."

"That's a considerable increase," I say.

Maugham is cool. "It is," he says casually. "But then you must . . . remember that I've held the stock for twenty years or more and that I've invested a few . . . pennies to improve it. Still, I do stand to make a handsome . . . profit."

"Do you suppose," I ask, "that the person who bought it from you today for two million would have any reason to expect a similar rise in the next twenty years?"

"What an interesting question," he muses, and adds: "I've no idea."

He drops us abruptly after lunch (whatever else happens, he never misses his nap) but later in the afternoon we are told that he is up at the pool. We go there—a long, long climb up a stone stairway. When I reach the top I am lightheaded and winded. How does he get up here? (Alan tells me, presently. He walks up, sometimes runs up —twice a day, every day.)

The enormous pool and its surround are like nothing I have ever known, and seem to have been there always. The area is bordered by lush vegetation and unusual flowers. Maugham is swimming and waves to us from mid-pool. When he emerges, he comes to where we are sitting and lies down to sun himself. I see an old body but a firm one, wrinkled but unblemished. I am glad that he does not notice my new Polaroid camera. Alan has warned me that WSM does not like to be photographed. The subject does not come up.

He asks about George Cukor. We tell him what we know of George's activity.

"He's a grand man," says Maugham.

We deplore the fact that George is not coming over. There had been a chance that he might.

"Why should he?" asks Maugham. "Unless, of course, it's for his work. As far as life goes, he's . . . made himself quite comfortable where he is. That's not easy to bring off when you're gadding about, is it?"

"I don't know," I said. "I'm quite comfortable *here*."

"I'm going to do my . . . dive now: Watch me."

He makes his way to the high board.

Alan tells us WSM does this dive once every day and adds, "I wish he wouldn't."

WSM stands, poised, at the edge of the board. I cannot resist the temptation, grab up the Polaroid, set it, and train it on the little phenomenon up there.

He dives. When he is midway to the water—I click. He hits the water, hard, surfaces, swims to the side, hoists himself out of the water and sits on the pool's ledge for a few minutes, recovering. Meanwhile, I time the exposure and tear off the finished picture. It is suprisingly good and clear. A diver in mid-air.

He starts toward us. I pocket the picture and stash the camera.

He sits down with us and asks, "Well, how did I look?"

The cue is irrestible. I take the picture from my pocket and hand it to him.

"Like this," I say.

Alan looks worried, Ruth disapproving. (She told me later she thought we were about to be asked to leave.)

He studies the photograph carefully for a long minute. Then he says, "My knees are crooked."

No comment about the wonder of this new camera, no reaction to having been caught unawares.

"They are?" I ask.

"Look here."

We study the print together.

37

He tears it in two, rises, and says, "I'd better do it again for you. Are you ready?"

He climbs to the top again, shouts down, "Now?" waits until I reply, "Yes!"—and dives again. I make a second shot.

This time he does not rest on the ledge, but comes directly out of the pool and begins to walk toward me swiftly. He reaches me before I have the damned picture out. He stands beside me, dripping, waiting. I just know it is going to be a spoiled one or a blur or a smudge or something. Will he do it a third time? Will he kill himself and will it be my stupid fault? The picture comes out and it is all right. It is improved photographically and the dive is arrow-like.

He takes it, peers at it briefly, and says, "Yes. Much better."

He hands the picture back to me (his interest in it is ended) and says, "Come along. Tea at four-fifteen."

He picks up his robe—a sort of kimono—and moves as he puts it on. By the time we reach the top of the stairway, he is gone. I have to keep reminding myself that this man is nearing eighty.

. . . We have just come back here after a tour of the house and grounds which followed tea. An experience.

"Actually, I owe my . . . possession of this . . . paradise to . . . sin." The final word is bobbled and he repeats it more clearly, "*Sin.*"

"How so?" I ask.

"Well, the whole of this Cap was owned at one time by the . . . King of Belgium, Leopold the Second. At least, the greater part of it was. He installed his . . . mistress here somewhere—there are differing views about exactly where—and because he was such a sinful man, albeit a religious one, he was afraid he might go to . . . hell. So he made a gift of this property to the Bishop of Nice and . . . built him this house. It's a Moorish construction because this particular . . . bishop had spent most of his life in . . . North Africa. I've no idea whether or not this . . . gambit kept Leopold out of hell. I should think not, but in the circumstances I'm . . . glad he was a sinner."

His bedroom is one of the most remarkable living machines ever. The basis of the arrangement is entirely utilitarian rather than decorative, although it is a handsome room. The bed-rest is specially designed; a shelf of books is within reach; the complex paraphernalia of sedentary living is all about—my impulse is to hop in and try it all. Dressing room, bathroom, all designed for convenience and comfort.

Finally, up to his study. It is atop the house, reached by a separate staircase. He explains, as we mount it, that he added on this part of the structure.

The room is large and spare. There is not much in it. One wall of books mostly by him. I am turned around and cannot get my bearings. I know we are high up, but I cannot see the view from any of the windows.

"Which way is Nice?" I ask.

"There," he replies and points to the wall of books. "I had the view blocked off. This room is for working, not looking."

It is the one room in the house without pictures, save one. Over a cabinet, far to the right of his worktable, is a portrait of a woman—head and bust. A round, adorable face; high color; red hair; saucy expression. She suggests immediately Rosie of CAKES AND ALE.

"Who's this?" I ask.

He looks at the picture for a moment and says, "The woman I loved."

Before anything more can be said, he moves to another table and says, "This may interest you."

May! It is his manuscript copy of THE MOON AND SIX-PENCE. It is bound. His hand is precisely what it is now: flowing, swift, economical, and attractive. There are corrections, cuts, changes, and emendations on the manuscript itself and on the facing sheets to the left (usually inserts marked with corresponding asterisks).

I examine it. "This is the first draft, then?"

"This is all of them," he says. "I wrote it so—" his finger moves down the page—"then went over it and . . . corrected it so, in red ink. And sent it off. Oh, yes, there were the boring . . . page proofs, but I only skimmed those and had friends help me. I have never read it."

There is a beautifully painted door which leads to a small terrace. He tells us that it is a door from one of Paul Gauguin's cabins in Tahiti.

"See here at the bottom—the stained part. That is where his dog peed on it. But it means much to me—having Gauguin's . . . door in my room."

The table at which he writes is outsize—I estimate it at about eight feet long. It is solid and two or three inches lower than average (to accommodate his short stature, I suppose). It is neat and tidy. I compliment him on this condition.

"Thank you," he says. "I accept that, because I look after . . . myself up here, for the most part."

We start down. I notice that he glances at the portrait of Rosie again.

Cocktails. He is surprised when we decline. He asks

if we want something else, suggests tomato juice. We accept. All this leads to talk of alcohol. He believes it to be an individual matter having to do with blood, metabolism, and so on.

"Winston," he says, "drinks a good deal and manages well. As for me, I am blessed by . . . nature with a fortunate mechanism. If I consume one drop more than I should have, I become violently ill on the instant. It's always been so. When I was a student—and on a pub crawl— one too many and I would be incapacitated for . . . days. It's a great bit of luck for me, that valve. I wish everyone had one. Actually, I've been drunk only three times in the course of my . . . life and each time I thought I was going to enjoy the experience and each time I was . . . disappointed."

. . . Dinner. The talk is of his pictures. He remembers vividly the details of the acquisition of each. He seems to have sought in every instance a non-characteristic work. Thus, the Degas in the dining room and the Toulouse-Lautrec in the drawing room are not identifiable on sight, other than by experts. He knows where each of the paintings is going when the time comes. He tells of the increasing difficulty of keeping them safe. Whenever he leaves St. Jean–Cap Ferrat for any length of time, the paintings are stored in the vaults of his bank in Nice. And of course, he explains, he pays regular fees to the Thieves' Union.

"The what?" I ask.

"Yes," he says. "The Thieves' Union. It has been in existence here on the Côte d'Azur for as . . . long as anyone can remember. When I first arrived in 1928, a committee paid a call. They were most . . . correct and formal and explained that my property would be exempt from

41

... molestation upon payment of a nominal fee. There was no profit in this, they insisted—not for anyone—but there were expenses involved."

"At home we call it 'protection.'"

"Quite so. Well, I told them that, as a matter of principle, I would pay ... nothing. They were extremely polite— we shook hands all round—and they took their leave. A few days later something was stolen from the house. I am not going to ... tell you what it was. The following week —something more—a lawnmower and a wheel from one of the cars. On the first of the month the same committee came again and made the proposal as though it had never been ... made before. This time I accepted. I have always paid them—the rates have gone up several times— and nothing has ever been stolen. Of course, I still put the pictures in the ... vault when I leave—it doesn't do to offer temptation."

[*The happy arrangement ended after a time. In 1960 there occurred a series of well-organized, professionally executed art thefts in France. A single haul from the Colombe d'Or at St.-Paul-de-Vence netted the efficient thieves over $600,000 worth of modern paintings. Not long after that, eight Cézannes valued at over $2,000,000 were stolen from an exhibition in Aix-en-Provence. Maugham's collection, one of the most celebrated and highly publicized in the world, seemed to be in line. It was at this point that he sent for Peter Cecil Wilson, of Sotheby's and began discussions about the possible sale of the paintings. The gossips put it down to a scheme whereby WSM would somehow do his heirs out of the collection. In fact, Maugham was attempting to protect his estate.*]

He smokes. He smokes heavily and enjoys it.

"It may be," he says, "that my lungs, having twice suffered tuberculosis, and twice . . . beaten the disease, may have reinforced themselves to uncommon sturdiness. In any event, I have no intention of . . . doing anything about it. There are few enough things out of which I can derive such great . . . pleasure at so small a risk. Worrying about it may make me ill sooner than . . . smoking itself."

1948. New York.

There we all sat yesterday, in that elegant, modern room in Margaret Case's Park Avenue apartment which might have been a page of her VOGUE come to life. (There is a pattern here, surely. The look of existence, the form, the cast—borrowed back and forth, forth and back from reality to her magazine, from the magazine to reality. I remember Thornton [*Wilder*] once confessing a weakness for scanning its pages. "When I die," he said, "I don't want to go to Heaven—I want to go to VOGUE!")

Anyway, there we were: WSM, Sam Behrman, Moss Hart, Ruth and Margaret and I. Anyone else? Well, yes, later—Leonora Corbett to mar the day with flip small talk and tired suggestive jokes. A fair performance but in the wrong play. Until she turned up, it was rare. Maugham, arranging the use of his New York time with care and economy, had asked for us and for two others who could not come. We were all, needless to say, flattered to have been invited by the remarkable old man.

He was at his best. We asked questions and he answered them without the slightest attempt at cleverness or quotability, and with no condescension or patronization.

43

I ask him if he sees any relationship between his interest in painting and music and his work as a writer, reminding him that Gertrude Stein said she learned to write in the way she wrote from looking at the paintings of Cézanne.

He says, "I suppose she meant something, but I'm ... damned if I know what it was. She wasn't a fool, but she most certainly was ... difficult. Too ... difficult for me."

"Never mind her. What about you and painting and music?"

"I've never thought about it much on the conscious level, but I suppose there is a ... relationship between one art and another. It's all a matter of ... form, isn't it? An attempt to put things in order. In storytelling—which is my profession—I know of only three ... designs. The first is a sort of up-down, up-down ... frieze. Not necessarily symmetrical, but up-down, up-down. Rather like a ... medical chart. Long works often use this line. Climaxes, chapter endings, up-down, up-down. Dickens had to ... do it, I imagine, because he was writing in monthly installments. I've used it myself, but with indifferent success. The other one is the ... line going straight up and ending at the top. Murder mysteries use this a good deal. I've never employed it. The last is that lovely crescent that begins down here and ... makes an upward curve and finally descends to the .. . level of its starting point. Most of the great French novels use this one. It's the one I feel most comfortable with. Those are the three designs or lines or shapes I know. I've ... never come upon any other."

"Don't many of your short stories use the second—the straight line moving upward to the climax or surprise or fillip or joke?"

44

"I suppose so. Yes. I was thinking of . . . longer works."

He was asked exactly how he went about writing. (Picasso says that when art critics get together they talk about content, style, trend and meaning, but that when painters get together they talk about where can you get the best turpentine.) Maugham carefully explained that he rises at eight o'clock every morning—no matter where he is—has his breakfast and so on, and at nine o'clock sits down and writes for four hours. (I recall having read about this in one of the autobiographical books— THE SUMMING UP, I think it was. In it, he stated that early in life he had been greatly impressed when he learned that Charles Darwin—working only four hours a day— had changed the course of civilization. Maugham wrote that since *he* had no such exalted goal in mind he saw no reason to exceed this schedule.)

Ruth: "Now, wait, Willie. Do you mean to say that no matter what time you go to bed, you get up at eight?"

WSM: "Yes."

Ruth: "But don't you feel tired sometimes?"

A pause.

WSM: "No."

Moss: "But what about those days when you simply don't feel like it?"

WSM: "If you live by your . . . pen, my boy, you can't afford such days."

SNB: "To hell with feel like it—what if you can't *think* of anything?"

WSM: "Oh, to be sure, that happens often. When it does, I sit there and . . . write 'W. Somerset Maugham' over and over and over again until something comes."

We talk of the depression engendered by public failure.

"I don't mean to . . . make light of it," he says. "It's

real and understandable, but one must learn to . . . take the blow, recover and . . . go on. We all have our ups and downs—people practicing the arts always have had. Remember that critics can often be right and so can the public. I've heard writers . . . rail against the critics and focus on the unfavorable reviews of their works, when they might have profited more by . . . focusing on the work itself. Had they done so, they might have learned more from the bad work than from the bad reviews. But that's . . . neither here nor there. In a lifetime of work, every writer produces some . . . inferior stuff. Balzac and Dostoevski and even Shakespeare—people are very . . . kind to him, they cut out most of what's awful. On the whole, I should say that the . . . mark of someone good is that up-and-down quality, provided the up is high enough. I suspect people who work on one successful . . . level for too long a period of time. It's a sign of . . . mediocrity. I'm sure of it."

Ask a stupid question and you'll get a stupid answer— so it goes in New Yorkese. But this afternoon I asked a stupid question of WSM and the answer was a beauty.

I asked, "Of all the writers in English you have ever read, which one do you most admire?"

He took time to reflect before he said, "I should choose a writing . . . creature of my own invention, one who never could have existed in reality. He would be a . . . man who combined Hazlitt and Newman. He would have Hazlitt's intellect and vitality and vision as well as Newman's . . . lovely sense of rhythm and music. That man, that procreation of these two . . . talents, an issue of the union of these diverse spirits, would have been, had he ever existed, the man whose writing of English prose I would have . . . most admired. Does that answer your question?"

"Yes, sir. It does."

Back to his plan. After he has written for four hours, he explains, he lunches and takes a short nap. Half an hour, twenty minutes, never more than three quarters of an hour. Now, he points out, he is ready for the world. The balance of his day—from about 2:30 P.M. on—is left for social life, business, reading, rewriting, galleys, study, medical attention, shopping or friends.

[*The system seemed so worthwhile, so practical that I resolved to adopt it at once. All this happened about eighteen years ago, and I still struggle with it. On the face of it, it seems simpler than simple to put aside, regularly, four hours out of each twenty-four for the activity which keeps you alive in every way. Yet how elusive those four hours can prove. There have been hundreds of days when I have worked for ten hours and a few when I have done even more. But I have never achieved that disciplined regularity which is essential.*

Four hours a day, he had admonished. Never more. But —note well—never less.

I cannot recall for certain, but it seems to me that he included Sundays, holidays, and birthdays. Yes. I remember now his saying: "Especially birthdays."]

He says, "I have known so many writers in my time— too many, I fear. I don't think it a good idea for writers to . . . fraternize with writers. It leads to a sort of inbreeding, don't you know, which in turn produces . . . idiots. It's far better to make friends with . . . fishmongers and steamship stewards and racetrack touts and harlots."

"Thornton makes a point of it," I say. "When he's living in Hamden, he gets up every morning and goes down to the corner drugstore to have his breakfast or to a lunch counter."

"Yes. A very good idea. Success in writing so often re-

47

moves the writer from his original . . . sources, and there's no avoiding other writers. If you try to . . . do so, they come at you. Many of them are charming and amusing chaps and I . . . find them interesting. In point of fact, I find all . . . people interesting. I don't like them, but I must admit they're interesting. I've met all sorts of . . . writers. There were those who wrote for . . . money—bloody fools I call them. I think you'll find that the average . . . plumber earns more than the average writer. Some, no doubt, write because they want to be famous, but there's nothing more fleeting than that. I could name you a dozen writers who were . . . famous during my lifetime—lionized, quoted, puffed up—and you wouldn't recognize a single name. If you did, you wouldn't . . . be able to tell me if they're dead or alive. Another sort I've encountered are chaps who want to be writers so they can . . . play the part. Pathetic, really."

I say, "I remember Edna Ferber addressing the graduating class of an acting school and telling them that their success would depend largely on whether they wanted to act or merely to be actors and actresses."

"Well said. I admire Edna Ferber. She's a true professional. I once had my . . . picture taken with her and the photographer didn't want us to pose, but wanted to make one of those . . . ridiculous candid shots. He said to us, 'Please talk, please say something,' and I heard myself saying to Edna Ferber, 'Our Father who art in heaven, hallowed be Thy name, Thy kingdom come, Thy will be done,' and so on."

"What sort of writer would you call her?"

"The best sort," he says. "She writes because she . . . must, compulsively. She couldn't *not* write, if you take my meaning."

"And is that your classification, too?"

"Good Lord, no. I've always found it necessary to . . . force myself to write. Your ideal writer has to force himself *not* to write. No, I'm simply one who . . . fell into it for want of something better to do and then . . . developed my talents and my aptitudes to a point where I was . . . pretty good."

"Pretty good?"

"Pretty good and later . . . very good."

"And now?"

"Good."

"Great, perhaps?"

"Good," he insists after shaking his head.

"Thornton Wilder says writing is 'a coy game you play with your unconscious.' Do you think there's anything in that?"

"Indeed. Subjective writing. That's the only . . . sort that's any good. I'm never sure what's going to . . . come out when I begin."

"But I've heard it said you think your things out pretty thoroughly before beginning to write."

"Quite untrue. Oh, I may have some notion as to characters and form and theme, but only in a vague and . . . most ephemeral sense. And ever subject to change. I've had . . . men turn into women in my . . . fingers, dramas become comedies, short stories become . . . novellas and novellas become . . . novels. And novels become . . . nothing. I surprise myself . . . constantly. That's what makes my . . . work so amusing—to me, at any rate. The element of self . . . surprise. It's how I can . . . continue to do what I do without going round the bend. Mind you, I'm . . . speaking entirely for myself. I don't think one can make . . . general rules about writing any more than one can make them about the practices of . . . love-making. What suits one might make another extremely . . . uncomfortable. Even unhappy. We must all . . . find our own way. I, for one, am still in the . . . process of finding my way after . . . decades of practice and effort."

He goes on. "I find it most . . . irksome that so many people think what I do is easy to do. I've no idea how others in my . . . profession feel about it, but I find writing . . . damned hard work. When I was gathering my . . . materials preparatory to writing THE RAZOR'S EDGE, I went to India. There I became familiar with various sorts of yogis and their work. One of them . . . told me that after he had sat meditating for an hour or so, he was so tired he had to lie . . . down and rest. Often he had to put himself to sleep in order to recover. And I thought to myself, 'Well, by God, if he feels that, no wonder the concentration required for writing is . . . tiring as well. And he doesn't even have to go to the trouble of pushing a pen.' "

1951. St. Jean–Cap Ferrat.

I ask him today if, in his work as a writer, he followed any rule or principle with regard to cutting.

"Yes," he replies without delay. "If it occurs to me to cut something, I cut it."

3 February 1949. New York.

This is a dictated report of our long dinner meeting last night with Somerset Maugham. As always, it proved to be stimulating, and filled with advice of the most practical sort which insists upon being heeded since it comes from within a remarkable creature who has successfully completed seventy-five years of a full, productive literary life.

We had dinner at Le Pavillon—the three of us—and began promptly at 8:00. We left the table at 11:25. So much was said that it becomes a considerable feat of memory to set down even the salient points. No use attempting to get them down in chronological order, or any sort of order at all, for that matter, but just as they come to me now.

Of course, we asked him about his new book, which has been announced for the fall. He explained that it was a book of some 435 pages and that it was an edited version of the notebooks he has kept with a certain amount of regularity from the time he was eighteen. He says at that time he began jotting down ideas and descriptions of persons and places, bits of dialogue, and scraps of information. This practice continued until he was seventy—that would make it fifty-two years. Why he stopped then, he does not say, nor do we ask. I should think he still keeps a journal of some sort—but that he chose to publish only what he had written to the age of seventy. After all, man is a creature of habit and, Maugham's statement notwithstanding, I cannot be persuaded that a man journalizes for fifty-two years and stops abruptly.

He goes on to say he has removed from the text most of the sketches and original jottings for books and plays and stories which he has since written.

GK: "I wish you hadn't done that. Nothing would interest me more than to be made privy to the genesis of a work and then be able to compare it with the finished product."

WSM: "But you're not the ... reading public, old fellow, are you? No, no. Including everything would have made the book far too long—I'm afraid it's too long as it is. I was ... quite right to omit what I did. You cannot shake my confidence."

He went on to speak of the practical value of his notebooks, pointing out that as time went on, ideas occurred less and less frequently. For the past few years, he says, he has been drawing heavily on his files and has been working out ideas formulated long ago.

With a certain amount of melancholy, he warns us to conserve our ideas, too.

WSM: "Yes, I know. You think this gay ... creativity will continue. It won't. Not even for you. It ... never has for anyone."

He told us how long it was since he had thought of an idea for a play, and went into detail about the development of his last three published books and of material in his notebooks.

(Although I do not argue the point at the time, I am not at all certain I agree with all this. I note it because he said it, and for the record. A great deal of first-rate work has been done by men in their sixties, seventies, eighties and, in the case of Shaw, nineties. This is not to say it was their *best* work, but in most cases it was the kind of work which could have been accomplished *only* late in life. Maugham might argue that these men, too, worked from earlier notes or notions. Who can say? Cervantes set down DON QUIXOTE late in life, but had the plan occurred to him earlier? Ask Thornton what he thinks.

On the whole, though, I see Maugham's point and, I suppose, accept it. I do not feel as desperately pessimistic about the effect of age on one's creative powers as he does. Still, notebooks and workbooks and journals would seem to be necessary and important elements in a writer's life.)

The discussion of saving ideas led him easily into the more concrete suggestion of saving money. He says it is not a question of being miserly or mean, but a responsibility to put by enough—if one can—to keep one comfortably alive in age.

He considers us extravagant and thus felt impelled to discuss the matter.

I got off a long, half-facetious spill (which I regret) on the subject of annuities as an anachronism in our time. About how, years ago, insurance agents would come and discuss with young men in their twenties plans for their old age and retirement schemes and savings patterns— against the time when they would reach the age of, say, sixty-five. I said that back then we listened seriously to such notions. But, I went on, suppose a man comes to me today and outlines a scheme whereby I pay him $123.40 a month and continue to do so for thirty or forty years—and then at that time the company—Prudential or Metropolitan or whatever—begins paying me $64.73 a month—why, I said, it is all too comical. Our times do not provide the stability which made such schemes sensible to our fathers. It is not the pattern of the day to plan a long-range future. The future is uncertain. And what about the quick rise and fall of the value of the dollar? What will a dollar be worth thirty or forty years from now?

He eats, loving it; and listens, hating it.

When I stop, he looks at me coolly and says: "You're exaggerating, of course, and I appreciate your attempt to entertain me. But the . . . fact is you are very foolish not to have a regular plan of . . . putting aside a certain sum for your use when you are old and unable to work, when your ideas and your energies have diminished and . . . prosperity is only a memory."

Unnerved by all this, I brush it aside and get on again, this time with part of a Joe E. Lewis routine. I tell Maugham how Joe, urged to save at least $10,000 a year for ten years in case of a depression, answers, "Sure. Fine. But then—suppose ten years pass—and suppose there's *no* depression? There am I—stuck with a hundred thousand dollars!"

Maugham laughs heartily at this, takes a sip of wine, and says: "You should take certain sums and . . . put them aside, in an insurance company." He stresses this idea of the insurance company several times in the course of the evening. He goes on to tell, at length, the story of Edward Knoblock. (Maugham is surprised when I identify him, correctly, as the co-author, with Arnold Bennett, of MILE-STONES.)

Maugham tells how Knoblock, an American, came to England to live and work. He had a number of literary and theatrical successes, among them KISMET. He bought a great house and lived in it brilliantly and beautifully and far beyond his means. Preoccupied with the grand life, with the capital-S Season, with the social swirl—he was unable to work well. He had a failure, another and another. Finally, he could not get a play accepted. Out of necessity and desperate for a killing, he produced several of his plays himself, using his own money. These, too, failed. Knoblock went broke and, Maugham relates with the fervor of an evangelist, lived out his last miserable years on the charity of his friends. (It is a Rowlandson print in words:

54

The Evils of Drink.) All scare copy—and it scared me. This was Maugham's intention, and he hit his target (me) bull's-eye. The fact that I am still recovering from a recent failure made me especially vulnerable.

[*I now recall the morning after that dinner. I was torn between continuing the Maugham-inspired plan of working from nine to one, and going immediately to a savings bank to open an account. I decided to work and go to the bank directly after lunch. I opened an account at the Seamen's Bank for Savings and I have it still.*]

I asked him about his new film, and he explained that an English company had made an omnibus picture out of five of his old short stories. He said he thought it extremely good except for the fact that they had in each case absolutely removed the point of the story. He seemed eager to talk about the business side. (He still regards me as a wizard.) He said they had paid him £25,000 for the rights to the five stories and had devised a way to make the amount tax-free. Something to do with transfer of copyright. Beyond me. He seemed proud and pleased to have pulled it off. I told him it sounded fine.

Ruth: "But is it of any real use to you, since you can't take it out of Great Britain?"

WSM: "That is unfortunate, yes. But I gave £20,000 to Liza." He laughs. "I must say, I did not . . . give it to her in the way she wanted to have it. I settled it on her. She may use the interest on the . . . sum and a certain proportion of it each year, for a time. Later on, when she's . . . forty, she gets the residue. This annoyed her enormously. She wanted to have it all right now to spend and . . . protested it wouldn't be of any use to her when she was forty.

55

She wanted it all . . . now. But I said to hell with that, and she took it in the way I wanted to . . . give it." He laughed again, in a stern way (if such a thing is possible).

I suggested he might have pointed out that at forty she might need the money to buy the beauty which she now has naturally. Surely Liza is one of the great beauties of the day.

Maugham looked up at me sharply and said, "By God, I wish I'd thought of . . . telling her that."

He told about his life at St. Jean–Cap Ferrat and said that, in his opinion, he lived rather too extravagantly; that the house was always filled with English friends and, since they could bring no money out of England for their holidays, he felt impelled to give them what he called "a good time." He estimated that his life there cost him about $25,000 a year. I checked him to make sure he meant dollars and not pounds.

He looked at me benignly and said, "Let me assure you, old boy, that I know the . . . difference between a . . . dollar and a pound."

The point was that $25,000 did not seem all that much in terms of the life he was describing—but I suppose in the economy of the Riviera it is high. Come to think of it, my friend GF has gone there to live and paint. He has a house at Eze-sur-Mer not far from Maugham's place and writes me that he does nicely (one wife, one child) on $3,000 a year. He could not do it here. I estimate that $25,000 a year at St. Jean–Cap Ferrat equals about $100,-000 a year in the U.S.A. in 1949.

I cannot remember, at the moment, how WSM cued into the subject, but all at once we heard him say, "Of course, the trouble is that you two live such a restricted life, and one not conducive to new ideas or views." He went on in this vein for some time, and suggested, "Why don't you go to Charleston for three or four months and see another kind of existence—another kind of civilization? Why don't you go to Reno? I was . . . talking to an American writer not long ago, and said to him, 'Why don't writers go to Reno? What a . . . marvelous place—filled with extraordinary characters—divorcées and gamblers and gigolos and cowboys.' I promise you it's an inexhaustible mine, a . . . bottomless well of material, and yet writers don't seem to go there. I'd do it myself, but then, I'm not an American, and I feel it would be far better for an American writer to cover that material. And do you know of a place called . . . Las Vegas in that area? A gambling city. It's new and burgeoning and fascinating. Why don't you . . . go there?"

[*I came upon the above some sixteen years later and tingled with gooseflesh. My new play,* THE SPITTING IMAGE, *is set in Las Vegas. Some time after WSM advised the trip, I went there for the first time. Exciting, yes; entertaining, somewhat—but as a locale it failed to interest me. It seemed unreal, esoteric, and not of general interest. But as the years went by, it changed and so, no doubt, did I. When I began to work with the characters in my story, they fell easily, naturally, and inevitably into the background of Las Vegas. Whatever happens, I owe this play to WSM and his influence.*

When I wrote to tell him all this and to thank him, Alan replied with the shattering word that contact was no longer possible. He said that "poor Willie" was barely conscious and that when he was—for brief spells—he was in spiritual misery.

George C. told us that when he was last in France he

57

phoned the Villa Mauresque and was told by Alan that a journey down would be pointless, since WSM would not be aware of his presence.]

Apropos, Ruth asked him whether or not his travels through the years were carefully planned for such purposes. Did he travel because he enjoyed it?

"No, no," he says. "Not much. Work was the real reason, perhaps the only reason. I was constantly searching for material, for . . . places to write about, for backgrounds, for new characters, and, most of all, for experience. If we had not been . . . quarantined for several days in 1916 at Pago Pago on a journey from Honolulu, I . . . never would have come across the people or the circumstances that suggested to me the short story RAIN—perhaps the most famous I've ever written."

What he was saying about us was perfectly true. About our "restricted life." It crystallized in an instant the wearing, deep-rooted dissatisfaction which I have felt for some time. A feeling of too comfortable sameness, a lack of color and excitement. He had put it in a clean, clear way, devoid of complex analysis, the statement of the problem itself suggesting the solution. All at once I thought, How the hell does he know all this? He sees us for a few hours every year or so. Maybe George Cukor chats with him about us, as one does of mutual friends—but how could Maugham have found so accurately the middle of the target of our trouble? I asked him.

GK: "What you say is true, old friend, but I wonder how you know?"

WSM: "I sense it, somehow."

He was as surprised by his knowledge as I was.

WSM: "It seems to me to be true. I suppose I see it in you. Remember, I am a trained and experienced observer of humans."

That was it. It is beginning to show. How we sit and where. What we say and how—all this begins to reveal the signs of a rutted and—yes—restricted same old existence. How right he is. And the way to change it is to do so. Suddenly. Today and tonight, not tomorrow. Whatever else happens, do something today to make it very different from other days. Cause a commitment that will spill over into the days and months—even years—to come.

[The change was not as swift and dramatic as I had hoped on the above hopeful day, but it did spark an eventual decision to go abroad for an extended stay. The following year my wife and I went abroad, lived in Paris for a time, worked and traveled. Out of this came her decision to revive THE MERCHANT OF YONKERS *by Thornton Wilder in London. A New York revival was out of the question. The play had failed seventeen years before and the cost of an American production was prohibitive. Re-titled* THE MATCHMAKER, *and staged by Tyrone Guthrie, it was a London success for a season, was brought to New York by David Merrick and The Theatre Guild, played over a year on Broadway and a year on tour, was made into a film, became, in a musical mutation,* HELLO, DOLLY! *and has affected, mostly for good, the lives of many.*

It all began with the shake-up evening with WSM.]

I asked him again about that morning routine of his because, candidly, it is giving me trouble.

He reiterated that, no matter what or where, he had his breakfast at eight and got to work by nine.

59

"But how do you do it?" I asked.

"I do it," he replied, "by *doing* it. Not by thinking about it or . . . talking about it or considering it or analyzing. Do you see?"

I heard myself say, "Yes, sir."

Ruth gave me a sign to get off this. For some reason the whole idea of work and new production is one which is touchy and irritating. Perhaps because he has recently come to the end of a piece of work and is not yet involved in another.

Following this line of thought, I asked, "What's next?"

"I am considering," he said, "a final autobiographical book. Different in form from the others. Essays, perhaps. People no longer write essays. A pity. It's such a . . . *nice* form."

I expressed the hope that he would write another play.

"No," he says, calmly but firmly. "I shall never do that. I shall most certainly . . . never write another play as long as I live—but then, that is . . . not so much of a promise, since I certainly shan't live very long."

"How *can* you be so sure?" I persisted. "How do you know that tonight, just before you go to sleep, or in the morning, as you're shaving, you may not be struck by the best idea for a play you've ever had?"

"I know," he said, "because I no longer *think* in the category of plays. Moreover, I have never been 'struck,' as you put it, by an idea for anything. It was more a case of . . . mining with me. Mining and refining. When I was interested in the theatre, I would turn up an idea for a play daily. Often two or three. Assuredly, most of them were . . . poor. But they were ideas. When I was interested in short stories, those ideas would . . . come to the surface.

And so on. No, no more theatre for me. With all its glamour, I found it a frustrating and maddening world, full of childish people—charming but childish. I adored them, but they often needed . . . spanking, and how does one go about spanking, say, Ethel Barrymore?"

We talk of Ethel. WSM was, he confesses, at one time hopelessly smitten with her.

He returns to the starting point. "No," he says sadly. "Never another play."

. . . There was I, sipping my single sugarless bourbon old-fashioned and trying to remember that one glass of wine would be all—and there sat the aged Maugham, tossing off a huge martini, another, wine, brandy, the works. Throughout dinner, cigarettes. After dinner, an outsize cigar. Me, rounding out my shaky first year of no smoking.

All this gave me pause, and I thought to pick up a tip or two from the great old man. I asked him if he thought his early years as a medical student and later as a young doctor had taught him how to live—that is, in the physical sense. Might this not have been a decisive factor in his longevity? The knowledge and experience, the clinical ability to diagnose, to recognize symptoms quickly, to care for his body?

His reply was in the negative. He said that he felt he owed his life today, from a medical point of view, to his discovery of an outstanding Austrian-Jewish doctor, now resident in the United States, named Dr. Max Wolf.

"Recommended to me," says Maugham, "by a . . . drunken neighbor of mine in the South of France. This is the same man who has . . . kept Elsie Mendl alive all these years. (Puff, puff.) Whether you think that is a . . . good thing or not. (Puff, puff.) But I must say this—it was indeed my study and training as a physician, and my work at St. Thomas's, which taught me all I know of human nature. I learned more about people than merely what their ... bodies had to tell. And what I learned—and which seems to me the most important of all the lessons—is that ... pain and suffering do not ennoble the human spirit. Not at all. Pain and suffering ... breed meanness, bitterness, selfishness, cruelty. It is only happiness which ennobles."

A little later it was strange, more than strange, to see Maugham's face change, and to hear his voice segue into another key, when the subject of Syrie, his wife, was introduced. Ruth knows Syrie far better than I do, but both of us have always found her to be a perfectly amiable and warm lady. We see no reason not to say so to him.

"Liza," he says, "has never shown the slightest inclination toward ... looking after herself or supporting herself in any way."

What's this? We were talking of Syrie a moment ago, now he's on to Liza. Is he getting tired? Potted? Should we stop? Or is it that he has decided to ignore the subject of Syrie? Not at all.

"This unfortunate condition," he goes on, "is entirely the fault of her ... mother, a foolish woman who has never been interested in anything really except ... social position. She is, and always has been, a snob. She brought Liza up to believe that nothing in life is ... more important than the right sort of marriage. I blame her not only for what she caused me to ... miss in my life, but for what I know she is going to cause Liza to ... miss in hers!"

With some effort and no little skill, we manage to steer him off this subject and onto a more palatable one. The house at St. Jean–Cap Ferrat. What about it?

"It takes twelve to run it," he says. "Twelve the year round. It is an extremely ... beautiful structure and a pleasant place to live, but it is a bad writing ... location."

"Why?"

"Because it is out of touch with the stream of life, with ... people, with happenings of import. As such, you see, it is ideal for rest or for retirement, but it is not a ... good place for a working writer to live."

"But don't most writers long for a getaway place—away from what goes on, so that they can work without distraction or interruption?"

"Oh, yes, now and then. For a time. I was talking of an abode, a ... permanent residence. No, the best imaginations want constant stimulation. Sights and sounds. I am impatient with those who make a ... mystical mystique out of an honest craft. Good God! Molnár wrote some of his ... best plays on the tables of coffeehouses in Budapest. Your Willa Cather sat in a ... luxurious apartment on Park Avenue and produced some of the loveliest prose in our language."

... He told (with innate British pride, I thought, his earlier comments on Syrie's snobbism notwithstanding) of Liza's several visits, lately, with the Royal Family at Balmoral. It all came about as a result of her having recently married Lord John Hope. Maugham relates that at Balmoral many card games are played—he does not know which ones, but he rather suspects it was gin rummy during this particular time. Liza, he reports, made a great hit with the King, who insisted that she play cards with him again and again. The Hopes were asked to stay on for several days.

When all this was reported to him by Liza, he said to her, "What a shame it has to happen in the present. In time gone by, you would surely have been made a Duchess, and even your poor old father would have managed an Earldom, at least."

... At dinner only one thing went wrong—almost wrong.

He had ordered smoked trout and I had ordered a white wine to go with it. When it was served, I tasted it. It seemed fine to me, but since I know so little about wine, I asked him if it was all right.

"Yes," he replied politely. "All right."

It was clear from his tone that it was something less than that.

"Are you sure?" I persisted. "Because if it's not, we can change it."

"Well," he said, "it *is* rather acid."

Le Pavillon is an expensive restaurant, and a fine one, and I am convinced that its owner, Henri Soulé, wishes to give satisfaction and appreciates having lapses called to his attention.

I called the wine waiter over and said, "We find the wine a bit acid."

He was immediately apologetic, took it away, and suggested another. When it was served, Maugham sampled it, pronounced it superb, and had plenty to prove he meant it.

The wine waiter expressed his regrets and whispered to me, "You were quite right, sir. I tasted it. It has gone bad."

For the main course, I had consulted the list of clarets and ordered the most costly one. (Not a good plan, ever.) It arrived and was served. WSM tasted it. I looked at him. He smiled and shook his head in a curious way. I tasted it, and, by God, wouldn't you know it? It was not good. What they call "corky," I think.

64

The wine waiter, watching us, saw at once that something was wrong. He held a glass up to the light, blushed, and whisked the bottle away. He brought a second bottle, opened it, sniffed the cork, and shook his head. What a night! The third bottle made it—more than made it. Even I could appreciate its exceptional bouquet, its delicious taste. Success.

The dessert champagne—Dom Perignon—was perfect as always.

[*There is more to tell in connection with the incident of the wines as related above.*

A year or so after this dinner, we were in England and began to hear from several friends about a comical routine Maugham had done involving us in a fancy restaurant. How we had taken him to dinner and—here WSM is said to have done a most amusing imitation of me tasting wine in the manner of a professional vintner; calling imperiously for sommeliers; making a fuss; sending back bottle after bottle until I found one to my taste; behaving, generally, like a charter member of the nouveau riche, a true parvenu!

I suppose I would have been justified in being properly irritated about this, since the facts are exactly as I stated them earlier. He was the one who complained in the first instance; all I was trying to do was to please him, to be a good host. The second difficulty had had nothing to do with me at all. So far as I know, I had never before sent a bottle of wine back—I would not know enough about it to do so— nor have I had occasion to do so since.

So WSM's sketch of me was as inaccurate as it was unjust—and, I might add, ungracious. In the circumstances, once he said the wine was acid, what could I have done other than what I did?

Why, then, was I not annoyed with him? Why did I

65

take him to dinner again and again as often as I could? Why do I forgive his behavior?

Because he was a storyteller. That was his life and work and business and vocation and avocation. It was impossible for him to retell anything exactly as it had happened, just as it is impossible for Picasso to produce a photographic likeness. Each of these masters needs to reproduce in his own vision; to give a subject meaning and interpretation, color and design, a personal view. Otherwise it is not Picasso and it was not Maugham. He was a novelist, not a journalist.

Suppose it was tough on his friends now and then. It was a price we had to pay. We had to take it and not so much forgive him as understand him. Certainly he made us all into characters, and turned our actions into routines. If they were to be entertaining routines, we had to grant him the license of exaggeration, even of invention. He needed to be fanciful if he was to be anything.

Further, the way he told it may well be the way he saw it; and although he may not have been telling the truth from my point of view, he probably was from his.

Rather than resent this practice, we should all be grateful for it. Think of the pleasure and excitement and enlightenment it gave us over the years.]

1953. St. Jean–Cap Ferrat.

At Les Rochers today WSM notices the many French grammars, verb drills, language cards and recordings. He teases me about my apparent efforts to learn the language.

"You will begin to . . . make progress," he says, "only from that moment when you realize that what you are attempting is ... quite impossible."

He himself spoke French before he spoke English. Yet there is no mistaking his pronounced accent. He knows the language well, perhaps as well as his own, but handles it cautiously, carefully; at arm's length, as it were—as though it were a trick cigar which might blow up in his face at any moment. He tells of other adventures with language, of how he has always made it a point to acquire at least a working knowledge of the language of the country in which he happened to be living. Thus, he has pretty good Spanish, working Italian, excellent German, and even a little Russian.

"The languages of the Orient, however, eluded me," he says. "Perhaps because they ... never seemed to be languages, really. Rather a succession of ... sounds with varied vibrations. Still, the Orientals and I ... communicated happily enough."

As he goes on talking about language and language study, he tells us something which I had not known: he was first produced as a dramatist in Germany. The play was called SCHIFFBRÜCHIG (SHIPWRECKED). He thinks it was done in Berlin somewhere around 1902 or 1903. A few years later it was published in London, in an annual of some sort, under the title MARRIAGES ARE MADE IN HEAVEN.

It interests me, all this, and I press him for further information. Was he around when it was produced? What did he think of it? Did it encourage him to go on as a dramatist? Who was in it? And so on. I see him frown and grow tense. His memory on the matter fails and I abandon the subject.

In a moment we are discussing language study once again and I ask for help.

He says, "We all of us . . . learn in different ways, of course. It's largely a question of aptitudes. Many musicians who can memorize whole concerti easily find it impossible to remember a . . . telephone number. Memory is a trick, in any case. Still, there does seem to be a single principle which guides . . . learning, and that is—repetition. We repeat our . . . multiplication tables over and over again. It is the way in which animals are taught, even though it sometimes takes a . . . dog years to learn what a boy might learn in an hour. And in the theatre the French word for rehearsal is répétition, isn't it? For myself, let me tell you what I have found to be the most useful . . . method. It is simply to read aloud the language you are attempting to acquire. Plain things are best. Newspapers or popular magazines, including the recipe columns and the advice to the . . . lovelorn. One should avoid high-flown stuff. Stick to the language of the ordinary . . . man living his everyday life. Take the newspaper, then, and begin to read it aloud. You may be mispronouncing . . . dreadfully, accenting impossibly and making no sense whatever. No matter. Continue to read aloud confidently and at the . . . top of your voice. Do this each day for an hour or more. The results will astonish you. What happens, don't you see, is that your *body* begins to learn the language—to speak automatically, as it were. Your tongue and . . . teeth and palate and ears and the whole . . . complex nervous system begin to respond. Speech is a physical thing to a great . . . degree, and once your organs of speech are adept, they will transfer their abilities to the brain."

I interrupt briefly to tell him of the theory of acting expounded by the great French actor Coquelin, who pointed out that a proper use of the externals could lead to inner feelings; that pounding on a table would eventually make one angry in the same way that one who is angry will pound on a table. This is a system much discredited and out of fashion at the moment, yet I know a good many players who employ it.

Maugham goes on. "You will find as you . . . continue to read aloud—not always understanding all of what you are saying—that certain constructions and . . . locutions and forms stay in your mouth. And soon you will hear yourself saying . . . something and know the ineffable joy of having your listener comprehend. You will have completed the cycle of . . . communication which is, after all, the purpose of language."

A little later he returns to an elaboration of this idea. "When I was beginning to . . . learn to write, I was told that one learns to write by writing, so I diligently performed each day or each . . . night, but often I was not at all . . . pleased with the result and, by way of a short cut, it occurred to me that I ought to copy the masters. Not so much as a matter of imitation, but rather as a . . . way of acquiring the sense of form and flow. You've seen art students in the . . . museums everywhere in the world sitting before masterworks and copying them. I myself had often observed this . . . practice and considered that it might be of help to me in acquiring the skill I was attempting to acquire. My principal models were Henry Fielding and Charles . . . Dickens, William Hazlitt and Cardinal Newman, Defoe and, above all, Anthony Trollope. I set about the . . . matter quite systematically. For a long time I put apart a certain period of my . . . working time for the purpose of copying out pages from the works of my masters. It was tedious . . . work, as I remember it, sitting there squinting at the propped-up book before me and transferring the . . . material to my pad. Yet, I feel sure that

I gained a great deal from this practice—some think I gained too much!—and I'm not at all sorry I did it. I don't know what my . . . brain learned from all this, but I am certain that my . . . body learned to write."

It certainly did.

I reflect on my own use of a system of repetition. When I was first trying to learn something about films with a view to writing and directing them, I spent long evenings at the Goldwyn studio running certain films over and over again; getting the original stories and treatments and first drafts and final scripts out of the files; studying them before looking at the finished product on the screen. I must have seen John Ford's ARROWSMITH forty or fifty times and Ernst Lubitsch's TROUBLE IN PARADISE even more.

We talk of Trollope and of his methods. WSM recalls that it was Trollope who said that the most important equipment for a writer was a large piece of sealing wax with which to affix his posterior to his chair.

And I recall an account of Trollope going up to London to pick up a rejected manuscript from a publisher, getting on the train to return home, laying the bulky bundle on his lap face down, and beginning a new book on the backs of the pages of the rejected one.

"There you have it!" cries Maugham. "A perfect example of the . . . needed spirit for a career in the arts."

Later we are walking in the garden and an afterthought stops him. "A pity, really, that so much time . . . needs to be used in acquiring other languages. If you wait two or three centuries, I'm sure that it won't be necessary."

"Why not?"

"Because by then I think it safe to assume that English will be spoken everywhere in the world, not exclusively, but enough for all practical purposes."

"What makes you think so?"

"Why, it's happening already, isn't it? One can get about quite . . . comfortably in many parts of the world speaking English. It's more and more spoken. Mind you, I think the language itself will change or be changed and to our eyes and ears will be something as . . . curious as the English of Chaucer."

"All right," I say. "I'll wait."

1954. London.

He makes a sweeping statement about the Italians which makes me impatient.

"But that's just a generalization," I protest.

"Perhaps so," he says, "but without . . . generalization there would be no . . . conversation!"

1950. New York.

During a pause in the conversation last night, WSM said, "I should like to tell you of two recent experiences in my life which have . . . moved me and touched me very deeply. One took place only the other day in New York, in the main dining room of the Plaza. I was dining there with a friend. The maître d'hôtel came over and presented us with a lovely bottle of Krug. He explained that a gentleman in the dining room, having recognized me, and being eager to extend his . . . compliments and his appreciation for the pleasure which my work had given him, had sent this handsome gift. I accepted it, of course, with gratitude, and asked him to tell me who the gentleman was, in order that I might be able to thank him. The maître d' said that the gentleman had . . . departed some time earlier and had given instructions that the champagne was not to be brought to me until well after he had gone. I can't tell you how affected I was by this great and anonymous . . . kindness.

"The second incident took place some months ago when I was traveling in Spain. I stopped for a . . . night or two in a charming hotel in Cordova. When I was ready to leave, I had my bags and so on put into the car, returned to the desk, and asked for my . . . bill. The clerk at the desk said to me, 'Mr. Maugham, for you there is no bill.' I couldn't imagine why this should be. The clerk went on to explain that the owner of the hotel had expressed such indebtedness for the edification—that was the word he used —which my writings had given him and considered it such an honor to have me at his hotel that he implored me to accept his hospitality . . . gratis this time and at any time in the future when I chanced to be in Cordova. In all the years I have . . . traveled, such a thing has never happened to me, which, perhaps, explains why I was so very stirred by the incident."

I said I could not be more surprised at his surprise and that I found it hard to believe this was the first time such a thing had happened. He assured me his memory on the point was accurate and, in any case, does not see why this form of recognition should be common.

I said, "But I've been given to understand that in Europe men of letters are respected and revered. In France they're given tax benefits by the government which amount to subsidies. And didn't I read, only the other day, an account of Ibsen coming into his habitual café at one o'clock to read the papers—and everyone in the room rising as he entered and being reseated only after the celebrated man had taken his place?"

72

"Yes," says Maugham, "I suppose that's true." He muses for a moment and says, "I saw him once."

"Did you? Where?"

"In a café in Berlin. He came in and sat down at the table always reserved for him. His stammtisch. I must say, he looked extremely angry, vexed, and . . . disagreeable. But then, of course, he *was* all those things, wasn't he?"

Talk of Ibsen for a time; Strindberg, Hauptmann—their influence. He tells of meeting Hauptmann once with Max Beerbohm in Rapallo.

. . . WSM: "One matures to the light touch of serious matters, don't you think? My own early writings, the one-act plays and short stories, were frightfully . . . grim and totally unrelieved. The first one to reach the stage was a piece called A MAN OF HONOUR. Very strong. And LIZA OF LAMBETH, my first published . . . novel. A slum book, rather advanced for its time, I believe."

Ruth tells of recently coming across a twenty-five-cent pocket edition of LIZA OF LAMBETH in the railway station in Philadelphia. When she got on the train, she saw that Bob Sherwood [*Robert E. Sherwood*] had bought a copy for Madeline [*Mrs. Sherwood*].

Maugham: "I'm very much in favor of cheap reprints. They widen one's readership so. Of course, from a . . . financial point of view it means little. We get—what is it? —a penny a copy. Well, even if you sell a . . . million, that's only ten thousand dollars."

It takes me a minute to check his arithmetic. I'm sure he's right, but I know he's wrong. No, he's right.

Ruth says, "I thought the picnic scene was just great."

Maugham: "The picnic scene. Forgive me. I haven't . . . read that damned book in forty years."

(I have noticed that this is nearly a mannerism. When-

73

ever an early work is mentioned he says he has not read it in forty years. Why forty? I wonder.)

He begins to talk about the writing of LIZA OF LAMBETH and of some of his other early work.

His routine in those days began with a full day at St. Thomas's. At 6:30 P.M. he would return to his lodgings and have what he referred to as "a combination high tea and dinner." Then he would sit down and write for as long as he could, which meant until he was exhausted, whereupon he would go to bed, rise early, be off for another day at St. Thomas's, until the evening again: eat, write, sleep, and so on.

It leads me to comment that apparently real writers, born writers, usually find a way to set it down, no matter how difficult the circumstances. I wonder if often these conditions cause the writing—the explosive power when the stored-up creative energy is released. Think of Faulkner working his shift as a—what was it?—stoker, watchman, engineer of some sort in a boiler room, and writing when he could. Melville at his customs job. Dickens, the court stenographer; Trollope, the Postal Surveyor; Wallace Stevens, the executive; Giraudoux, the diplomat; Thornton, the schoolmaster; Maugham at the hospital.

"I can't say that my life was hard, really—except that I was early and often with no . . . money whatsoever."

Ruth asks, "Is that why you began to write, then? To make some money?"

Maugham: "No, I don't think so. I think I'd have been a writer in any case, but, of course, if I'd had . . . money I'm sure I'd have written much differently."

We are soon onto OF HUMAN BONDAGE.

Maugham says, "Decent people often say to me, 'Why don't you write another OF HUMAN BONDAGE?' and I reply,

'Because I've only lived one life. It took me thirty years of living to possess the material for that one work.' "

I ask, "But what about the thirty years that followed?"

He thinks for a moment, as though reviewing them, and says simply, "Well, the next thirty weren't . . . quite so fruitful."

1958. St. Jean–Cap Ferrat.

The butler: "What wine, sir?"

WSM: "The Château Margaux, '41. Just a moment." (To Ruth): "Are you still off wine?"

Ruth: "Yes."

WSM (to me): "And you, too?"

Me: "I'm afraid so."

WSM (to the butler): "Open a half-bottle, then."

The butler: "Yes, sir."

WSM: "I'm not . . . mean, you know, but I am . . . frugal."

1948. London.

He comes in tonight and says to Ruth, almost at once, "Stand up and let me look at you, darling. It has reached me that you have become one of the . . . ten best-dressed women in America."

"I haven't heard about it," says Ruth.

"My information is . . . *never* wrong," he says. "My name is Ashenden."

Ruth stands up. He clucks about awhile and adds, "My information *was* wrong. You are surely one of the . . . nine."

She is wearing her anniversary-gift emerald. WSM be-

75

comes a loony music-hall turn as he looks at it, does a take, puts his head closer, pretends to be blinded, and so on. Wonderfully comic and skillful. (It bears out once again the notion that novelists are actors within.) He drops his act and discusses the emerald, then other emeralds, then *all* emeralds, with knowledge and wit. Africa, India, emeralds.

He wants to know our immediate plans. Ruth tells him we are on our way to California to work on ADAM'S RIB with George and Spence and Kate. He says he has heard all about it from George and that it sounded expert and funny.

"I shall go to see it," he promises.

He talks of YEARS AGO [*an autobiographical play written by my wife*] and asks Ruth if it is all true.

"I admired it so much," he says, "but I don't know if I should praise you as a playwright or as a . . . memoirist."

"Why not both?" asks Ruth gaily.

"Very well, then, both."

I interpose an anecdote. "Thornton says he once asked Gertrude Stein, 'Gertrude, tell me. Why do you write?' and that she answered at once, flinging her arms wide, 'Oh —for praise, for praise, for praise!' "

My loyal Ruth responds. As for WSM, I swear the sound which came out of him was "Harumpphh!"

Memoirist. The word echoes in my ear. Is there such a word in English or is WSM doing what bilingual people often do: interchange words?

"Is 'memoirist' a word?" I ask him.

"Of course."

"French or English?"

He thinks, but only for a split second. "English," he says.

"I've never heard it before."

"Well, you have . . . now."

He seems touchy. I tell him about John Steinbeck's reply to an editor who objected, "But, Mr. Steinbeck, there's no such word!" "Never mind," replied Steinbeck. "If the book's a hit, there *will* be."

Maugham laughs hard at this, then does a surprising thing. He makes me tell it again so as to be sure he has it right.

"I shall want to . . . repeat that," he explains. "Thank you."

We bounce back to YEARS AGO. Ruth explains that she believes the play to be true in spirit and in character, knows it to be largely based on actual incidents, but does not claim anything like word-for-word recall.

"Yes," he says. "I should have . . . known all that without asking. It's a . . . fine play—no, better than fine—it's a *human* play."

There is discussion of the play as an expression of the great American theme of opportunity. He speaks of America and Americans with warmth and gratitude.

He says, "It may be that Europeans sometimes have a . . . poor opinion of Americans because the Americans they meet are—or used to be—of a special sort. Moneyed and snobbish."

He tells the following anecdote: Lloyd Osbourne, the adopted son of Robert Louis Stevenson, was living at Antibes one summer with his wife, Ethel. A famous Ziegfeld beauty by the name of Ruby De Remer came to Antibes and got to know the Osbournes.

She entertained them again and again, sent flowers and gifts, and was far more deferential and polite than any American the Osbournes had ever met.

77

They noticed that she always called Mrs. Osbourne "Lady"—but let it pass as an Americanism of some sort.

One day, at the beauty parlor, Ruby and a friend met Mrs. Osbourne. Ruby introduced her as "Lady Osbourne."

"But I'm not 'Lady' Osbourne," she protested.

"You *must* be!" insisted Ruby. "Isn't your husband '*Lord*' Osbourne?"

1960. Beverly Hills.

Charlie [*Charles Brackett, writer and film producer*] tells a Maugham story. Apocryphal? Does it belong here? Lady Cunard, he relates, once entertained WSM at dinner. Directly following, WSM announced he had to leave. Lady Cunard protested.

Maugham said, "I must get to bed if I want to keep my youth."

Lady Cunard said, "Oh, but why didn't you bring him? We would have *loved* having him!"

[*Years later, sitting alone with WSM, I repeat the above and ask him if there is any truth in it.*

"*Yes,*" *he says,* "*some. It was a joke I'd heard at the . . . Garrick and told to Lady Cunard. I suppose she then repeated it, casting me in the major role. I see her point. It's better—more . . . telling her way.*"

"*And you don't resent her having done that?*"

"*No, no—having practiced the art of elaboration and substitution all my life, I should be the . . . last one to take offense. We all use it. Didn't Eliot name it—rather neatly, I thought—'The Objective Correlative'?*"]

17 July 1951. St. Jean—Cap Ferrat.

Longevity is largely a matter of luck, if not wholly so. Consider WSM here. Seventy-eight in January. A life far from simple or still. The hazards of illness (he has had two bouts with tuberculosis), of travel (he has been damn near everywhere), of dissipation (men and women, much drinking and rich eating and smoking and partying), of worry (wife and daughter and other complex relationships)—yet here he is, hale. He is working away daily, Alan tells me, on his TV project. There are motion-picture plans in the works. Last night he talked at great length about the lecture he has just completed and which he is to deliver in London in October.

[*This memorable address*, THE WRITER'S POINT OF VIEW, *a milestone in WSM's life, was delivered on Wednesday, October 24, 1951, at the Kingsway Hall, London, under the auspices of the National Book League with enormous success.*]

He is now, he says, in the process of making the corrections. He reads late into the night, not for pleasure, but researching his next essay. He does not tell us what the subject is. Cocktails before lunch, before dinner; wine with both meals; brandy and cigars afterward. Climbing the steps to the pool every day—some days, when the weather is especially warm, more than once.

And last night, showing us all over Villefranche, clambering about the hills, streets, and back alleys and odd byways.

Sitting at the café in the port, he talks of the long trip to Egypt which he is soon to make. He has not decided about which parts of the journey to fly.

He says, "I should hate to . . . miss certain things and there are others one *should* miss."

Luck. The tiniest slip last night speeding up that dangerous road with a show-off chauffeur and all the keeping of the rules and diet and vitamins and eight hours' sleep would have helped not at all. Think of the millions of such moments in his long life, in his full time.

Nowhere in the world is there better food than at Maugham's house—he sees to it. Yet, last night he insisted upon taking us up to the Château Madrid on the Middle Corniche. It is a famous restaurant perched on a hill overlooking the Cap Ferrat peninsula. Sitting at a window table, you have the illusion of being in a hovering helicopter. We have seen it from below, but have never been there.

Ruth hates those high winding roads and tells Maugham so.

"I get frightened," she says.

"You won't be," he assures her. "I'll see to it."

When we assemble in the courtyard, the butler appears with a tray bearing four glasses.

"What's this?" asks Ruth.

"Something to take your . . . terror away," says Maugham.

"I don't drink."

"I know you don't, but drink this. I'm a . . . doctor, remember."

We drink. It is a considerable prescription.

The driver, eager to prove he can handle this American car as well as anyone, drives too fast, recklessly, and ought to be arrested and I keep hoping he will be—but we sing French folk songs all the way and arrive at the Château

Madrid happily. What the hell was *in* that glass? Our host does not tell.

We order consommé and lobster. The consommé comes and goes. We wait. I can see WSM getting restive and I try all sorts of talk to divert him and put him at ease. But he, accustomed to swift service, is impatient and after half an hour sends, magisterially, for the headwaiter. The headwaiter comes over and bows and Maugham says: "What are they . . . doing? *Catching* that lobster?"

I must say, I had expected something more sparkling from the lips of this ranking man of letters.

The headwaiter does his standard sickly grin, shrugs, and, with a couple of "Tout de suites," moves off.

The lobster, when it finally arrives, is no good and Maugham says so.

"What the hell," says Ruth. "We came for the view, didn't we?"

Unfortified for the trip down, I take the driver aside and tell him that I do not like the way he drove up and would he please drive down more carefully, because my wife, etc. He scowls. I tip him. He smiles and drives down as though pushing a baby carriage. WSM tells him to go a little faster, please. The driver say, "Oui, m'sieu"—but does not do it.

We stop in Villefranche (shades of Scott Fitzgerald!) for coffee and sightseeing, then back to the Villa Mauresque late. I am tired and highly stimulated.

1951. St. Jean–Cap Ferrat.

Last night he urges us to read Edmund Burke. "There," he says, "is a use of the English language. I never realized how abundant are its riches until becoming

... familiar with the writings of Edmund Burke."

On another occasion he recommended Anthony Trollope. I recall to him that Trollope was one of Woollcott's passions as well.

"He carries you to his next page," says WSM. "Is there anything more important for a storyteller than that?"

"Yes," I say. "Not to let you down at the end."

"I never ... do," he says.

1954. London.

He is smoking more than ever before. I notice it and mention it.

"Yes," he admits, "I'm trying to ... make up for lost time."

"How do you mean?"

"Well, last year I fell ill and my ... doctor made me promise to stop smoking for at least three months. I stopped and after a few days found myself ... more miserable than I'd been in years. I enjoyed nothing. My rhythms were ... shattered and my reflexes insulted. I turned as mean as cat's meat, but the ... blighter had frightened me and I continued to abstain. After a month I thought I would die of the ... deprivation sooner than of the danger. Still, I persisted. He'd not only frightened me, but *successfully* frightened me. I quit on the fourth of January and smoked ... not at all until the fourth of March. That was two-thirds of the way through, and I gave it up. I didn't feel ... disgraced any more than a Channel swimmer does who makes it two-thirds of the way across. That damned doctor assured me that if I stopped for three months I'd never wish to ... smoke again. He was wrong. I wanted it . . . more and more. So, as you see, I'm smoking again. I feel no ill effects, my sweet . . . nature has returned, and all is well."

"But maybe if you *had* stopped for three months, you never *would've* wanted to smoke again. Now you'll never know."

He is stony. "Don't be a . . . bloody bore," he says.

"You're like a movie producer I know in Hollywood," I persist.

"Heaven forbid," he says.

"He'd had a severe heart attack and said to me, 'Dr. Prinzmetal told me I could go back to the studio and work if I promised him that I'd lie down three times every day for an hour each time—once in the morning and once after lunch and once around five or six o'clock before I went home. I tried it for a few days and it knocked the hell out of my schedule. So you want to know what I did? I called up Dr. Prinzmetal, I got him purposely in the morning when he was real busy in his office, and I gave him a fast heart-to-heart. I said to him, "Listen, Doctor, how would this be? Instead of lying down three times for an hour each time, I'm willing to lie down five times a day—not three, *five!*" So he said, "That's even better." And I said, "But as long as it's going to be five times, how about if I just make it a half an hour each time?" And you want to know something? The schmuck *went* for it!' "

WSM smiles at first, laughs a little, and is suddenly sober.

"And you think I'm . . . like that?"

"In a way, yes. You set up this contest with the doctor and you beat him at it. You outsmart him, as you would in a bridge game. But who's the loser?"

"Shut up," he says, and lights a cigarette defiantly.

1958. St. Jean–Cap Ferrat.

He and Alan tell us, with a certain macabre glee, about their bonfire nights.

They sit before the fire in the sitting room evening after evening, with cartons and boxes full of old papers, notes, letters, documents, fragments. First acts, unsent letters— and so on.

WSM examines each item and nine times or so out of ten hands it over to Alan, who puts it on the fire.

"I find it . . . salutary," says WSM.

"I find it wicked," I say boldly.

"So?"

"Yes. There goes up in smoke an important part of the history of contemporary literature."

"Steady."

"I mean it. You may not always be the best judge of what ought to be destroyed. Oh, sure—personal stuff or anything you feel might be wounding or damaging—"

"Mind your . . . business," he says.

Then, as though to put me properly in my place, he tells of finding an unproduced, unpublished four-act play the other night.

"I didn't burn that at once, did I, Alan? I saved it out, took it up to . . . bed with me and read it. Damned good. It made me . . . laugh a lot. We burned it the *next* night."

"There must be another copy somewhere," I say. "It'll turn up."

"Are you trying to get a rise out of me? You're not succeeding. Save your breath to cool your . . . porridge. I remember the circumstances ever so clearly. I chanced to meet Charles Hawtrey at the Atheneum one afternoon. I

admired him so much. He asked me to . . . write a play for
him. I was a fashionable . . . dramatist at the time, still I
was pleased and flattered and told him I would think on it.
A few months later I surprised him by calling round to see
him and delivering my manuscript. We had a drink in his
. . . dressing room and he was full of bubble and excitement. We parted. You can imagine how astonished I was
when I heard nothing for days. A week went by. He rang
me up and asked me to come by. I did. He was all enthusiasm for the play and for his role and . . . talked of other
players and so on endlessly. Yet, I knew something was not
as it should be. After a very long time he tentatively suggested a small, unimportant change. I nodded. Then another. I agreed. Now he uttered a line he . . . wished to
insert. Not bad, you understand, but not *mine*. I demurred
and told him I would take it under advisement. He made
further suggestions, a good many—he was an extremely
creative man—but by now I had stopped listening. When
he had done, I picked up the . . . manuscript and said I
would give his ideas consideration. We parted. I was, as
you can imagine, greatly irritated. In the morning, however, I called myself a fool, decided I was making too . . .
much of a trifle—after all, a production by Hawtrey would
ensure success and pad my purse—he was then the most
popular player in London, with an enormous following. I
sat down at my desk and opened the . . . manuscript I'd
collected from him the night before. One sight of a single
page with his scribblings, and parentheses indicating cuts,
and substituted words—I remember two lines turned about
so as to put the joke word at the end—easier for the player,
I take it, but destructive to the style—and I was soon at a
. . . boil. I destroyed the manuscript and all the other copies
save one—for my files. That was the one we put into that

85

flame a few nights ago. Odd. I saw Hawtrey many times after that and we remained . . . good friends until his death —but he never . . . mentioned my play again. Nor did I."

I ask if some of the material he is so systematically destroying might not be of value to an eventual biographer.

He says that's just it. There is to be no biographer and no biography. Ever? Ever.

"Why not?"

"Because I don't . . . wish it."

"But what's to prevent someone from doing it anyway?"

"Nothing. But they'll get no assistance from me or from my . . . bones."

[*He must have changed his mind about this, because I note that three books have been published since that time —all, apparently, with his full cooperation:* W. SOMERSET MAUGHAM *by Karl G. Pfeiffer* (*1959*); SOMERSET MAUGHAM *by Richard A. Cordell* (*1961*); *and* THE TWO WORLDS OF SOMERSET MAUGHAM *by Wilmon Menard* (*1965*).]

Talk of the letters begins. WSM lived for the greater part of his life in a letter-writing world. People wrote to one another continuously. Even after phones were in common use it was considered more polite to write.

He has gone into the legalities of it all and says that, according to British law, the letter itself—that is to say, the piece of paper—is the property of the recipient. But the contents of the letter remain the property of the writer. Mrs. Patrick Campbell could not publish her correspondence with Shaw because Shaw would not grant his permission. She had her letters (I remember her pulling a handful of them from her handbag one day in New York and showing them to me) and he could not reclaim them

—but he could prevent them from being published and he did.

"I'm going to ask all . . . my friends to return my letters to me," says Maugham.

We are silent.

"My work will speak for me, I hope, as . . . long as anyone is interested."

1954. London.

Maugham says this afternoon that Voltaire's CANDIDE is his touchstone. I ask him to elaborate. He says that whenever he is ready to begin to set down a piece of fiction—short story or novel—he rereads CANDIDE to remind him that it is possible to be good as well as light, lucid as well as philosophic, witty and graceful and (did he say brief?)—anyway—as well as classic. That is what makes it his touchstone. He reads it in French. He suspects that his influences are mainly French.

1950. New York.

He says, "Imagine it. I was . . . walking along the street today—Madison Avenue, I think—when a strange woman stepped up to me and inquired, 'Mr. Maugham?' I tipped my hat and nodded. She . . . touched me and said, 'I want to thank you for hundreds of . . . wonderful hours of entertainment,' and off she went. Now, you must admit that's better than any . . . possible fulsome review in a literary journal."

He goes on. "I'm having a grand time not only because I'm . . . making pots of money out of the . . . television and the film, but all my expenses are being paid somehow. It has been explained to me, but I don't understand it and I've no intention of . . . trying to do so. Of course, if I were paying the expenses, I'd make . . . damned sure I did understand. And I'm having a splendid run at cards, too. So you see, all is well."

He has been shopping. "I love to shop in New York," he says. "It's by far the most . . . varied, rich, and complete bazaar in all the world. I dote on Macy's and Bloomingdale's, especially the adventure of the . . . escalators. Recently, in one day, I bought pajamas at Macy's, grand tinned goods at Gristede's, a . . . Renoir at Rosenberg's, and at Max Schling's some seeds for golden bantam corn. How can anyone . . . deprecate a city where such a . . . day is possible?"

October 1954. London.

WSM has many friends here, as well as his share of detractors. The latter make much of his residence abroad, although they are perfectly willing to think it charming in others—Max Beerbohm, for example.

It is said of him that he likes only the very rich. I can testify that this is not true.

He is accused of being a snob. Hard to say. What, exactly, is a snob? It means one thing at home, another here, and in Paris—where the word is adored (pronounced "snawb")—it has a meaning of its own. By certain definitions, yes, I suppose he could be called that—and would readily admit it, I think.

Today xx attacked his patriotism. Look who's talking! He claims that Maugham is actually "homeless, stateless, and rootless."

He goes on.

"That's not a home in France, it's a museum he lives in, a safe. And all that travel—he loathes it, actually. It's a tax dodge. If he stays here for more than a hundred and eighty-three days, they'll nab him—or in France—that's why he flits so."

I hear righteousness in the tones, but envy as well.

January 1943. New York.

I am on a two-day pass and feel liberated. Why, then, do I want to do nothing more than hang about the apartment and do next to nothing?

We arrange books. I come upon a strange one, THE SALMAGUNDI BIRTHDAY BOOK—a Victorian relic, and one of Ruth's treasures.

A beautiful old binding; blank pages for signatures; and facing pages upon which are printed sentiments—two for each date, one for the man and one for the lady.

The messages are no more reliable than fortune cookies, but even those give you a jolt now and then. Although these are drawn from the works of hundreds of authors and poets from Matthew Arnold and John Donne through Victor Hugo and Percy Bysshe Shelley to William Wordsworth and Edward Young, there are, peppered throughout, some saucy items.

Mine (November 24) reads: "I will not choose what many men desire, because I will not jump with common spirits, and rank me with the barbarous multitudes.—Shakespeare, THE MERCHANT OF VENICE"

Close enough.

Ruth's (October 30) says: "She was a lovely young

woman, more sentimental than accomplished, wanting the polish of a person often in society, but full of character.—Hawthorne"

I say to her, "Why didn't you show me that *before* we got married?"

I turn to January 25—Maugham's.

It reads: "A young man with gray deliberation, cold and systematic in his plans, and all his plans were evil. —Lamb"

In this copy the words "A young" have been crossed out. Over them is written "An old" and the passage is signed: "W. Somerset Maugham."

June 1962. New York.

Holy God. It has happened. WSM has written and published a personal (*too* personal?) memoir of his life with Syrie. The meeting, the affair, the pregnancy, her divorce, the pressures, the marriage and its subsequent pains.

For a long time now there have been rumors and intimations of a private notebook which Maugham is said to be continuously writing and which is to be published after his death. Some say he works on it daily and keeps it under lock and key. Others claim to have seen these notebooks on a shelf over his bed. It is said that he sets down his feelings and opinions about anything and everyone and everything without restraint of any kind. Someone close to him told me once that this was to be WSM's last great joke—a bomb timed to explode after his final departure.

Like most rumors, it appears that these were not entirely accurate, although they were based remotely upon fact.

The bomb has been exploded. Accidentally? What caused it? Why now? These revelations (SHOW, July, 1962) are shattering, blush-making, shabby, sordid, embarrassing, and absolutely enthralling. It goes without saying that they are stunningly written. For my taste, it is the best writing he has done in years. Fine writing comes of deep feeling, and this account is the residue of long-smoldering passion.

In publishing this material, WSM has placed his friends in a difficult position. One is forced to take sides. You are either for him or against him. We are told that in England, where the material (in a somewhat bowdlerized form) was published in THE SUNDAY EXPRESS, the greater number of his friends and acquaintances and even readers have turned against him. Certain doors—important doors—are closed to him forever. Many intimates threaten to cut him dead. His behavior has been described variously as outrageous, reprehensible, larky, courageous, ungentlemanly, insane, madly funny, bitchy, campy, and completely justified.

What table talk it provides! What altercations it has provoked!

The upper crust is horrified at this breach of conduct by a man who is not only the very model of a British gentleman, but—good Heavens!—a Companion of Honour.

The complex dichotomy of private versus public behavior is here represented. To some guardians of manners and morals it does not matter what you do so long as you do it in private and keep it to yourself. A gentleman may kiss, but he may not tell. Not even if he tells it well?

This last point is what complicates the matter. Syrie, who is so badly used in this article, is dead and cannot defend herself, cannot tell her side of the story. In fact, no one can. Only two persons ever knew the truth—rather, the facts—and only one is here to tell. Thinking this one layer deeper—what would it matter if Syrie *were* alive? What would she do? Say? Write?

Remember when WSM published CAKES AND ALE in 1930 there was great feeling in certain literary quarters that he had libeled Thomas Hardy by drawing him uncomplimentarily and naming him Edward Driffield. (Hardy had recently died, which to some compounded Maugham's misdeed by adding cowardice to cruelty.) Worse, the portrait of Mrs. Hardy was not complimentary. Still worse, he had pilloried Hugh Walpole by caricaturing him as Alroy Kear.

Maugham denied it at the time, insisted he had met Hardy only once and did not know him well enough to draw him, but this was considered by the objectors a backing down.

A passionate Hardy defender named Elinor Mordaunt then dashed off a 300-page riposte in the form of a novel. It was called GIN AND BITTERS and contained a murderous portrait of Somerset Maugham. Alas for the author, it was a wet firecracker. In these things, it is not right or wrong which matters, but skill. Not truth, but talent. CAKES AND ALE was and is read, GIN AND BITTERS is forgotten.

(That saying Pop used to repeat: "There are three sides to every story—yours, his, and the truth.")

In a certain sense, Maugham has a perfect right to disseminate his side of the affair, since there are a good many unofficial ones about.

The details of the marriage itself, for example. I have heard on many occasions, and with only slight variations, this said-to-be-true version: that Syrie was pregnant, came to New York, and asked WSM to marry her. He refused.

Edward Sheldon [*American dramatist, 1886–1946*] sent for him and convinced him to do the right thing. Maugham agreed. A ceremony was held at the Hotel Brevoort. Maugham kissed his bride and went off to the South Seas with Gerald Haxton.

But hold. In WSM's account, he agrees to marry his pregnant girl friend, but cannot, since her divorce from Mr. Wellcome is not yet final. So he goes to Tahiti (yes, with Gerald Haxton as secretary-assistant) to research THE MOON AND SIXPENCE. Upon his return, he leaves Haxton in Chicago, returns to New York, and marries Syrie in New Jersey. Their child is (I cannot make it out from his narrative) one or two years old. His chronology is probably accurate. Moreover, if he says they were married in New Jersey, I believe they were. Ethel Barrymore once told us about attending the wedding at the Brevoort —perhaps she meant the reception following. History is tricky, memories grow dim, fact and fancy intermingle.

He once said to me: "My wedding lacked not only ... sentiment, but what is more important ... glamour. I remember that immediately before the Judge in New Jersey married us he ... fined a drunk; and immediately after, he fined another."

Time. I hardly knew Syrie, but the Syrie I knew was a quiet, diffident, sweet lady—with great ability in her field of interior decoration. In WSM's account we get a wild gadabout, breaking homes and hearts and causing havoc simply by being a dazzling demi-rep.

Before one weeps over the picture of the betrayed girl in trouble, it is well to remember that Syrie was thirty-seven when they were married. The drama was entirely adult.

Still, I do not feel it is my business to take sides, to

judge, to moralize. He did what he wanted to do, perhaps what he had to do.

[*When my novel* BLOW UP A STORM *was published, someone at Random House dug out a quote of mine from somewhere for the jacket: "To find a self, to express that self, and to take the consequences—is the pattern of a creative life." I do not remember writing it or saying it, but I am willing to stand by it. This work of WSM is a manifestation of the creed.*]

I do not believe he is demented, or under influence or pressure. He is an old man aware of impending death and he wants to set the record straight. His sense of order has always been highly developed.

Ruth has solved the problem in her own way—by refusing to read a word of this stuff. She loves Maugham and does not want to be tested. (She did not always love him. When she first met him, in 1928, she found him cold and cruel and forbidding. Later he changed—at least, to her. I once heard her say to him, "Why weren't you always as nice as you are now?" And he replied, "I always was. You simply couldn't see it. Your vision has improved, I'm happy to observe.") She feels close to him. He has been a good friend over the years and in many places and circumstances. In England, in New York, in Chicago, in Beverly Hills, in France.

In England he asks her to go to Brighton with him, where, he claims, Ruth Chatterton is ruining his play THE CONSTANT WIFE. After the performance my Ruth says to him, "Ruth Chatterton is wonderful. It's the play that needs fixing."

He tells this and laughs and says now that both Ruths were right.

In Chicago, 1940, Maugham is visiting on British government business. Ruth is there, playing in HERE TODAY and celebrating her twenty-fifth year on the stage. Jones, eleven [*Jones Harris, my wife's son*], comes to Chicago to spend the Christmas holidays. A party is arranged. Ruth, Jones, the Lunts, Maugham. A great success.

At midnight WSM rises and says gravely to Jones, "I believe the time has come for all those under sixteen and over sixty-six to retire."

In Beverly Hills he takes Ruth to concerts at the Hollywood Bowl, to dinners, and to parties, helping her over a bad patch of time.

Once he finds on her bookshelves in New York a first edition of OF HUMAN BONDAGE. He inscribes it warmly on the flyleaf, then turns to the title page and under the printed author's name writes: "W. Somerset Maugham." He returns the book to the shelf, having quietly and practically increased its value.

In France he urged us to come to St. Jean–Cap Ferrat, helped us find a house to rent, and proved, for the many months we lived there, a warm and helpful neighbor.

Remembering all this, Ruth is not so quick to want to judge him. Perhaps a lapse—very well, it is *his* lapse. He is doubtless prepared to take the consequences. She remains his friend.

Me, I do not know what I think or feel about all this. I do know that it is one hell of a marvelous piece of writing.

[*There were later developments, perhaps triggered in part by the publication of this material. He quarreled with Liza and, in an attempt to disinherit her, made a number of clumsy, ill-advised moves. He tried to adopt Alan Searle.*

Liza brought a suit to prevent this. The French courts voided the adoption. He sold some of his pictures. Again Liza made a claim and again Maugham's plan was frustrated. He kept trying gambit after gambit—but, so far as I know, he did not, in the end, have his way.

According to our correspondence with Alan, WSM at the end was a broken, bitter, miserable old man—bereft and abandoned by all his relatives, defiant and remorseful by turns. An unhappy ending indeed.]

There is more in this series of articles to come, they say, worse than this. I wonder. It seems to me he has gone about as far as he can go. Why did he? For an answer, I take him at his word—that he wanted to say what he felt he had left unsaid.

1954. London.

He says, "I'm going to tell you something . . . privately which I can't very well say publicly at the peril of seeming ungrateful or unappreciative or ungracious; and that is that I find this Grand Old Man stuff excessively . . . irksome. I don't in the least feel like a Grand Old Man, but to say so would . . . spoil the fun and I shouldn't like to be a spoilsport. We British are fond of our old people. We like to dress them up and applaud them, whether they're kings or queens or prima donnas or painters. If they're old, they're good; like a Stradivarius or an antique—valuable. The French tolerate them—the old, that is—which seems to me more . . . sensible. The Americans ignore them, more sensible still; and some African tribes simply throw them away, which . . . seems to me the most sensible of all. Don't you see how embarrassing it is to have attention

called to one's age and at the same . . . time one's infirmi-
ties? Mine are not all my . . . fault. I can't help my fading
sight, or my poor hearing, or my wrinkled crocodile skin,
and I . . . dislike having attention called to any of these
things. In point of fact, what old people would like best of
all would . . . be to be left alone. But one can't say that.
Now, can one?"

July 1962. New York.

The August issue of SHOW is out and breathing
is easier. This installment, the final one, is less personal
than the last, more general. Yes, there is a sum-up, but it
is sort of philosophical and neither private nor acrimo-
nious. It is also, thank fortune, the end.

A question arises: how did SHOW get these publication
rights? It is a handsome, classy publication, all right, but
it is also new. Its circulation cannot be impressive, not yet.
Why, then, of all possible outlets, is this the one? Can it
be that other magazines—MC CALL'S, LADIES' HOME JOUR-
NAL, COSMOPOLITAN, THE SATURDAY EVENING POST, RED-
BOOK, and so on—rejected the material on the grounds of
subject matter? I would like to know. Was it fear of libel?
Or was it a plain, simple case of money? SHOW is rich, I
gather, and may have bid the most.

I have heard harsh words spoken on the subject. I have
heard WSM called a "cad." When I commented that it had
been some time since I had heard that word spoken, the
reply was "Well, in this case, there *is* no other word!" As
I understand it, the meaning is opposite to "gentleman."
And the meaning of "gentleman"? Never mind reaching
for the dictionary—what does it mean? It has been defined
as "one who never, knowingly, inflicts pain." Will that do?

In this instance, I am afraid that my friend WSM *did* knowingly inflict pain—upon Syrie's friends and, more importantly, upon his daughter and indirectly upon his grandchildren.

[*In time to come he was to deny Liza as his daughter. At this, even his closest friends had to bite on the nail. This was going far indeed. When did he decide to take this foolish position? He had acknowledged her as his daughter for forty years or more. Even in the notorious, abusive* SHOW *articles he made constant references to "our daughter."*

It all had the air of an angry old man flailing about desperately, carelessly, with an eye to victory only, the spoils at any price.

Now comes the matter of advice. I know that he usually disdained the idea of "experts," yet in matters involving such complicated elements as wills and estates and taxes and inheritances one would think that advice should be sought. Can it be that he got (and accepted) bad advice? I cannot believe that a man so civilized and intelligent— to say nothing of crafty—would plunge into lawsuits and countersuits on his own whims or impulses. Can it be that he was being fleeced again somehow?

In family dramas the facts are hard to come by. Who knows?

A story about WSM and Liza and her husband made the rounds some years ago. I heard it a dozen times from different people, each time in a slightly different mutation.

This is how he himself told it to us:

"Liza came down here with John a while ago. They had an idea—rather brilliant, actually—of how to avoid excessive . . . death duties. I like John. He's not only in-

telligent, but wise. The scheme involved . . . turning over much of my estate now. I would retain use of it, you see, but legal provision would have been made for its . . .transfer. I declined. And when Liza asked, 'But why won't you, Pa?' I said, 'Because, my dear, I have . . . read KING LEAR.' We all had a good laugh over that."

Please note well the final line. What he said he said as a joke. Usually, when the story is repeated, Lord John Hope and Liza are somehow characterized as cleverly scheming and WSM as outfoxing them. Neither color is true. Their idea was probably sensible and practical and the sort of thing rich families do all the time in all countries. WSM was being cantankerous and selfish, but tried to remove some of the strain with a joke—and a damned good one, too.

I recall another occasion when he refused to turn over sums to Liza on the spot. At that time his conscious concern was for her good.

He may have been a careful man, but he was not stingy. He gave great gifts and made countless bequests—among them, the much coveted Somerset Maugham Award.

This prize of about £500 is given annually to a British writer who has published literary work of outstanding promise. It is administered by a committee of the Society of Authors, Playwrights and Composers.

Maugham has stated that the purpose of the prize is to encourage young writers to travel and acquaint themselves with the manners and customs of foreign countries. The candidate must be a British subject by birth, under thirty, and must agree to spend not less than three months outside the United Kingdom, using the prize money for the journey.

It has proved to be an important and valuable stimulus

to contemporary British writing and would not exist but for the thoughtfulness and sensitivity and generosity of WSM.]

1958. Nice.

A mauvais quart d'heure tonight at the Villa Mauresque develops into a mauvais deux heures.

I had been talking about Thornton and the countless debts I owe him. He has been a kind and firm master and has done more for me, I suppose, than any other man.

I go on to say that, despite his enormous popularity and literary standing, he seems to me less appreciated in America than he should be. And I wonder in passing whether this might not be a result of the fact that he is not and never has been a politically aware man. He has always been a scholar and a teacher, an academic person rather than a social one.

WSM lights a cigarette with swift, nervous, birdlike movements. "I don't see that that has ... anything to do with it."

I had meant to pose a question, not to provide an answer, but somehow the discussion gets away from me. "But isn't a writer supposed to reflect his times?" I ask. "Wasn't Chekhov politically aware? Wasn't Dickens? Isn't Ernest Hemingway? And what about—?"

This is as far as I get.

Maugham is on his feet. "Rubbish!" he shouts after a good deal of difficulty in enunciating the word. Then, not completely pleased with the force of it, he rasps out a second, higher reading, "*Rubbish!* This idea of writers being politicians and pundits ... nauseates me. Politics is a profession and so is writing and I don't see that they have any real connection unless a writer is . . . foolish enough to choose a political figure as a character. Or unless a political figure is misguided enough to attempt to write. I've done what I do for a very . . . long time and I can assure you that I know what I'm talking about."

"I'm sure you do."

"Oh, are you?" he drips. "The trouble with these well-meaning creatures who get themselves all involved in . . . causes of one sort or another and allow their feelings about such things to spill over into their work is that they . . . run the risk of becoming swiftly outdated. Causes change, don't you know, and so do issues. And if these are substituted for lasting things, the works themselves become old newspapers and . . . magazines. Look at Wells and . . . Galsworthy. Oh, yes, it's true enough that Dickens used every sort of situation and condition, but that's not what made him great, nor is it what makes his work live. We don't much care about the social implications or the injustices on the statistical scale." (His passion is such that his stammer has disappeared. Strange, because as a rule when he gets excited the stammer gets worse. Now he enunciates even so difficult a phrase as "statistical scale" with apparent ease.) "I'm a storyteller and I don't feel I need to apologize for that. It's a perfectly honorable calling. I don't need to pretend that the stories I tell are going to cure the ills of the world or influence men to be good rather than bad. If it happens, let it happen. Some of my stories may well have the opposite effect and make good men bad, but I'm afraid that can be no concern of mine. I must tell the stories that occur to me as I feel them. I've no objection to anyone getting involved in anything or, as the new chaps like to say these days, engagé. But I think it dangerous to get it mixed up with one's work."

101

"Yet you became an intelligence agent and got ASHEN-DEN out of it."

He is thrown, but only for a moment. "That was an accident, dammit! During a war it is quite impossible to remain uninvolved and, in any case, I might not have used the Ashenden material if I hadn't contracted tuberculosis and been sent away for a long time."

I see that we are going to get nowhere. He is not all wrong about this, but not all right, either.

It began with talk about Thornton, but Thornton soon became a euphemism for WSM. When I asked the question about the possible lack in Thornton's make-up, WSM read it as an implied criticism of himself. Had I thought this out beforehand, I would have avoided the reference. It was careless of me and I regret the blunder.

He is often referred to as cold and hard, detached and unfeeling. I do not find him so. He seems to me to be sensitive, perhaps oversensitive, full of feeling and capable of deep emotion.

1954. London.

Maugham: "When I was a dramatist, I worked in a most methodical, diligent way. I gave a month to the writing of each play and followed a rigid schedule of an act a week and a week to revise."

Impressive, this. Still, I wonder if it would have been possible had he attempted a more ambitious sort of play than the ones he produced. Not a word against THE CIRCLE, OUR BETTERS, THE LETTER, or THE CONSTANT WIFE—but, in a sense, they are stories written to be acted rather than read. Could ST. JOAN have been written on his schedule by anyone? Or MOTHER COURAGE? Or DEATH OF A SALES-

MAN? Well, hell. Arthur [*Miller*] told me DEATH OF A SALESMAN was written in six weeks of concentrated effort. That is not so far from four, is it?

August 1953. St. Jean–Cap Ferrat.

We gave a dinner last night for Maugham. Since we are not equipped for entertaining here, it took some doing, but it was worth it. WSM and Alan. Claudette and Jack [*Dr. Joel Pressman, husband of Claudette Colbert*]. Lee Shubert and Marcella [*Mrs. Lee Shubert*] drove over from Cannes. In all the years of Maugham's activity in the theatre, and all the times Mr. Lee has been to London and worked and done business there, bought and sold theatres and produced plays, they had never met. They both looked forward to the meeting.

They meet and are warm friends at once. The rest of us become audience as they reminisce and talk of the old days. Of Charlie Cochran and Charlie Dillingham. Of Ethel Barrymore. Finally, they hit upon Billie Burke and the years fall away. It is clear to those of us listening that each one is talking of a woman he once loved. But time has turned the passion gentle, and they are able to exchange their remembered excitements sweetly. Two tough old birds, but the nostalgia evoked by the memory of this adorable girl turns them into canaries.

Maugham has much to say about Billie Burke. She appeared in his play MRS. DOT in 1910. It was produced by Charles Frohman and played at the Lyceum. A few years later, again Frohman and again the Lyceum, she played in THE LAND OF PROMISE. About six years after that she did a third play of Maugham's, called CAESAR'S WIFE.

103

This one was produced by Florenz Ziegfeld and played at the Liberty Theatre.

These plays were all considered successful, although not one of them played a hundred performances. Things were different then.

[*In Billie Burke's memoirs, she writes*: "*With* MRS. DOT *I met Somerset Maugham, its author. Today, Mr. Maugham lets on that he is a 'very old party,' but judging from the few happy times when I have been fortunate enough to see him these past years, he is still a very handsome man. He was known and is known now as a British writer, but to me he has always seemed French. Indeed, he was born in France and learned French before he spoke English; and he was Parisian instead of Bond Street in elegance; always with his swallowtails and striped trousers, piping on his coat, smart gloves, a stick, beautifully made shoes, a gray top hat with a black band, and his briskly clipped mustache. And he had great smoldering brown eyes. Ah yes, Mr. Maugham, so you had, and I was a little in love with you, sir.*"

Now it comes out. Billie Burke was a little in love with Maugham and he more than a little in love with her. Another case of bad timing.]

After dinner we go down to the town square where a long-advertised fair is in progress. Nothing could be tackier or cheesier or dustier or more charming. We make the rounds, throw the balls, shoot the guns, spin the wheels, buy the confections, and have a real good time.

We lose Mr. Lee for a while, and find him over by an ice-cream stand buying ice cream for every loose urchin in town. Later we come upon these same kids trying to sneak into the performance by wriggling under the tent.

Mr. Lee prevents them from doing so and, although he cannot communicate with them in language, makes it clear that what they are doing is sinful in the extreme, takes them around to the front, gives them money, and stands over them as they buy tickets and enter.

"I'm not sure they wanted to see the show, Mr. Lee," I inform him. "I think they just wanted to sneak in."

Mr. Lee is dead serious. "They shouldn't do that," he says.

1950. New York.

WSM on the phone this morning: "I'm sorry I didn't call you as soon as I arrived, but the fact is a . . . butler I sacked burned my address books. All of them. It was the . . . bastard's revenge. He was with me about twenty-five years and after he had been with me for about a . . . year, I saw that he wouldn't do, but somehow it took me a while to get round to sacking him. I'm a . . . bit sorry. After all, one can acquire a new . . . address book and, if necessary, new friends to . . . list in it. It's going to be . . . more difficult to find a new . . . butler."

August 1943. Washington, D.C.

Ruth is back from Edgartown, Martha's Vineyard Island, Massachusetts, and has a lot to tell. What interests me most is what she has to tell about Somerset Maugham and about seeing him there. What an odd place for him to be! Ruth thought so, too, and asked him how come. He replies that last summer he sought a quiet place by the sea where he could work. Because of gas rationing, the beach for bathing and a cinema had to be accessible by foot. Opportunities for bridge games desired but not required. And the chance of pleasant company from time to time. Good food. He wrote these specifications to a number of friends and to a few travel bureaus. He consulted the newspapers and wrote for descriptive brochures. After a term of study, he decided to try the Colonial Inn in Edgartown.

"It proved to be," he tells Ruth, "exactly what I wanted. And so I have returned *this* summer."

There is something characteristic in this methodical approach. It is how he writes and eats and lives.

Ruth notes that he follows a fixed, unvarying schedule. He rises early, breakfasts in his room, and writes until lunchtime. He tells her, briefly, something about his present work and says that it is "scholarly." He winks at the word.

[*The work was* THEN AND NOW, *scholarly indeed. A historical novel about Machiavelli and his play* MANDRAGOLA *and a Maugham fancy of how it came to be written.*]

Last summer he lived in one room. It was the only aspect he found inconvenient. He is not accustomed to sleeping, eating, and writing in the same room, but he explains to Ruth that he is "rather hard up" at the moment. Most of his assets are abroad and unavailable. He lives here on what he earns (after taxes) and has to provide for Liza and her children as well. His publishers and friends, too, are generous and kind, but he feels it would be wrong to take more than he needs. Thus, last summer he took only one room at the Colonial Inn.

This year the management has insisted that he have a sitting room at no extra cost. He has accepted gratefully.

106

[*I heard him, in later, easier years, relate this many times. He was moved by the warmth and hospitality of America, and by the many small kindnesses shown to him in the United States across the years. His impression is made up of countless small things such as this rather than any one large or seemingly important event. It is interesting to consider that it was during that first one-room summer at the Colonial Inn that he was completing his last major work of fiction—*THE RAZOR'S EDGE. *He had come full circle—from the weary young aspiring medical student sitting in his bedroom writing* LIZA OF LAMBETH *to the weary old great novelist sitting in his bedroom writing* THE RAZOR'S EDGE.

At that party at the Plaza in 1949, a silly fat woman we all know pressed close to him, spilled some of her Bloody Mary onto his lapel, and blew smoke into his face as she gushed, "Do you know what my favorite is? The one about Isherwood. Christopher Isherwood? What's it called? Wait a second. Don't tell me. RAZOR *something.* A RAZOR EDGE! *What a book. How long did it take you to write it?"

WSM, unperturbed, replies, "Sixty years."

"Really? Excuse me."

And she is gone. Where? To repeat the information to someone? Or to ask Aldous Huxley how long it took him to write whatever?

I admire the courtesy and patience of WSM, developed over the years.]

Ruth reports that in Edgartown he lunches in the hotel dining room, usually alone. Then he goes up for his nap. At the same hour every afternoon, dressed in his bathing clothes, a beach robe, and sandals, and carrying a sling

107

bag, he walks down to the penny ferry (about two blocks), crosses over to Chappaquidick, and makes his way to the beach. After a time there (the length depending upon the weather) he returns to the hotel and changes. Ruth says he seems to wear almost the same outfit every day: slacks, foulard, and an old blue blazer. He plays bridge until going up to change for dinner, which he has at the Edgartown Yacht Club.

Then to the movies. He goes every single night. Fortunately, they change the program daily. It does not matter to him what is playing. He goes and buys his ticket and sits through it. To kill time, I suppose. To rest his mind, perhaps. At any rate, this is his routine.

(I think of Gertrude Stein, buying used books by the bushel at church bazaars, then reading through them, rocking away. And of Artur Rubinstein, who goes to a movie, sometimes two, on the day of a concert or recital. A delicate thing, the artist's mind, which needs rest and relaxation and understanding, especially by its owner.)

He invites Ruth to dinner. She explains that she is in Edgartown to see her young son, who is spending the summer at the Harborside Inn with his governess. Maugham nods sympathetically, and that is all. I ask Ruth if it did not occur to him to include Jones in the invitation, perhaps even Jones and Miss Ryan. Ruth's guess is that it did occur to him but that he rejected the idea. He knows Jones and likes him, but apparently it does not suit his mood at the moment to have dinner with a small boy. So Ruth's meetings with him are confined to a few trips over to the beach and a number of afternoon chats.

He asks her again. Again she explains and declines. She has left Washington and her new, Army-confined husband in order to spend this time with her son. Two well-organized, disciplined, single-minded creatures have crossed. WSM has met his match. Ruth does not lunch or dine with him. They understand each other.

WSM likes Martha's Vineyard enormously. It is pleasant and tranquil. He suffers few interruptions and there are no distractions other than those which he chooses or invents. The lovely little library is only three or four doors away and he makes use of it. He is comfortable here, reasonably contented, extremely productive, and finds that he and the atmosphere are suited, one to the other.

("I have observed," he once told me, "that I work well in salubrious climates—a physical manifestation which has shaped my life. It has dictated the location of my home in Cap Ferrat and driven me again and again to the South Seas. Once, shortly after my marriage, I went to Atlantic City and wrote most of THE MOON AND SIXPENCE there.")

Ruth says that, so far as she could see, he was absolutely alone. Gerald Haxton is seriously ill at Saranac. WSM is deeply concerned about him and his condition, stays in close touch and does what he can.

[*Haxton, Maugham's secretary-companion, did in fact die in November of the following year.*]

It is my guess that Maugham is going to live for a very long time. Barring accident, how could it be otherwise? He takes great care of himself and puts his own interests and health and welfare and comfort in first position of priority. This is not to suggest that he does not respect his obligations. He does, but not at the expense of his major energy or concentration.

109

July 1951. Villa Mauresque.

At cocktails this afternoon, I am the first one down and WSM follows almost immediately. He is chipper and gay and begins to tell me about a comical letter he has just received from Noël [*Coward*]. He sticks on a word —snaps his fingers so violently that I fear he may break them—puts down his glass and punches his palm. The word, stuck, will not come. He blinks and switches to another word. I can tell because the first consonant of the first word was "p" and now he is struggling with "m." This defeats him as well. He throws up his hands and brings them down in an oh-to-hell-with-it gesture. He is annoyed and says, "Oh, bbbb—" And now *that* will not come. For the first time in my life, I decide to help him out.

" 'Balls'?" I suggest.

He looks at me disdainfully and speaks with no effort at all.

"No, no," he says calmly. "I was going to say 'bugger.' "

It makes us both laugh. He goes on and finishes the Noël story easily.

Since we are still alone, I ask him if he relates his urge to write, in any way, with his stammering. Might it be, I suggest, that since he had early difficulties in expressing himself orally, he learned to do it literarily? After all, it was a way in which he could express himself easily and gracefully without being troubled. His pen has never stammered. He replies that he has thought a good deal about this and has come to the conclusion that what are called gifts—whether for writing or painting or music—are, in all probability, introspective refuges or escapes of one sort or another.

He goes on. "I am no longer self-conscious about it, or even . . . conscious. One gets used to oneself, don't you agree? Now and again I regret the inconvenience . . . caused to my listeners, but I have long since given up being vexed with myself. Why should I be? I do my best. This seems to be . . . my way of speaking. That is all."

Guests arrived at this point and the subject was, of course, closed.

One more thing about the stammer. You come in, the conversation begins, you are aware of the speech defect, troubled by it, embarrassed a little. All at once it passes. You forget about it completely. You have never been aware of it. Content has conquered form. You have become accustomed to it as you might to a foreign accent. Special, charming.

January 1950. New York.

A letter this morning from WSM. It contains a thank-you for our birthday cable. I note that the letter is dated January 26. He received the cable on his birthday, January 25. I remember him telling us once long ago that English people of a certain class always dealt with their correspondence as soon as they received it. This would seem to bear it out.

The letter contains some further teasing about the business of sending some wine back at the Pavillon.

He continues:

Dear Ruth, I am credibly informed that you're now one of the ten best dressed women in America. I suppose you tell Garson—as all wives do—that the dressmakers dress you for nothing. The proper answer to that is my eye and Betty Martin. In his place I'd put a detective on you. You girls, there's no holding you, but even though you may be morally delinquent I send you my love and to Garson I say this: Keep a stiff upper lip or else buy her her clothes yourself in Macy's bargain basement.

July 1953. St. Jean–Cap Ferrat.

An hour of money talk tonight. More than an hour. I can see Ruth becoming impatient. I try, several times, to change the subject, but he will have none of it. He still thinks I know about financial matters. He is determined to find legal ways to avoid taxes, to get the better of the Bureau of Internal Revenue and whatever it is called in England and whatever it is called in France.

I try to tell him that I am craven in such things, over-conservative, scared; that we usually get a refund each year; that we declare paper clips when returning to the States—but he thinks I am fancifying. He presses on.

After a time Ruth says, "Good Lord, Willie! There *must* be more interesting things to discuss. What on earth did you worry about in the days before income taxes?"

"A nagging wife!" he belts back.

The answer has come like a whiplash, as though the subject is always close to the surface of his feeling.

Having thus disposed of her question, he lights a cigarette and returns placidly to the matter of Swiss corporations and numbered bank accounts.

November 1945. New York.

George Cukor is to direct THE RAZOR'S EDGE. There is some difficulty about the screenplay. Zanuck is not happy with what has been turned in so far. WSM arrives in California. He stays with Cukor in George's guest room. George is most discreet and does not feel it right to pick brains, so he barely mentions the day-to-day struggles at the studio. WSM is the one who brings up the subject. This work means a great deal to him, more than any of us suspected. He thinks of it as being, perhaps, his last major work. No matter what the critics or the public thought of its philosophical content, it is profound and meaningful to him. It says as much as he has to say. He asks George finally, point-blank, to let him read the screenplay. He reads it. He is horrified. The picture, however, is scheduled and will shoot. He offers to write a new screenplay gratis. George conveys this to Zanuck. Zanuck can hardly refuse. WSM sits down and begins to write. He writes in longhand, slowly, methodically, but steadily, and finishes the screenplay. Irene Burns, George's secretary, types it. George reads it and thinks it great. He takes it to the studio. They agree. WSM has the handwritten manuscript bound, inscribes the title page, and gives it to Irene as a gift.

"It may be worth something one day," he says.

From the studio he will take no money at all. Zanuck feels indebted and wants to give him something.

"Very well," says WSM. "He can give me a picture."

How it is arranged, I do not know, but there are pictures and pictures and someone has to decide exactly what sort

113

of picture. A $30,000 picture? An $80,000 picture? It comes down, finally, to a $15,000 picture.

December 1945. New York.

WSM tells us today of his troubles in finding a picture that he likes, that he wants to have, and that will cost exactly $15,000—no more, no less. He does not want it to cost less because then the studio will be getting an advantage. He does not want it to cost more because he resents having the transaction turn into an expense. Eventually he finds a picture. He is content. The studio is content. Everyone is content.

[*Something happens. What, I do not know, and it is none of my business. George Cukor did not direct* THE RAZOR'S EDGE. *Somewhere in the shuffle that screenplay of Maugham's was abandoned.*

As to the picture, it came down to a choice between a painting of the harbor of Rouen by Pissarro and a snow scene by Matisse. Maugham was attracted to the first not only because of its art, but because of its association. Flaubert was born in Rouen and wrote MADAME BOVARY *in an apartment on the harbor there. It struck WSM that Flaubert must have lived with this view while writing his masterwork.*

Still, after consultation with experts, WSM chose the Matisse because it was a better buy. But the memory of the Pissarro haunted him and some time later he traded the Matisse for it.]

114

August 1953. St. Jean–Cap Ferrat.

Looking about the luxe in which he lives leads to several thoughts today.

I tease him about having solved all the problems of creature comfort. How does all this relate to his writing life? Does it help it or hurt it? No, he insists, he is organized and practical.

I remind him that Thomas Wolfe once said, "My trouble is, I can find plenty of girls to go to bed with me, but I can't find any who can read my handwriting."

June 1950. Faraway Meadows.

Bob Sherwood and Madeline are spending the weekend here with us. At lunch yesterday there was talk of what plays might be worth reviving. Ruth spins out her theory that the shelves are filled with big hits if only someone will take the trouble to lift them down and put them on properly. I tell of having seen a beautiful revival of Maugham's THE CIRCLE during the war. This leads to talk of other Maugham plays, and all at once there is spirited conversation about OUR BETTERS. I have read it, but the details do not come readily to mind. Bob and Ruth and Madeline agree that its most recent American production, although it had Ina Claire and Constance Collier, left something to be desired, and that it should have had a greater impact. In any case, it has not been done for a long time, and I make a note to have a look at it as soon as I can. As soon as I can turns out to be in the middle of last night. One of those damned no-sleep fits came upon me. I got up, wandered about for a while, went downstairs, and started

115

to look for something to read. I came upon a copy of Maugham's SIX COMEDIES, which contains OUR BETTERS. I began to read and, as I finished the first act, found myself still standing there, the book in my hands, facing the bookshelves. I took it out to the kitchen, where, with a glass of milk, I had the second act. I was pretty excited by this time, and went out into the big sitting room to finish it. I did so at twenty minutes to eight, and there was no point in going back to bed before breakfast. So I went over and let the dogs out and walked and thought about this remarkable play.

I suppose what we were talking about yesterday was a part for Ruth. I am not sure whether or not OUR BETTERS would serve this purpose, but what is important is the fact that I have read and digested an absolutely first-class play, with bite and satiric content, with matchless character drawing, constant surprise and wit and grace and lucidity. In short, a model of its kind.

Madeline has breakfast over at the cottage, but Bob comes over to have his with us. Elsa makes buckwheat cakes and Newport sausages. I tell Ruth and Bob about my nocturnal adventure. Bob is anxious, at once, to refresh his memory of the play and so is Ruth.

Who can tell? Something may come of all this.

[*Nothing did.*]

August 1953. St. Jean–Cap Ferrat.

I wish I could understand his interest in bridge. It is more than an interest. It is a sort of passion, a narcotic. He gets bored easily, but never, apparently, when there is a bridge game in progress. A few nights ago we were all invited over to Charlie Monroe's. (Our neighbor.) Mrs. Monroe used to be an actress named Anne Swinburne, married to Gus Schirmer. Now she is the wife of this unbelievably rich man who has renounced his American citizenship and become a citizen of Monaco—a monégasque.

There are reasons—I shall not go into them here—why WSM likes to make fun of Monroe. He tells of the time Charlie was solicited for a contribution to the British-American Hospital in Nice.

Monroe declined, saying: "Why should I? I'm never sick!"

Alan reports that one evening Monroe discoursed for an hour about the distribution of his wealth—so much in Canada, in timber; so much in the States, in real estate; so much in South America, in tin, coffee, and rubber; Mexico, gold; Switzerland, cash.

Shiny with excitement, he turns to Alan and asks, "Have you got much money?"

"Not a sausage," says Alan cheerfully.

"That's too bad," says Monroe. "Because if you had some, I could tell you what to do with it."

WSM does not like Monroe. Why, then, does he accept his invitations and go to his home? Why, to play bridge. They have damned good bridge at the Monroes'.

He hurries through dinner and makes his way directly from the dinner table to the bridge table. It begins. We leave hours later and the game is still going on. We go over to say goodnight. He mumbles something without looking up. He is winning. Or losing. What does it matter? He is enthralled.

July 1960. New York.

Maugham has said or written somewhere that the possession of money is like the possession of a sixth sense; and that it is the most important of the senses, since it is the one which makes it possible to use the other five to the full.

He seems to subscribe to the sentiment of Harold Rome's song "I'd Rather Be a Rich Man with a Million Dollars Than a Poor Man with a Pocket Full of Dreams."

July 1953. Les Rochers, St. Jean–Cap Ferrat.

Spencer Tracy is here with us and what a joy it is to have him. He is one of the few original thinkers I know. He says what he thinks, not what he has read or heard someone else say. He makes up his own mind, and he has a mind to make up.

He arrived on the *Constitution*, and we drove to Cannes to meet him. The ship was to dock at 7:30 A.M. We thought we had better be there in plenty of time, so we set out at six which meant getting up at five. But the drive was pleasant and the look of the country absolutely new at that hour. We reached Cannes far ahead of schedule, had coffee in a bar, and proceeded to the dock. Right on time we saw the ship come in and, soon after, the small tender carrying the passengers who were disembarking at Cannes. As it came into sight, we saw that great American head, with its white thatch, in the bow of the tender looking something like a classic figurehead. It was grand to see him, and he seemed happy to be here after all the in-

118

decision about should he come or not and several changes in plans and arrangements.

We drive home, stopping on the way at Cap d'Antibes because Spencer wants to. Having heard about it and read about it, he wants to see it. We stop at Eden Roc, more coffee. He creates a sensation around the hotel and its grounds, with practically everyone greeting him, saying, "Bonjour, M'sieu Spen-*saire!*"

We reach Les Rochers. By this time we are all over-heated and go immediately to the water and dive in. We are swimming about happily. Spencer turns out to be an accomplished and powerful swimmer. At one moment, floating on his back, looking up at the lovely towers of Les Rochers, the incomparable sky, and luxuriating in the celebrated Mediterranean, Spencer spouts a whale-like stream of water.

Ruth shouts, "Isn't this great?"

Spencer replies quietly, "Well, it's no more than what we deserve."

Since that morning everything has been going beauti-fully—until last night. I do not understand it, but the se-quence of events is as follows: We told Maugham that Spencer had come to spend some time with us here. A few days later he invited us all up to dinner. Without consulting anyone, I accepted. At lunch I announced that we were going up to Maugham's to dinner the following evening. I was certain that Spencer would be interested in seeing Maugham and the Villa Mauresque and especially the paintings, since that is something Spencer knows about. In fact, he has been doing some painting himself. I was therefore startled to hear Spencer say casually as he wolfed his salade Niçoise, "Not me."

I did not fuss about it too much at the time, since I

know that Spencer is not devoted to the social ramble. After lunch, while we were doing the long walk around the peninsula, I brought the subject up again, and Spencer said, without further explanation, "Thank you very much, but I don't want to go."

It is always difficult for me to know when Spencer is joking. He is such a consummate actor that even after all these years of friendship he can fool me easily with pretended anger or joy. Sometimes he will recite a long account of an adventure and, when I have been properly bowled over by it, will reveal that the whole thing was an invention.

I put his refusal down as one of his elaborate jokes and said no more about it. The following day as we began to make definite plans to go up the hill, it became increasingly clear that Spencer had no intention of joining us. I phoned the Villa Mauresque late in the afternoon and said that Mr. Tracy was not feeling well. Maugham was sympathetic and solicitous, asked if there was anything he could do, would we want him to send his doctor down? I said we were sure Spencer would be all right, but perhaps we should cancel dinner. Maugham said no, we were to come along. I did not think his invitation had full enthusiasm, but he is a routined man and clearly did not want to have his evening upset.

I kept thinking that at the last minute Spencer would come along, but he did not, and we went up alone.

After breakfast this morning we were telling Spencer about our visit and about the fascinating things which had occurred. He seemed eager to hear it all.

(Ruth interposed a story about being here in the South of France in 1928, staying with Woollcott and Harpo and living the Riviera life. Charles Brackett had the villa next door. Woollcott and Ruth and Harpo would go to dinner parties and events and the next day describe them to Charlie. Charlie plunked for being invited to some of these affairs, eventually was. Now the four of them went off, and the next morning Charlie said, "I liked it *much* better when you went without me and described it all in the morning.")

Breakfast is over and we sit about.

I say, "Now that it's done, Spence, will you *please* tell me why you wouldn't go?"

"I don't like him," said Spencer.

"Why not, for Heaven's sake?"

"I just don't."

"You mean you don't like his writing?"

"Did I say that? I love his books and his stories. I've read them all."

"Well, then, why wouldn't you be interested in meeting him?"

"I've met him," said Spencer grimly.

"Oh?"

"Oh."

Ruth asks, "And you didn't hit it off?"

"Well," said Spencer, "I'll tell you. A few years ago I was making DR. JEKYLL AND MR. HYDE with Ingrid Bergman. Vic Fleming was the director. That damned part was something that had haunted me for years. They used to play the play a lot when I was a kid in stock, and it always bothered me that the transformation was so overdone and unreal, so corny. I'd read the book and it seemed to me to be a marvelous study in schizophrenia. The idea of two personalities was fascinating to me—of course it would be to any actor—but blowing it out to the point of big false teeth and putty noses and scraggly hair . . . God,

121

there used to be guys got themselves up looking like orangutans for the Mr. Hyde part. And I thought for years about the possibility of doing it with acting only and not with the laying on of hands of all the Westmore brothers. I'd seen some remarkable feats of acting by now—small actors become tall and tall actors, by the force of their talent, seem insignificant. I'd seen people become almost invisible on the stage—and pretty common fellows become convincing kings and noblemen—gents become bums— and it wasn't only costumes and make-up, it was *acting*. And for a long time I'd had this idea that DR. JEKYLL AND MR. HYDE could be done realistically, believably. That the portrayal should be that of a *personality* change, not so much a *physical* change. Well, I used to talk about it around and nobody was much interested, but by this time I'd gotten to be well set at Metro and a few of the pictures had done okay and I was in a position to do pretty much what I wanted. So I talked it over with Fleming and he was nuts about the idea, and we decided it was worth doing. The studio agreed and then damned if we didn't get Ingrid Bergman, who was the hottest thing going at the time, and it was on. We studied the book and Johnny Lee Mahin did a hell of a good screenplay, and pretty soon we started shooting. Well, one day George sent a message that Somerset Maugham was visiting him and was going to be coming over to the studio that day, and could he bring him onto the set. We had a strictly enforced 'no visitors' rule because of the rugged work, but hell, if Cukor asks can he bring Maugham, you don't say no, do you? So we didn't. That day it happened to be one of the wild Mr. Hyde scenes, where he has the girl locked up and she's trying to get away. Now, visitors on the set make me nervous enough, but *Maugham*, you can imagine. Anyway, believe me when I tell you that we played the hell out of that scene, and I could see, back of the camera, George standing with this little guy and one or two others. When it was over, I sort of expected some applause. Instead, there was a little laugh. It was a print and we knocked off while they changed the set-up. George introduced me to Maugham, and we talked for a minute. Pretty soon they left, or started to leave. I took George aside and said, 'What was so funny?' George said, 'Funny?' And I said, 'That laugh.' And George said, 'Well, while we were watching the rehearsal, Maugham asked me what you were shooting, and I told him it was DR. JEKYLL AND MR. HYDE. And then while you were doing the scene, he looked at me and asked, "Which one is he now?" ' "

Spencer took a swig of coffee, put it down, and said, "And that's why I didn't go up there last night."

Genius is difficult. I still do not know if this is really the reason, used as a reason, or simply a joke. Probably I shall never know.

Spence did not seem to mind when we all laughed at the punch line. In fact, he laughed himself. But then there is always the fact that he did not go up to the Villa Mauresque last night to have dinner with Somerset Maugham.

September 1953. St. Jean–Cap Ferrat.

WSM is in a reminiscent mood tonight, and directly after dinner we return to the great parlor. From one of the shelves on the wall he begins to pull down old theatre magazines which have been there, bound and apparently untouched, for a long time. He talks of the time when he had four plays running simultaneously in London.

As he tells the story of how it all came about, he finds the pictures of the productions and reviews and accounts and interviews. His face is flushed. It is still exciting to him.

Think of it. LADY FREDERICK at the Court Theatre, MRS. DOT at the Comedy, JACK STRAW at the Vaudeville, and THE EXPLORER at the Lyric. All successes with the exception of the last, and that, he says, just missed. But for a time there were four—a record unexcelled until now, we all agree.

He finds and shows us the famous cartoon in PUNCH drawn by Bernard Partridge showing a billboard advertising the four Maugham plays, and in front of the billboard, nervously biting his nails, stands William Shakespeare.

Later he gives Ruth a book and inscribes it: "To Ruth Gordon, that promising young dramatist, from a dramatist long on the shelf."

April 1959. New York.

A note this morning from WSM from the Plaza in answer to the flowers we sent him. It reads:

Ruth my angel,
What makes you so good and sweet and how the hell does poor Garson manage to cope with it? I couldn't and I tell you right now that I withdraw the offer of marriage I made you the other day.

Thank you for the flowers and they are so well chosen—white to symbolize my innocence of the wicked ways of the world; and mauve to remind me that all are not so unspotted as in my childlike fashion I like to think. Perhaps there is a lesson here that you

124

think I should do well to ponder. Well, I will.

Darling, I do think it's sweet of you now that you are rich and famous and flashing with jewels not to forget the friends of your humbler days.

Bless you.

Willie

April 1954. London.

It has been a tremendous evening. The best in many ways we have ever had with Maugham. Now it is very late, and I am a little drunk. A little? Well, say half drunk. What does that mean, half drunk? It means not completely out-of-hand drunk, but somewhat elevated. Ruth has gone to bed. There is no point in my doing so because I made the mistake of brandy. That, along with the too much coffee, is going to stave off sleep for some time.

Maybe it is just as well, because it gives me an opporunity to set down an account of tonight while it is still fresh in my wavy mind.

I hope I am going to be able to read this scrawl tomorrow. I am afraid to use the typewriter in this small house. It can be heard almost everywhere. No matter. If I cannot read it, Ruth or Miss Monier-Williams over at the office will be able to do so.

We are living in this dandy house at 29 Charles Street, about two blocks from Berkeley Square. It is owned by a rich American lady, Natalie Hays Hammond, and she has done it beautifully. It may be too expensive for us, but Ruth is happy here. The house comes partly staffed, which makes it especially convenient. The location is ideal. A few blocks in one direction, Claridge's. A few blocks in the other, the Dorchester. A two-minute walk to Shepherd's Market, a charming place to shop. It is quiet. Sometimes too quiet. I have also taken rooms to work in at a place called Chesterfield Court, which is in Curzon Street, around the corner. We have settled in.

This dinner for Maugham and Alan has been planned for some time, about ten days. We and Mrs. Ball, our cook, have gone to considerable trouble to provide the proper repast for that particular and fussy Old Party. I am confident that he is not going to be disappointed. At about 4:30 Maugham phones to say that Alan has a cold, that it has become progressively worse, that he is now sneezing his head off, has a considerable temperature and a headache.

I say how sorry I am and ask if there is anything we can do or send. Maugham says no. There is a long pause, and I say nothing, since I feel he is probably about to say something else but is having trouble getting it out. We mumble back and forth until finally, after a long pause, he says, "I don't suppose you'd . . . want me alone."

God damn it, I was clearly supposed to have suggested this long before, but it did not strike me that that could be in his head.

I yell, "Of course we would!"

The odd thing about all this is that he meant it. For some reason he thought we might prefer to postpone the whole thing. As things have gone, it takes me a considerable time to persuade him that we really do want him to come alone. He checks the time again. I offer to call for him.

He says, "No, no. That won't be . . . necessary. I know exactly where it is. I once lived right round the corner from you with Syrie. In Chesterfield Street. I shall enjoy visiting my old . . . quarter. I'll stroll over, then, at about seven-thirty."

He arrives punctually, is much taken with the house, and immediately wants to see it all. All includes the basement, servants' quarters, the kitchen (where he spends some time examining everything on the stove and talking things over with Mrs. Ball). Upstairs, into the dining room, the closets, admiring the fireplace in the hall, up again to the bedroom floor, and up to the top to the separate apartment complete with kitchen. On the way down he wants to know the rent, the conditions of the lease, and do we have any idea as to what she paid for the house and what she might take for it now. We are able to answer some of these questions.

Downstairs, he asks for a martini and I take great trouble in preparing it. Esther brings up the exceptional toasted, salted almonds which Mrs. Ball makes.

Maugham smells them and shouts, "Oh, good!" He reaches in, grabs up a handful and begins to bolt them. "Good Lord," he says. "We used to have these on holidays when I was a boy in Whitstable."

I bring him the martini. He takes a sip of it.

"Is it all right?" I ask.

"No," he replies. "It is not."

"Oh? What's the matter with it?"

"It's not . . . cold enough. A martini should be very cold."

I pick it up and start out.

"What are you going to do?" he calls after me.

"I'm going to make it colder."

"And just how do you . . . propose to do that?" he asks.

"Remix it," I explain. "With more ice."

"That will make it . . . weaker," he objects.

127

I am ready to throw it at him, but instead I say, "Well, please tell me what to do."

He rises and says, "I'll show you."

We step out into the library, and there he gives me a short but concise lesson in martini-making. We start from scratch, chilling the glass, chilling the shaker, measuring, and mixing the ingredients carefully by shaking, not stirring. Finally, and only for a few seconds, adding a great mass of ice and giving the whole thing a couple of final shakes before pouring. It has all been so fascinating that I have one too, although it is not what I usually have. He is right. It makes all the difference.

[*From that time on, I could always prepare a satisfactory martini for Mr. Maugham. Years later I was able to improve upon his instruction. I had visited some serious drinkers in Pennsylvania who were so jealous of the strength of their martinis that they would not allow ice to make contact with the ingredients at all. They prepared shakers of martinis and put them in the deep freeze for an hour or two. When they were served, they were ice-cold and full strength. I relayed this important intelligence to WSM. He tried the method immediately and reported to me that he was greatly indebted, adding that it was the only thing of true value he ever learned from me.*]

We talk about food in London, and I ask him whether or not he agrees with me that it is or can be excellent. Has this always been so? Have things changed?

He says that it has usually been possible to find excellent food in London at a price, but never, he adds, have costs been so far out of the reach of "mortal men." He discusses several of those fancy, fashionable restaurants in Curzon Street where, he says, the food is superb but—and this is his phrase—"obscenely expensive." I cannot imagine that while he is in London he ever pays for a meal. He seems always to be someone's guest, but, whether he is paying or not, he is aware of what things cost. Paraphrasing Oscar Wilde, Maugham knows the price of everything and the value of everything. He is conscious of expenditure because he has worked hard all his life to earn. He is interested in my talk about my days as a Western Union messenger, when I computed the cost of everything in terms of how many telegrams had to be delivered to pay for it. At a cent and a quarter a message, it meant so many for a hot dog, so many for a Coke. He says he used to think in terms of so much a word or a story. One story would cover expenses for a month, and when he found it necessary to discard material, he thought of it in terms of discarding time and time was money.

We had a hell of a lot to drink tonight, but we ate so much that we did not get as potted as we might have. We did get plenty loud and over-garrulous, though. Fortunately I became wildly indiscreet and asked all sorts of questions which might have occurred to me had I been sober but which I surely would not have asked. For example, I ask him if he considers the London theatre homosexually dominated or controlled.

"Partly," he replies.

"Would you say principally?"

"No."

"Would you say that this influence is growing or diminishing?"

"Growing, I should think."

"Well, do you consider this a good thing or a bad thing, or don't you think it matters one way or the other?"

"I think it . . . most unfortunate. And something which

should be checked, if possible."

"Why?"

"Because it spoils the ... women, don't you see? It makes them hard and rather cynical. When there is no ... premium for femininity, it fails to develop properly."

Together, we consider the truth of this. How few feminine or, say, sexy actresses have been developed in the past fifteen or twenty years in the British theatre. We list the girls who have become important, who have become stars. Talented, attractive, interesting, full of personality, but damned few of them who could be called girl-girls.

... Later I ask him if, in his opinion, he has been a good father to Liza.

"I swear I ... tried to be," he says grimly.

"But that isn't what I asked you."

"I'm quite aware of that. I think I was as ... good a father as she and the circumstances permitted me to be. I've always provided for her and for her children when that was necessary. I haven't demanded any loyalty or ... duty. I care for her. But remember, she was always somewhat torn. And, whatever others might have thought or might think, I always considered her mother a bad influence upon her."

I ask him if he would have liked to have had more children.

"Yes," he says, "I suppose so. They are extremely interesting and ... teach one a good deal. They teach one about one's self—things not possible to learn otherwise."

Moving from the particular to the general, we talk of parenthood, of the complex parent-children relationship.

I ask, "What would you say was the principal requisite of a father?"

He thinks for a moment and replies, "To set a ... good

example. Nothing more."

"Do you think you did that with Liza?"

He thinks for far more than a moment and says, "No."

Somewhere along the line I say, "May I ask you an indiscreet question?"

"Good Lord," he says. "I was just thinking it was about . . . time for a *discreet* one."

"How many times in your life," I ask, "have you proposed marriage?"

"Once," he replies.

"Oh," I mumble disappointedly.

He catches the sound and says, "What?"

I comment, "Well, that's not very exciting, is it? You proposed once and you were married once."

He looks me in the eye and says, "Would it make it more . . . exciting for you if I explained that the woman to whom I . . . proposed refused me?"

"Yes, it would," I say.

And he tells about his one great love affair.

[*In a preface to* CAKES AND ALE *written twenty years after the book's first publication, Maugham writes,* "I like CAKES AND ALE *because in its pages lives for me again the woman with the lovely smile who was the model for Rosie Driffield.*"]

He tells, feelingly and movingly, of meeting this woman (Nan, in real life), of knowing love for the first time, of thinking with her that it was a passionate burst which would burn itself out in a few weeks. Instead, the affair lasted for eight years.

Then, quarrels and complications, and indecision as to marriage. She goes away and does not tell him where she has gone. After a time he begins a desperate search and traces her to the United States, to Chicago. He is prepared now, buys a ring, goes to Chicago, finds her, and proposes. She refuses him. He is stunned, can scarcely believe it. He thinks it a joke, a tease of some sort.

She says simply, "I can't marry you."

"Why not?" he asks. "Are you already married?"

"No," she replies, "I'm not."

"Do you love someone else?"

"No."

"Do you love me?"

"Yes. With all my heart."

"Do you believe that I love you?"

"Yes."

"Then why?"

"I can't marry you."

He says his doctor's mind immediately leaped to the clinical, especially since he knew Chicago to be a rough, tough town.

He asks her frankly, "Are you ill?"

"No," she replies, "not at all."

"Will you think about it? Will you reconsider?"

"I can't," she says stubbornly.

The mystery made him impatient. He shouted at her. There was a scene. It was no use. They parted.

He says that many, many years later she told him that what had happened was that when he finally proposed to her, she had just learned she was pregnant by another man. A casual thing, an accident. But there it was.

I do not think I have ever seen tears in Maugham's eyes until tonight. But as he comes to the end of this account, there they are.

"She never had the child," he says dully. "She had a

miscarriage. But our moment had passed. Yes. She . . . died only two or three years ago."

After a long pause, he says, "I often wonder what course my life might have taken had it not been for that . . . freakish happenstance."

[*A small mystery. In the preface to* CAKES AND ALE *he writes of her: ". . . by the time I wrote it she was dead." This was in 1930. On another occasion he wrote that she did not die until 1948. In the above account, he places her end at 1951 or 1952. What the hell?*]

. . . In CAKES AND ALE, when Edward Driffield celebrates his seventieth birthday, the narrator comments, "An uneasiness passed over the world of letters. It grew evident that there had lived among us all these years a great novelist and none of us had suspected it."

I ask Maugham if Edward Driffield was indeed modeled on Thomas Hardy. The question makes him impatient.

"Oh, I don't know. I've denied it and admitted it and denied it. There . . . might have been some small thread of him in the fabric. In any case, what does it . . . matter?"

"It doesn't matter at all," I reply, "except that there seems to have been a change of cast. When you wrote the book, you played the part of the narrator and now, I think, you're playing Driffield. It's like a play that's been in the repertory for a long time and the girl who was the ingénue now plays the character part."

"I like character parts," he mumbles.

"Life imitating art, and all that. Would you like to talk about it?"

"No."

. . . Later, very late for him, he begins to talk of taking his leave. I suggest we walk him home. He protests and says it is not at all necessary, he has spent a good part of his life walking about the streets of London and can find his way easily. I tell him I am not concerned about that, but that we would enjoy it.

"In that case," he says, "come along."

(Privately, I am concerned for his safety. We are both nicely crocked by now and the streets are very in-and-outy in the neighborhood. There are curious cul-de-sacs and odd drops.)

We leave 29 Charles Street, turn left, walk about half a block, and turn left again into Chesterfield Street. We walk. He stops. There is a great, gaping space. A building has been torn down and a new one is being constructed. He stops at the fence in front of the new construction, looks about, seems confused, goes quickly to look at the number on one side of the new construction, hurries over to examine the house on the other side, comes back and says, "Yes. This it it. This is where I lived. With Syrie. Right here." He points with his cigarette. "In this space." He stoops down to look under the fence. Lower, lower. He spends a considerable time in this cramped position. We bend down, too. There is nothing to see. Only space. But it means something to him.

We walk on, slowly, turn right, and in a few minutes have reached the Hotel Dorchester lobby.

As we part, he frowns and says, "I'm so sorry for Alan. Sorry that he had to miss this. But then, if he'd been with us, I suppose I'd have said much less."

I say, "I know damned well I'd have asked much less."

"Quite so."

He looks at Ruth and winks at her before kissing her cheek.

As we shake hands, he leans forward a few inches and

says to me, "D'you suppose I shall . . . hate myself in the morning?"

He turns quickly and walks extra-erect through the deserted lobby to the lift.

March 1958. Nice.

Last night up at Maugham's I begin, for some reason, to talk of Gertrude Stein. Noël, absolutely vicious on the subject, calls her work "literary diarrhea." I defend her. Maugham, in between. Strangely, he never knew her well, never read her much, but understands that she was perhaps a greater influence than generally supposed.

I make the point that she has much to teach writers in the way of freedom, let-go. I trace her history from her studies with William James at Harvard; her work at Johns Hopkins; the early experiments in automatic writing, and what effect that had on literature. The odd idea that she, working along one revolutionary line, and James Joyce, working along on another, hardly ever met, although they were both living in Paris. When they did meet, they were rather disapproving of each other. She, not terribly interested in his work; he, not at all interested in hers. So it goes.

We talk of influences, of the debts writers owe to other writers, of the special qualities possessed by some.

From Thornton Wilder, for example, one can learn the value of depth. From Maugham, lucidity. From Gus Eckstein, simplicity. From Gertrude Stein, freedom. From Mark Twain and Benjamin Franklin, much about the roots of the American language; and from Cardinal Newman, Adlai Stevenson, E. B. White, E. M. Forster, Dashiell Hammett, Churchill, Frankfurter, Shakespeare and Shaw, something of the mystery and majesty of the English language.

January 1954. London.

I have just read CAKES AND ALE again. Again. I have no idea how many times I have read this book. More, I should think, than any other. Books have a way of becoming friends, yet there are few I have gone back to time and time again. I never return to this one by choice or design. What usually happens is that I pick it up, begin to read it, and am unable to stop. It has that compelling beat, that move forward, that magnetism which is perhaps the most desirable thing in storytelling. The fact that I know, somewhere within me, what is going to happen next does not interfere with my enjoyment. I am able to play the game and pretend that I do not know. That is not necessarily the standard of enjoyment anyway, is it?

(I think of the story of Toots Shor standing in the lobby during the first intermission of Maurice Evans' HAMLET and saying, "You know I'm the only sonofabitch here who doesn't know how this thing is gonna come out?")

Children are the best audience for stories, and they like to hear the same one over and over again. They react in the way they are intended to react, whether with laughter or shock or fright or surprise or tears, time and time again. Storytelling is an art, and so is story-listening, and so is reading. CAKES AND ALE is a surpassing piece of work.

This time something strikes me. Why not make it into a film? I do not mean that *I* should, but that someone should. I am certainly not the man to work on it in any department. I begin to think of Larry and Vivien [*Laurence Olivier and Vivien Leigh*]. Vivien would be immense

136

as Rosie, and Larry a perfect director. To adapt it for the screen, Terry Rattigan? Noël, Emlyn [*Williams*], Peter Ustinov—good Lord, there are a great many. If Larry cannot undertake it, Carol Reed. Maybe Larry would be willing to do a kind of cameo as Edward Driffield—creating one of his tremendous old men, with Vivien at her most enchanting. My heart begins to pound. All I want out of it is to see it. I am going to do something about this.

February 1954. Notley Abbey.

I talk to Larry and Vivien about CAKES AND ALE. Their reaction is instantaneously affirmative and enthusiastic. We cannot understand why it has not been done before. Larry is going to look into it, perhaps talk to Korda [*Sir Alexander Korda, British producer*]. Now I have a sick feeling that the rights are not going to be available.

February 1954. London.

On the telephone today with WSM I tell him about the CAKES AND ALE notion. He is delighted. I am to drop over and discuss it with him tomorrow.

February 1954. London.

I ask WSM how it is that CAKES AND ALE has never been done as a film. He is relaxed and philosophic about it.

"Well," he says, "when it was written, about twenty-five years ago, it was considered rather ... daring, and the cinema people were terrified of doing anything which smacked of immorality or which might run afoul of the censors. I'm happy to learn that time has caught up with it. Vivien will be . . . marvelous, won't she? What a pity Larry's part is not a better one. Do you really think he'll play such a small role?"

"Well, if he doesn't, you can play it."

"Yes, I would be rather . . . dashing, wouldn't I?"

"At least it would stop people from saying you caricatured Thomas Hardy. The joke will be that you were really writing about yourself all the time."

"I always do."

There is more talk on the subject of CAKES AND ALE, but although he is pleased at the prospect, I do not feel any excitement. I wonder if it is simply that he is not all that interested in films, or if too much time has gone by, or if he is less than keen about seeing Rosie personified by an actress. I decide to open it up and ask him.

"No, no," he assures me. "It's none of those things, and in any case, the money to be made is a . . . compensating factor. It's simply that, for some reason, not a single one of my works has ever . . . translated well into the cinema."

I mention John Cromwell's production of OF HUMAN BONDAGE with Leslie Howard and Bette Davis.

"Yes," he agrees somewhat grudgingly, "that was fairly effective in some parts and . . . quite successful, I believe. But it seemed to me a sketch of my book, a sort of extract. Too much was . . . missing, for my taste. It had been edited brutally."

"But a film can't run on indefinitely," I argue, "and certain adjustments have to be made."

"Oh, I see that . . . perfectly well," he said, "but you can't expect me to be . . . satisfied, can you?"

I point out that since CAKES AND ALE is much shorter than OF HUMAN BONDAGE, it may be possible to film the entire story, leaving out practically nothing. This pleases him, and he lights another cigarette.

We begin to talk of all the material which has been developed out of his original work. It is staggering. The plays, the pictures, the musicals.

I learn, to my surprise, that he did not like the play RAIN. He thought it a poor job of work and was sorry he had ever allowed it to be done, despite the fact that it was a great success in New York and in London and was made several times as a film and done as a musical show as well.

"No," he says. "On that subject I have only to say that I think it a ... very good short story."

He recalls that he happened to be in Hollywood doing some film work when the book of short stories containing RAIN was published. Living in the same hotel with him was John Colton, who read it and said to Maugham in the lobby one day that he thought it would make a play. Maugham says he liked Colton, who was not doing very well at the time.

In a moment of generosity he said, "Well, go ahead and do it, if you like."

They shook hands. Within a few months the book had been widely circulated, the story was popular, and other people saw dramatic possibilities in it. There were many extravagant offers.

Maugham says, "I let the handshake stand."

I ask him if he would be interested in working on the screenplay of CAKES AND ALE. His response is immediate and vehement.

"Not at all," he says. "That story is entirely too ... personal. I have no wish to delve into it again. I shan't

139

even . . . go to see it."

"Oh, you'll go to see it, all right," I say confidently, "because it'll be surpassing, and *everyone* will want to see it."

1954. London.

At tea with WSM today I express my embarrassment over my ineffectual efforts to get CAKES AND ALE launched.

He is especially kind and understanding.

"Please don't . . . trouble your head about it. These things take time and come when they come. I am a stoic, you see, in addition to . . . being a cynic. Alan got out some files the other . . . day and we discussed the question of THE MOON AND SIXPENCE, which was made into rather a good . . . film a few years back. That book was written in 1919 and a . . . couple of years after that an American company took an option on the film rights, held them for a while, and dropped them. People would . . . talk to me about it from time to time—just as you've been talking to me about CAKES AND ALE—but nothing whatever came of it. Some years went by and a woman—I think her name was Ellis—wrote a play version. It was produced in London and although it was not a great success, it was well enough received. Leslie Banks was in it and so was Harry Ainley. Again I heard from the film people. A while after that, a number of my things were done on the films: RAIN with Gloria Swanson and then a . . . talkie of THE LETTER with Jeanne Eagels and Herbert Marshall. Once more there were options on THE MOON AND SIXPENCE and once more they were dropped. The difficulty seemed to be . . . censorship. RAIN was done again with Joan Crawford and

Walter Huston, I believe, and a film was . . . made of OUR BETTERS.

"The woman who'd done the MOON AND SIXPENCE play version . . . wrote and asked me if I would allow it to be done at a . . . small theatre in California because she was certain that that would . . . lead to a sale of the film rights. And so I gave my consent. Charles Laughton saw it and . . . got in touch with me. I kept saying yes and getting messages from the . . . various studios. Then OF HUMAN BONDAGE was made and Garbo was planning to do THE PAINTED VEIL, but . . . nothing whatever happened about THE MOON AND SIXPENCE.

"In 1939 I finally sold the rights to . . . Warner's and a good job too, because I . . . needed the money. But it was not made until the war was on—and then by someone else, not them—but it turned out . . . very well for everyone. So that one, you see, took about twenty-five years to . . . find its way to the screen. By this calculation CAKES AND ALE ought to be . . . ready soon. Isn't it grand I'm such a . . . patient man?"

April 1954. London.

Supper last night with Vivien and Larry. I bring up the subject of CAKES AND ALE. They still think it would be a fine idea, but somehow not much has been done. What is worse, I begin to feel that nothing is going to come of this after all. Is it inertia? Is it the absence of a strong personality to act as the catalyst? (This is where an on-fire producer comes in handy.) Have there been difficulties about the rights? No, not so far as anyone knows. Has anyone dampened their enthusiasm? No. It is merely that other things come up, other plans are made, other

141

projects elbow in and time goes by, and passion fades.

I suppose more good ideas have not happened than have happened. Most babies never do get born. I am deeply sorry about this one, though. It would have been such an interesting baby.

[*Even now, in 1966, it seems surprising to me that this outstanding work of English fiction has never been filmed. Certainly it will be one day. Consider how long it took to get around to* TOM JONES.

I have no recollection now as to the details of the melting away of the CAKES AND ALE *scheme back then. I know that I did not press it beyond the original proposal, since I was not to be directly involved and it began to seem embarrassingly pushy.*

I saw WSM many times after that, and he never mentioned it.]

September 1953. St. Jean–Cap Ferrat.

There is talk tonight about writers and their notebooks. I tell WSM about the rumor that he has one, running to several million words, in which he has set down precisely what he thinks and feels about all his friends and enemies and relatives, places and things and happenings, and that there is further a report that these confidential notebooks may not be published until some time after his death.

I ask him if this is true.

He says, "Partly."

I wait for him to amplify, but he does not do so. He has decided to be cryptic today.

We go on to talk of other notebooks and journals. I tell

142

him how I was forced into the habit by Thornton, who insisted I commit something to paper each day.

I ask him if he has ever heard the advice that every author should write a journal and make certain never to read it.

He laughs at this and says he thinks it a clever remark but ill-advised. He claims to have made great use of his notebooks, aside from the fact that he published a part of them not long ago.

I tell him about my interest in the notebooks of Henry James, the impressive account of struggle in shaping and reshaping material, how one idea becomes quite another, the endless self-examination, and the work toward discipline. He listens to all this coolly.

When I stop, WSM says, "I am not interested in Henry James. I never . . . liked him, nor what he wrote."

This seems to end that part of the discussion.

[*It may have been because of the above, and further conversations on the subject, that the case of Maugham vs. James became one of the few mysteries I have ever attempted to unravel. I wondered what could have caused this bitterness. On the face of it, it would seem that Henry James and Somerset Maugham were two men of a piece: both gentlemen; fastidious writers, travelers, social lions, and extremely industrious. I should have thought they would have liked each other and admired each other's work.*

With James long gone, it is almost impossible to find out what, if anything, happened between them. I have delved into this, spending far too much time on it. Maugham has said and written a good deal about James, but the other side of the coin is very nearly blank. In

143

March, 1914, an article entitled THE YOUNGER NOVELISTS by Henry James appeared in THE TIMES LITERARY SUPPLEMENT. *Another version was later printed in a collection of his literary criticism under the title* NOTES ON NOVELISTS. *In it he discussed eight of the outstanding younger novelists, including Hugh Walpole. (A strange choice, perhaps; less strange when you consider that Walpole was a close friend to James.) The other seven mentioned were Joseph Conrad, Maurice Hewlett, John Galsworthy, H. G. Wells, Arnold Bennett, Gilbert Cannan, Compton Mackenzie, and D. H. Lawrence. There is also an important reference to Edith Wharton. The name of W. Somerset Maugham is conspicuously absent, although by this time he had written and published* LIZA OF LAMBETH, THE MAKING OF A SAINT, THE HERO, MRS. CRADDOCK, THE MERRY-GO-ROUND, THE BISHOP'S APRON, THE EXPLORER, THE MAGICIAN *and had achieved enormous success as a dramatist. Twelve of his plays had been produced. Could James have been sticking on this point, that Maugham's major success had been as a dramatist and he was discussing novelists? Maugham was about to publish* OF HUMAN BONDAGE, *but James could not have known that. Could it have been that James was consciously or unconsciously jealous of Maugham's success in the theatre? It is generally agreed that, more than anything else, James wanted to succeed as a dramatist and wrote many plays, but never a success. In 1895, in connection with his theatrical ambitions, he suffered a trauma from which he was never to recover. It had to do with the famous, disastrous opening night of his play* GUY DOMVILLE.

In later years the work of Henry James became the basis of a great many theatrical successes: BERKELEY SQUARE, *based on* A SENSE OF THE PAST; THE INNOCENTS, *based on* THE TURN OF THE SCREW; THE HEIRESS, *based on* WASH-

INGTON SQUARE; THE ASPERN PAPERS; THE WINGS OF THE
DOVE; *and others. Yet he himself was never able to trans-
late his work into acceptable theatrical form, and here was
this young flash turning up and knocking off play after
play, to the point where he had four running simultaneously. Could this have troubled James? Whatever it was,
it was something. They gave each other offense, and
Maugham never forgot it. Despite this, they seem to have
developed a relationship of sorts. They met often. In 1910,
when WSM went to America for the first time in his life,
he journeyed to Cambridge, Massachusetts, for the express
purpose of calling on James, who was trapped there at the
time. Before his brother William died, some six months
earlier, he had made Henry promise to stay in Cambridge
with the widow. Not for purposes of consolation, but in
order that the two would be together when William attempted to communicate from the beyond. Why Henry
and the widow had to be together and why in Cambridge
has never been explained. Nothing happened. The lines
were down, even for so exceptional a communicator as
William James.*

In his essay SOME NOVELISTS I HAVE KNOWN, *Maugham
dissects Henry James as a man and as a writer with the
concentration and cruelty of a small boy removing the
wings and the legs from a hapless fly.*

*It has been said that the character of Elliott Templeton
in* THE RAZOR'S EDGE *is based upon Henry James. Perhaps.
But Maugham, in the essay, has done more than hide his
dislike in a fictional character as he did when he wrote
Hugh Walpole as Alroy Kear. Here he says plainly what
he thinks and what he thought of Henry James and why.*

*Maugham must have felt a curious satisfaction on the
night he stood before the Royal Society of Literature and*

delivered his lecture on THE SHORT STORY. *Somewhere he found a way to take a further swipe at Henry James. In discussing form and content, he talked of the triviality of so many of James's themes and of the elaboration of the treatment. And he ended his remarks on Henry James by saying, "He was like a man who should provide himself with all the paraphernalia necessary to the ascent of Mount Everest—in order to climb Primrose Hill."*

George Cukor recalls WSM saying, "Men treated Henry James like a god, and the poor brute began to behave like one."

The rebuttal, the other side of the debate is, alas, missing.]

We talk of other writers' notebooks—Chekhov's, and Ibsen's, and Proust's, and Mark Twain's.

WSM says, "In a day when letter-writing was more ... fashionable and part of the daily life, a good deal of journalizing went into letters—Dickens', for example, and Trollope's. Now one scarcely writes or receives personal letters. In my day, no proper young Englishman or Englishwoman would consider beginning the day's activities until all letters were answered, all invitations dealt with, gifts acknowledged, hostesses thanked, and bills paid. I myself still bear the ... burden of this dull discipline."

We return to talk of journalizing, and Maugham tells us about Jules Renard.

"He was a minor writer and, in a lifetime of work, produced no more than a single remembered book—POIL DE CAROTTE—but he kept a careful journal and wrote it day by day. When it was ... published, it proved to be an astonishing document and it, more than any of his works of the imagination, will earn him a ... permanent place

146

in French literature. He draws, without primarily intending to do so, such a ... fascinating portrait of his time, of the people who inhabited it, and of all the happenings of the day, that it ... becomes not only enthralling but invaluable."

Summing up, he feels that a notebook or a journal is of immense importance. To him, the constant act of writing, of exercising the writing muscles, is indispensable. It is equivalent to a pianist's practicing, or to a ballerina's going to daily class. A writer, he says, must write and record and describe and express constantly.

1954. London.

A rich and unexpected trouvaille tonight. We talk of Terry's play SEPARATE TABLES, which is at the St. James's—and all at once WSM is reminiscing about another night at that same theatre: "It must have been somewhere around the ... beginning of 1895. George Alexander was on the crest, and Henry James—I suppose he was about fifty at the time—was fashionable. So it was an important event. I can't remember all the other ... players, but of course Alexander was in it, and Irene Vanbrugh, one of the Terrys, too—I don't recall which—and it played at the St. James's. I can't imagine how I—an impecunious medical student—got to that first night. It was one of the ... grand ones, and, sitting up there with the gallery gods, I saw the carriage folk come in. There was H. G. Wells, and Arnold Bennett, and that American woman who wrote and acted. What was her name?"

Ruth supplies it. "Elizabeth Robins."

"Quite. And several ... Terrys, George du Maurier, and I remember the thrill of seeing John Singer Sargent

147

in the flesh, and Mrs. Humphrey Ward. And of course there were the ... critics: William Archer and A. B. Walkley and Clement Scott and a new one named George Bernard Shaw. He had been, up to a few days before, a music critic and had just ... begun to cover plays for Frank Harris on THE SATURDAY REVIEW. GUY DOMVILLE must have been no more than the ... second or third play he reviewed. They said that Henry himself didn't attend. He was entirely too ... nervous, and so he went to the Haymarket, nearby, to see Oscar Wilde's new play, AN IDEAL HUSBAND. I thought the first act of GUY DOMVILLE went well enough, but in the second, things became ... dull, whereupon the audience grew restless and there was a good deal of coughing. The play was laid in the 1700's, consequently the costumes were odd. There were some that seemed ... bizarre indeed. One of the actresses entered under an enormous chapeau. The audience began to ... laugh, and from somewhere a voice called out, 'Where did you get that hat?!' Of course, this set some of the others off. A little later there was a ... drunk scene—quite embarrassing—and that went not at all as intended. Henry later cut it from the play, but—too late. The audience ... got out of hand. Toward the end George Alexander, playing the leading role, said something like 'I'm the last of the Domvilles, m'lord,' and a voice from the ... gallery cried out, 'And a bloody good thing, too!'

"They say Henry came in through the stage door as the play was ending. He'd no idea it had gone badly or that the audience had been restive, had even shouted. So when the curtain calls were being taken and a few voices began to call 'Author! Author!' he responded. George Alexander must have been ... most upset, else he wouldn't have brought poor Henry on, but there have been other theories.

148

H. G. Wells wrote somewhere in telling about it that he believes a spasm of hate for James seized Alexander. At any rate, Alexander took him by the wrist and pulled him right out onto the stage with him. Booing and hissing and catcalling began. Henry stood there with his mouth wide open. You saw he wanted to move, but he was rooted. He made a sort of gesture. I can't describe it. It was rather like . . ."

Maugham shrugs his shoulders and makes a movement of his arms, as though to say, "What the hell, I'm sorry," or something of the sort.

"Then he turned suddenly and ran off the stage with Alexander after him."

How odd that Maugham, not yet a writer, not yet a dramatist, should by coincidence have been present on this historic, blistering, nightmare night.

What I am thinking is this: Could it be that he had somehow made this fact known to Henry James, and if so, would this not have upset James? In any case, twenty years passed, and when James wrote his article for THE TIMES LITERARY SUPPLEMENT, he deliberately snubbed Maugham. And so began, as far as I can make out, a feud which lasted for two lifetimes.

1958. Nice.

"Ruth, my dear, what do you think of this?" he asks. "I had a letter from a . . . lady in America. She said she'd read many of my . . . books and clearly I am a sage who knows everything about everything, especially love."

"You probably do," says Ruth.

"But wait. She was a pragmatic . . . party and wasn't

writing simply to compliment me, but to get some . . . free advice. She wanted to know, first, how to get a . . . man and, second, how to . . . hold him. Alan picked the letter out of a . . . basketful and showed it to me because he thought it . . . would amuse me. Or perhaps he was simply teasing me. But I decided to reply and so I . . . wrote her and said, 'The only way to get a man is to be sexually attractive and the only way to hold on to him is to be . . . sexually satisfactory.' She never acknowledged . . . my advice, although I can assure you I was absolutely in earnest. Do you agree with it?"

"Not entirely," says Ruth. "It's not as simple as you make it out to be. It's a much deeper secret than that."

"Such as?"

Ruth smiles. "If I told you, it wouldn't be a secret any more, would it?"

WSM shakes his head sadly and says, "I might have . . . known."

January 1954. London.

We get to talking about the war and about Intelligence. He wants to know more about what I did. The minute I mention the fact that I was attached to the OSS, he begins to question me sharply about methods and notions. Even at this late date, almost ten years after my discharge, I am terrified of a slip of tongue, so I bumble along, saying practically nothing. However, we do talk about various Intelligence methods, and he tells about the brilliant notion the French had of censorship in World War I, which was simply to throw all mail and communications into bags, put them into warehouses, let them stand for two or three weeks, then send them on. The idea being that Intelligence, like fish, is good only if fresh.

February 1949. New York.

WSM says: "I'm especially fond of the old Plaza. People find the hansom cabs out in front a quaint anachronism, but I must say they seem perfectly . . . natural to me. And I find it one of the few hotels in New York in which I can work. I've no idea why this should be so."

"What have you written here?"

"Well, for one thing, my story THE COLONEL'S LADY. Odd, that. I scribbled a note long ago—I can't remember when or where, since I failed to date it or place it—but I was getting together selections from my . . . notebook for publication and in an envelope I came upon this . . . note. I thought about it in my . . . bath one morning. I was living here at the Plaza and that day I . . . began to set it down. It went very easily. It should have. The . . . damned thing'd been gestating for over forty years. I got enough out of that story to pay my . . . bill, which was, I'm sorry to say, a . . . large one, so it all worked out . . . neatly."

He has seen only three things in the theatre on this trip: A STREETCAR NAMED DESIRE; KISS ME, KATE; and THE MADWOMAN OF CHAILLOT.

He says about A STREETCAR NAMED DESIRE that he thought it rather good as he watched it, but that his admiration for it has grown daily and hugely in the interim. He admires Marlon Brando enormously. He thinks highly of Tennessee Williams, "a true dramatist," and wants to know all about him.

He uses the word "agreeable" to describe his reaction to

151

KISS ME, KATE, and even our table-pounding enthusiasm for that work fails to raise his estimate. It remains "agreeable" and I gather it failed to live up to his expectations. Evidently, he had heard a great deal about it and wanted more.

On THE MADWOMAN OF CHAILLOT he is mild, although he says he admired Bébé Bérard's décor very much and thought the play well acted, especially by Martita Hunt.

I mentioned having read the interview in which he stated that he has really come to America to get a Mixmaster and a girdle for his cook. He insists this is quite true and that he has turned the project of acquiring the Mixmaster and the girdle over to Doubleday, Doran and Company. (That is what he called it, although it has been simply Doubleday and Company for a long time. Still, he came with the company through George Doran, and I suppose it will always be Doubleday, Doran to WSM.)

He tells us a long story which surprises us. About how he always has on his person a number of sleeping pills sufficient to put him out for good.

"I can imagine," he says, "any number of circumstances in which I should prefer oblivion to the . . . prospect before me."

He thinks it an outgrowth of his wartime flight from the South of France, when he made his way to England on a collier. During this time, he relates, he had provided himself with several ampules of instant-death poison in case of capture or emergency.

Salvador Dali stops by the table and they exchange "Cher maîtres." We remark on the beauty and elegance of the phrase.

(Later, as we are leaving, Maugham stops at the bar to thank André for an excellent martini—shaken—and their exchange of compliments ends with André saying, "Merci, maître.")

Ruth eats only four of her oysters. Maugham leans over quickly and gobbles up the remaining two. He adores oysters, he says, especially with the "exciting red sauce you have here in the States."

"Of course I'm partial to oysters. Remember I was a boy in Whitstable, one of the great oyster centers of the ... nation. Oysters were one of the few things—the very few—I liked about Whitstable."

For salad, he orders hearts of lettuce. We try to dissuade him, telling him there are other varieties far better. No, this is what he wants. Cold, firm, white hearts. He says he tries to eat the food of the region he is in.

In the course of the evening he talks of life: "Amusing"; of death: "Nothing"; and a good deal about religion. It has been important to him always. He reminds us that he was reared in a clerical atmosphere. (His guardian at ten was his uncle Henry Macdonald Maugham, Vicar of All Saints' Church in Whitstable, Kent.) As he grew older, he continues, he came to know more and more of the world and of its beings, of the complexities of life, and of the infinity of both past and future. He considered what an infinitesimal part of the universe the earth is—one tiny grain of sand, no more—on miles of limitless beach and he could not persuade himself that a single intelligence could be responsible for all this, let alone control it. He therefore came to the conclusion that the philosophy of materialism was the only one which man's reasonable nature could honestly accept.

We drove him home, all of us still talking on many subjects, trying to gather up loose ends, finish points, and answer arguments against the racing clock.

He invited us to come and stay with him in France. I experienced, in the last few minutes, that same wave of sadness I had known upon parting from him last year. Will we ever see him again? His attitude and his continuing vitality are constantly reassuring, but he is, after all, in his seventy-sixth year and one must accept the inevitable.

He kisses Ruth. I kiss him and say, "I hope that the God neither of us believes in will bless you and keep you until our next meeting."

He pats my shoulder, kisses Ruth once more, puts that little black homburg smartly on his head, and starts up the Plaza steps out of the snow. Halfway up, he turns and sees us still standing there watching him. He comes back.

"Did I tell you you've given me the best evening I've had in New York?" he asks.

He goes again without waiting for a reply, and this time does not look back.

1954. London.

Someone last night was being bitchy about Lady Colefax, the London hostess.

"She's nothing but a lion hunter" is the complaint.

"Yes," says WSM, "but what would happen to the lions if there were . . . no hunters to hunt us?"

November 1944. London.

With Guy [*Guy Trosper, American writer*] last night to the Haymarket to see THE CIRCLE by Somerset Maugham. John Gielgud plays Arnold, and the direction is by William Armstrong.

I had expected to see a dutifully done revival of a nice, old-fashioned British drawing-room comedy put together by John and Binkie [*Hugh Beaumont, head of H. M. Tennent, Ltd., British theatrical management*] for a bunch of otherwise unemployed players who have nothing better to do just now.

How wrong I was! The play is superb and this particular production matches it.

First, the physical side. The theatre was made for it. Is this where the original production opened?

[*Yes.*]

Next, the décor. I could smell that room. It was done by Sybil Colefax and John Fowler: interior decoration, set dressing, furnishings, and props. Surpassing. No wonder they are somebodies.

As to the clothes—that is what they were. Clothes, not costumes. (By H. W. Luker.) Moreover, they went with the players and the players went with them. The result was people, persons—not actors and actresses.

Yvonne Arnaud and Leslie Banks looked at each other and you believed every word of the scandale which was then revealed. A girl named Rosalie Crutchley, excellent. As for John, I have never seen him better.

The play might well have been written this year. I am reminded of something Thornton once said: "Every masterpiece was written this morning."

Not that THE CIRCLE has such lofty aspirations. Still, who is to say? When those words "masterpiece," "genius," "great" begin to be tossed about, I usually turn off my hearing aid. I only mean to indicate that there is not in this work the slightest suggestion of its being outmoded, outdated, or anything but of the moment and about the human race.

155

It is a great success and the audience was spellbound. Having recently arrived in England, I am not yet accustomed to the London theatregoing routine. This performance began at 6:15 and was over at about 8:30. The idea is to get everyone home before the blackout. The business of alerts and air-raid warnings takes some getting used to. In fact, there was an alarm during this performance. It was dealt with by the third or fourth layer of consciousness so far as the actors and audience were concerned. I may say it got my full attention for a while.

This la-de-dah sort of play would seem an odd choice for this time and place until you get here. Then you understand. The top attraction in town is the ballet. It appears that what is most desired and appreciated is design and form and order and beauty.

A play such as THE CIRCLE—stylish, graceful, winning—makes it. Above all, it has the attractive theme of continuing, continuous time—life goes on, we grow older, the human drama happens, then happens again—existence is a permanent performance—like the Windmill Theatre's sign: "WE NEVER CLOSED."

One regret—that Maugham will not see this cherishing production of his fine play. I am certain it would have meant much to him and would have given him great pleasure. I must write him about it.

October 1953. St. Jean–Cap Ferrat.

WSM says this afternoon that he did not fly until 1940, when he was sixty-six years old. His first flight was from Paris to London during the war. The plane he was in flew very low over the Channel, so as not to be mistaken for an enemy aircraft. From then on he got the idea, he says, and has flown everywhere. Until that time, he explains, he did not think it worth the risk.

[*He wrote many articles during this period, and they were widely published. I suppose René Clair saw some of them. There was in 1939 and 1940 much bitter feeling between the British and the French, and it found its way later on to Beverly Hills, where he and René clashed. He had written slightingly about the French war effort, and sensitive Frenchmen were miffed. He wrote articles of the same sort about the British, but that does not matter to people of pride, such as the French.*]

May 1954. Bulbridge House. Wilton.

Here we are in Old England. At about four o'clock this afternoon we stepped across the threshold of time and into the past.

We are weekend guests of Lady Juliet Duff, along with WSM and Alan and Arthur Macrae (in my opinion, the wittiest man in London). Also present: Simon Fleet, a most agreeable young man who has been with Juliet for some years. They were both wonderfully kind to me here in England during the war and I owe them a great deal.

Ruth and Juliet have been friends since 1936, when Ruth came over and did THE COUNTRY WIFE at the Old Vic.

Juliet and WSM have been friends, he tells us on the London station platform, "for a thousand years or so."

This is an English country weekend in the traditional sense. It may be that if one looks too closely the veneer is a bit dull, surfaces are cracked, and fabrics raveled—but the form is here and the manner. Our bags are taken up.

Tea is ready and important. By the time we reach our rooms, everything has been unpacked, hung up, put away, arranged. (Later, every piece of soiled laundry is taken from the room—washed, ironed and returned. I can only assume that this goes on all night, considering the schedule.) Maids are assigned, and valets. Life is lubricated. There are biscuits in the bedrooms, and bowls of fresh fruit and vases of fresh flowers and current periodicals from various parts of the world. A selection of the newest books, carefully chosen.

The scheduled routine of life here moves in the manner of a slow carousel. You can get on or off or stay off at will.

Breakfast is served upstairs or down. (Ruth stays up, I go down.) Walks are arranged, gardens are tended, "elevenses" (tea or coffee or bouillon), drinks before lunch, lunch, naps or no, trips into town, tea, bridge? conversation? up to dress; evening clothes are laid out, the valet in to help or just to hover or remove the used clothing. Cocktails, dinner, port. Brandy, coffee. Conversation (more spirited now)—then slowly we peel off one by one— up to bed.

You get the feeling that you are a player in a popular classic, your part is large or small, important or not—there is no audience, but the show must go on. It is a show, a ritual, a way. It is exceedingly pleasant and restful. And, in a way, deadly.

After dinner tonight (a spectacular repast; the notion of no good food in England is absolutely erroneous) Juliet and Ruth leave us. WSM and Alan and Simon and Arthur. The port is passed. I decline as quietly and unobtrusively as I can, but I sense their faint disapproval. In this drama (pageant?) I have muffed a line, and it makes the other players uncomfortable.

158

The tone of the talk changes. Men. Club stuff.

WSM turns to Alan and says, "Tell them the one about the lorry driver in the pub."

He laughs already. When he stops, Alan dutifully complies.

"A lorry driver stops at a country pub and goes into the saloon bar. The barmaid comes over and says, 'Evenin', loov.'" (Alan's accents and characterizations are immense.) "'Evenin',' says the chap. 'What's your pleasure?' she asks. 'Beer and buggery,' he says. 'What's *yours*?'"

WSM laughs again, although he has doubtless heard it told many times. I think he must be laughing at our strange reaction rather than at the joke itself. The attempted titillation strikes me as arch. I am uncomfortable. I hate jokes anyway.

WSM: "Oliver Messel told us a remarkably amusing anecdote about Juliet."

Simon: "About the ball in Berlin?"

WSM: "Yes."

Simon: "It isn't true, you know."

WSM: "Tell it, Alan."

And Alan relates that some time before the war the very tall, imposing grande dame Juliet and a party of friends were in Berlin. That was the city in those days for far-out excitement and raffish entertainment. Among the more sedate enterprises were drag nightclubs and Lesbian cafés. There were variations of these where boys and girls intermingled and the kick was in not knowing for certain if the beautiful girl you were dancing with was a boy or vice versa or versa vice. There were places where people brought, dined with, and danced with animals; and others frequented by the misbegotten and their eccentric partners.

159

Juliet and her friends were told of a great fairy ball which was to take place and, since she had not only money but influence, they were able to gain admittance. They dressed up in their best and gayest ball dress and were off. Crowds and noise and masks and madness. Shortly before midnight a dance began. Juliet and one of the young men in her party began to dance and, as they did, noticed that one couple after another was leaving the floor. The dancers were thinning out. When only six couples were left, they saw a group of judges wearing badges moving about, studying them. Before they realized what was happening, there was a crash of cymbals and a roll of drums, and Juliet was led to the stage and presented with the prize for wearing the best drag of the evening.

We laugh, but not much.

Simon repeats, "It isn't true, you know."

WSM (impatiently): "Oh, what does it . . . matter? It's a singularly amusing . . . story!"

. . . Saturday. We pay a call on the Pembrokes, taking a further step backward in time. If at Juliet's we were in the nineteenth century, here we are in the eighteenth at least. Even the air seems old. The castle is weary. Anachronisms abound. We make the tour. It would have meaning, I expect, for a student of English history—which I am not. Our hosts are polite and proper—but definitely aristocratic and, to my eye, badly misplaced in time. Even the grounds and gardens are treated as commoners. The trees wear period costumes, the hedges are antiques, and damned if the sky does not seem to contain colors and designs belonging to another civilization. Some may find comfort in this charade of the past, but I am uneasy. I am glad when it is time to go.

Back to Bulbridge House by way of Stonehenge. When

160

this plan is announced, WSM and Alan exchange a look. Alan signals calm and the trip is under way.

As we get into the car, WSM mutters to me, "I hate sightseeing."

He smokes incessantly and intransigently fails to look at what is pointed out by Juliet and Simon.

We reach Stonehenge and walk about while Juliet discourses on the subject with enormous knowledgeability. WSM smokes. I find myself standing beside him.

"I *loathe* sightseeing," he says.

Photographs are taken, rocks are touched, exclamations are made. We get back into the car.

As we do, I overhear WSM whisper to Ruth, "I abhor sightseeing."

Stonehenge was a bust today, at least with W. Somerset Maugham.

. . . Tremendous talk at dinner tonight. World War I and WSM's missions for British Intelligence. Nothing, I suppose that he has not written, but it is quite another thing to hear it all from him.

You begin to see what is meant by the classic British phrase "muddle through."

For me, having recently read ASHENDEN, OR THE BRITISH AGENT for the first time, it is a heady experience—a rare opportunity to observe how the actual happenings were transmuted by this inspired storyteller into his marvelous narratives. In this case, truth may be stranger than fiction, but fiction is better.

He eats as he talks and talks as he eats with the long-experienced manner of an accomplished diner-out. He plants the necessary background and information with skill, so that one cannot distinguish between background color and lighted fuse.

161

He makes his main points as clear as can be, and uses understatement for punches, tags, and endings.

Above all, he seems to enjoy the telling and takes pleasure in the effect of his stories on the listeners.

By the end of dinner, during the savory (anchovies on toast), the emotional temperature is high. The adventure stuff seems to have come to an end and we are beginning to move into the political aspects of his activities. Now, to my dismay, he moves straight to the bridge table, where—joined by Alan, Simon, and Juliet—a game begins. We are invited. Ruth declines and when I say, "I don't play bridge," WSM looks at me as though I have just said, "I don't wash."

Ruth and Arthur and I go for a long walk. In a way, I am glad of it. A chance to digest the talk as well as the food.

We go up. Ruth reads. I write.

. . . Sunday. Breakfast is elaborate. There is far too much to eat, and so we eat far too much. After breakfast the polite withdrawals for a time, followed by a ritual reading of the Sunday newspapers. Here there are only the posh ones as a rule, but, in deference to the weekend guests, this morning there are also THE SUNDAY EXPRESS and THE SUNDAY TELEGRAPH. Still, the principal interest centers around THE SUNDAY TIMES and THE OBSERVER: the book reviews, the film and television reviews, the art and dance articles, the theatre reports. There are also the editorial pages and assorted features, especially the arcane crossword. Sections are exchanged, arguments are sparked, disagreements are fed; it is all extremely pleasant. Somewhere in the midst of all this the inevitable tea comes once again.

. . . WSM does a charming thing this morning. While Ruth is having breakfast in her room, he sends his valet over with an envelope. Ruth opens it and finds two clippings—one from the SUNDAY TIMES and one from THE OBSERVER. They are the reviews of THE ACTRESS, which opened in London earlier this week.

[*This was the film version of her autobiographical play* YEARS AGO, *directed by George Cukor for MGM, starring Spencer Tracy and Jean Simmons.*]

Maugham has pasted little pieces of paper at the top of them and has printed "MAUGHAM'S PRESS CUTTING SERVICE, LTD." with an invented address and curious markings, so that they resemble the items one gets from a clipping bureau.

We talk about it at lunch. He is delighted by the good reviews and says he wants to see the film, although he now seldom goes to the movies.

"They hurt my eyes," he says.

"I shouldn't think they'd hurt your eyes more than the television set," I say.

"No, I don't suppose they do."

"Well, then?"

"There's a difference, don't you see? I have to . . . *go* to the cinema. The . . . telly comes to *me*."

Ruth shows the clippings to Juliet and the others. I am curious to know how he knew about preparing them.

"Do you have a press-clipping service?" I ask.

"Oh, no," he says. "I did, long ago. When I was a . . . dramatist I thought I might have something to learn from the press comment. So I subscribed to a cutting service and alternated between the joy of being patted upon the head and the anguish of being . . . birched. But I kept it up for some time. Then I began to travel widely and the post would catch up with me only from time to time at . . . prearranged places. Quite frequently it was three or four months before these cuttings reached me. By then, I was surprised to learn, they seemed to matter not at all. They had lost their . . . force somehow. A review, whether good or bad, seemed to affect the day it was published, then faded swiftly. I gave the whole thing up."

The crossword puzzle is a great event. Juliet, having solved thousands of them, begins to run through it like a breeze. As for me, I fail to understand the questions, let alone the answers. Everyone pitching in, the puzzle is done in record time.

I get the feeling that these Sunday publications are leaned upon, lived upon, in a way that ours are not.

Later. Tea is worth describing. Talk about the Japanese tea ceremony! The routine here is every bit as exact, prescribed and executed. Three tables are rolled in at about a quarter to four by the butler and two maids. One table holds the tea service itself; the second bears the scones and sandwiches and croissants; the third is laden with biscuits and pastries. Juliet pours gracefully, beautifully, elaborately, and there is a hell of a lot of eating.

(I have a theory about the ubiquitous British common cold. Every country has its popular ailment. In America it seems to be the headache. In France it is liver trouble. In England it is the common cold. It has been most frequently related to the weather, the damp of the island, the fog, the cold. I relate it to the tea, or, more specifically, to the acidity caused by the tea. Consider our secretaries, Jennifer and Yvonne. I notice that their midmorning tea usually consists of five or six cups each, with the same amount consumed later in the afternoon. They have already had tea for breakfast. Sometimes a biscuit with the morning tea, always pastries with the afternoon tea. If it is true (and I believe it is) that the common cold is brought on by hyperacidity or flourishes in a condition of hyperacidity, it would seem here to be traceable to the consumption of these gargantuan amounts of tea. This evening, after dinner, WSM and Alan and Juliet and Arthur were all sniffling away. But we are creatures of habit and there is no use going on about this to them. It is a sure way to become a bore. Watch it.)

Monday. May 1954. London.

On the way home in the train this morning, we all sit together in a compartment and, naturally, talk of the time we have just spent.

We agree that Juliet is an exceptional woman.

Maugham says, "She's one of our . . . proper aristocrats, you know. Her mother was the great Lady Ripon who brought Diaghilev and Nijinsky to London. What a . . . beauty! Juliet is not much now in fashion, and some of the newer blokes fail to appreciate her. But she's made a very real . . . contribution to her time. She's been extremely helpful in making marriages, as it were, in the arts. She's so modest and self-effacing one forgets she's a woman of considerable accomplishment. Did you know she speaks Russian fluently—as well as French and German and Italian? And has often advised on translations? And so on?"

This certainly surprises the hell out of me, and I ask him how it came about. He relates that her husband—or was it her father?—was in the diplomatic service, posted to Russia. So she learned Russian in preparation for the trip. When she got there, she continued to study diligently. She ended by knowing Russian, which was a great help during both wars when she was called upon to act as interpreter on many occasions.

I remember my first meeting with her. She was in uniform and had something to do with one of the arms of civil defense or disaster control, or ran a canteen—I cannot remember precisely. I do remember that I took her to lunch at Claridge's. The uniform was threadbare and she looked bone-tired, but she was gay and in great spirits and helped me to adjust to wartime London, and I admired her then as I do now.

[*Lady Juliet Duff died in London in 1965 at the age of eighty-three.*]

January 1966. Beverly Hills.

I spend an hour or more browsing in Hunter's fine new bookshop today and scanning the catalogues. There is a profusion of Maugham stuff and I buy a few things which I do not have here with me. Waiting for my change, I study the charts of current best-sellers displayed on the counter. The Maugham books I have bought were written thirty to fifty years ago and I cannot help wondering how many, if any, of the current list will be subjects of such a transaction thirty to fifty years hence—that is to say, in 1996 or *2016*!

1958. Nice.

A long discussion tonight about Spain, for which Maugham has tremendous feeling. It may be because he is especially admired and appreciated there and is, in fact, one of the country's most popular authors. It may be that he likes the look of it, the atmosphere, the tempo and mood, or the food. Whatever it is, a vibrant sound comes into his voice whenever he speaks of Spain. I recall that he did some of his first writing there. That autobiographical novel—never published—in Seville. What has he written about Spain? THE LAND OF THE BLESSED VIRGIN. DON FERNANDO. CATALINA. What else?

He speaks of his love for Spain.

Noël: "Yes. But what have they ever produced, really?"

Maugham (reverently, with a world of meaning): "Spaniards!"

He urges us all to go there.

At the end of the evening he gives me a copy of DON FERNANDO and inscribes it: "To Garson, a little book to take with him when he goes to Spain. From his friend William Somerset."

[*Curious that "William Somerset" seems to be all right, but I shall never forget the time I made the mistake of calling him "Somerset."*]

29 November 1954. London.

Dinner with WSM last night in his rooms at the Dorchester. Four of us only. He and Alan, Ruth and I. WSM has been ill—a liver ailment of some kind—and reports he has scarcely been out of the hotel for the past two weeks.

Nevertheless, he looked well and was in extra-good spirits, if a trifle weak. I am not surprised to see him fade as the evening proceeds. We arrived promptly at a quarter of eight and left at ten-fifteen.

Ruth had heard that he no longer follows his usual practice of going to the country every weekend. He says the report is quite true, and explains that his doctor has told him to stay put.

Ruth, teasing him, asks, "Did your doctor really say that, or are you just using it as an excuse to get out of going to the country?"

"Not at all," he replied. "My doctor reminded me that I am in my eighty-first year, and that I should rest for at least two days each week. In my case, it works out that Saturdays and Sundays are best for this purpose."

. . . Gertrude Stein. I cannot remember how we got onto the subject, probably by way of discussing Thornton. I tell WSM something he does not know, which is that Thornton is a disciple of Gertrude Stein. WSM is greatly surprised at this, since he fails to see any stylistic connection. He begins to talk about Gertrude Stein, says that he met her only a few times and that she always seemed to him "just an old Roquefort cheese."

I tell him it is lucky for him Thornton is not in the room or he would have to answer for that last crack. Thornton has revered her since he first knew her: an expatriate, living in Paris in the '20s, being charming and articulate and gregarious. She had a great deal to do with molding the style of Hemingway, Wilder, Fitzgerald, and others less known. They in turn (especially Hemingway) begot a whole new generation of American writers and writing.

I repeat what TW has often mentioned: Gertrude Stein's dictum that writing is a series of spiritual exercises leading to the eventual amputation of the audience.

WSM looks at me with faint disgust and says, "Would you mind repeating that in words of . . . two syllables, so that I can understand it?"

168

I play the game, take him seriously, and do so.

He says, "Well, if people want to . . . do that, they have a perfect right, but they have no right to expect . . . me to read it."

I ask him if he is now or ever has been a man of superstition.

He thinks it over and says, with some surprise, "No, I can't say that I ever have . . . been addicted to superstition." A few minutes later he revises this, saying, "As you know, I have always been . . . fond of playing cards. When I had a great run of bad cards, I used to think this meant my . . . play would succeed, and if I had a run of good cards, I used to think my . . . play would fail."

I ask, "And did it ever work out so?"

He replies, "I suppose it must have to some degree, for me to have . . . continued making the connection." He goes on to rationalize, "I suppose there is a certain logic in it. One can't have only good luck or only . . . bad luck; so if luck was running well in one direction, I assumed it was . . . going to be bad in another to make up for it."

Ruth brings up the matter of that trademark sign of his (on his gate at the Villa Mauresque, on all his books, and on much of his stationery). She asks if this is not a manifestation of superstition, since she has been told it is a sign to ward off evil. WSM says he has never thought of it in that way. He uses it because it is interesting and decorative, and says, "It was used by my father before me." This is something we did not know. He goes on to relate how his father found the mark in North Africa over a hundred years ago.

He stops in mid-sentence, looks out the window into the distance over Hyde Park, and muses, "Think of it. My father has been dead for over seventy years."

... He tells us that OF HUMAN BONDAGE was less than a conspicuous success when it was first published and that it took some time for it to get going in Great Britain. In fact, it was not until after its American publication that it took hold. I ask him if he has any idea as to the reasons for this.

"A case of ... poor timing, I expect," he says. "You must remember that I had the ... misfortune to publish that book in 1915 and so found myself in competition with another and rather more ... meaningful saga called The Great War. At that time it was the occasional material, that which ... concerned itself with the events of the time, which had immediate popularity. I'm afraid the struggles and ... problems of my characters seemed remote and obscure and unimportant. Trifling. More and more, I perceive that the ... trend of things matters ... much. There are those who can instinctively recognize the right moment, a ... most enviable gift." He lights a cigarette, during which a further detail strikes him. "It was Dreiser in America—what on earth was his ... Christian name?"

"Theodore."

"Quite! Theodore Dreiser who helped my book enormously. He wrote about it and ... talked about it endlessly, with great enthusiasm. He was, I'm told, in a strong ... position at the time and his words had weight. I've always thought it sad that I never could bring myself to finish a single one of *his* works. It makes me ... seem an ingrate, but in fact I've always felt greatly ... indebted to him."

... He gets to talking about Georges Simenon, whose work he admires enormously, although, I gather, on strictly an entertainment level.

I tell him of Thornton's admiration for Simenon and

his work; of Thornton's meeting with Simenon in New Haven when Simenon was living in Lakeville, Connecticut; and something of Simenon's disciplined work methods.

All of this is of great interest to Maugham, who says that Simenon told him the following story: "I always wanted to be a writer, and I began very young. I suppose I was sixteen or seventeen when I wrote my first story. I was audacious enough to send it to Colette, who was then the editor of LE MATIN, a literary review in Paris. I did not hear from her for some time, and so went round to see her. 'I have read your story,' she said to me. 'Take it home and simplify it.' I took it home and worked on it, then took it back to Colette. A few days later she sent for me and said, 'I've read your story again. Now go and take the literature out of it.' I worked on it some more. It was returned to Colette a third time, and when I went to see her again she said, 'Now take it home and simplify it further.' I was about ready to give up in complete discouragement, but decided to have one final go at it, and did as she advised. When I returned this time, she read it and said, 'Very well. Now I would like to engage you to write a story every week for this publication.' And so I did, for well over two years. Imagine what I owe to Colette. How kind of her it was to have taken the trouble to have taught me so much, not only about writing, but about myself. She showed me how to find the best in myself by digging deeper and not settling for the superficial spill."

. . . I notice the television set in his room and ask him if he is still addicted.

"Not terribly," he says. "I find it rather . . . poor."

"Not terribly?" cries Alan. "Why, he's a regular telly-boy. Worse than ever! We sit there looking at it by the hour, with our eyes streaming."

WSM has recently been interviewed on television and the program is being much discussed. He was apparently impressive, although he claims it was absolutely off the cuff and unrehearsed.

(I wonder what he did about the stammer, which was worse last night than I have ever known it to be.)

... There is, naturally, much talk of THE MATCH-MAKER. Ruth reports to WSM the strange contradiction in Thornton, who claims that critical comment means nothing to him, but appears to be rather let down by the failure of one of the critics to appreciate what he was getting at in the play.

She asks WSM to elaborate on something he talked about briefly last spring—his relationship to his critics.

"Oh, well," he says, "it's been so many years since I read any review of my ... work that I hardly remember."

I envy him as I consider that business in New York of waiting up for the reviews—the cliff-hanging, bone-crushing suspense. They arrive, at which moment they appear to be all-important. It is only after some time has passed that comment falls into its proper perspective. The work is either successful or not to whatever degree, and the importance of the immediate reaction fades into the background. In time there comes to be a prevailing opinion, which is what matters. Not what one particular person, whether private or professional, has said or thought, but what the color of the whole is.

I am suspicious of those who claim to be uninterested in critical comment. There was long a legend that Alfred and Lynn never read reviews, but in fact they often do. I would have thought Thornton only mildly concerned, but on this production we find that he is greatly involved. I suppose he knows that Gertrude Stein's idea of amputating the audience is correct theoretically, but I doubt he works it out practically, even if sometimes he thinks he does. It is like smoking. Thornton has the idea he has practically given up smoking, but I watch him puffing away while telling how he smokes scarcely at all.

All the above is discussed to the great interest of WSM. He is curious about the working methods of other writers, and wants to know about Thornton and Simenon. He is interested in Hemingway and Faulkner. He admires both, Faulkner more. I would have thought it the other way about.

He responds with excitement to the recital of Simenon's calendar working method of concentrating on writing for three weeks out of each month—morning, afternoon, and evening, beginning early each day, working on fresh material until one chapter has been completed. In the afternoon, revising; in the evening, reading, studying germane material, walking, meditating, preparing. Early the following morning, 5:00 A.M. or so, down to the study for the next chapter. This for three weeks, and then a week off to leave the working place and routine. When he lived in Lakeville, Connecticut, he would go to New York, usually to the St. Regis, see friends, attend to business, go to the theatre, to concerts, films, dinner parties, and so on. After a week of this, back to Lakeville and the routine. Once Thornton met him in New York and asked him to attend some special event—I forget what it was.

Simenon was dismayed and said, "Oh, how unfortunate. On the twenty-ninth I go back to work."

... We talk a good deal about the difficulty of being self-employed. The moment you go to work for someone, you feel that you must perform conscientiously and work full hours and give the employer his money's worth. Being self-employed, you are more inclined to be lax and less disciplined. WSM says this has been true in his case, and that had it not been for editorial pressure on the part of Ray Long and Herbert Mayes and others, he might not have produced as much or as well. There have been cases when he contracted to provide a certain number of stories, working against deadlines, and, he says proudly, "I always made them."

He is delighted with my recounting of a recent statement made in an interview by William Faulkner: "I work only when the spirit moves me. Fortunately, it moves me every day."

We discuss the mnemonic devices which various writers use in order to find their way to their work. After all, it is one thing to live in the day-to-day world and another to move into the world of the imagination. A bridge is needed to take one across.

A writer gets up in the morning, has his breakfast, reads the newspapers, eventually goes to his desk. Now he must find his way into the world with which he is dealing, to the characters which he is creating and controlling. It cannot be done with a snap of the fingers. Willa Cather, they say, would go into her study and read a chapter of the Holy Bible. We remind WSM that he has said he sits down and starts to write and, if he can't think of anything to write, forms his name over and over again, the physical act of writing priming the pump of creativity. Thornton has told us of Hemingway, at the end of a day's work, deliberately breaking the points of all his pencils. The following morning, there they were before him. With a sharp pocket knife he would begin, carefully, to sharpen the points on all the pencils. By the time the last point was sharpened, he was ready to begin his work.

All this interests WSM, but he constantly challenges, wants to know how we know, where we heard it, are you sure, and so on. He is not after information, he is after *accurate* information.

...He has been to see Peggy Ashcroft in HEDDA GABLER and has admired her performance enormously. He is not keen about the play any more; thinks it one of the most difficult acting parts ever written, and believes that Peggy brings it off brilliantly.

Ruth tells him she often considers getting together a production of JOHN GABRIEL BJORKMAN.

He furrows his brow and says, "JOHN GABRIEL BJORKMAN. I haven't read it in thirty or forty years, but I seem to . . . remember I admired it very much." All at once he begins snapping his fingers. "Wait now, wait now, isn't he a . . . businessman of some sort?"

"Yes."

"Hasn't he been to prison, and—wait, here it is! He . . . paces. We hear him . . . pacing upstairs."

"Yes, that's it."

"Oh, a very . . . fine play."

I note the remarkable use of memory. Further, I am interested in noting exactly what does stick in recollection. In this instance, the colorful dramatic effect of the offstage sound of a man pacing up and down. What one remembers about THE GIRL OF THE GOLDEN WEST, say, is the splendid theatrical device of the blood dripping down from the ceiling, revealing the hidden, wounded man up there. You remember the cavalry charge in the film HENRY V, and so on. Great theatrical experience is made up almost entirely of moments.

175

1955. New York.

Dinner with Dick Adler tonight. He tells about his visit with WSM in the South of France last summer.

Dick is working on a musicalization of OF HUMAN BONDAGE and had gone there to confer with Maugham, who takes a great interest in the project.

Dick flew up from Rome, having cabled on ahead. When he arrived at the Nice airport and was deplaning, he was surprised to see a large group of reporters and photographers. He wondered whom they were meeting, since he had not recognized anyone on the plane. As he approached the airport building, he saw Maugham standing with Alan and the newspapermen. The whole group came forward and greeted him. There were questions and answers and photographs. During this, Maugham turned to Dick and said, "Why, my dear boy, I'd no idea you were so . . . celebrated!"

(There is a further point of interest in the account. It is an example of Maugham, the practical professional, in operation. He must have made it a point to inform the press; otherwise how could they have been there?)

1953. St. Jean–Cap Ferrat.

Title talk this afternoon up at Maugham's. We agree that titling is a unique gift and that Scott Fitzgerald possessed it. All his titles are near perfect: TENDER IS THE NIGHT, ALL THE SAD YOUNG MEN, THIS SIDE OF PARADISE, THE RICH BOY, DIAMOND AS BIG AS THE RITZ, and so on and so on.

"Were they all his, do you suppose?" asks Maugham.

"I believe so," I reply. "I once had occasion to discuss this very subject with him, and he took great pride in this ability. He said he had even provided Zelda, his wife, with the title for her only published novel, SAVE ME THE WALTZ."

"Isn't that fine?" says WSM. "The title, I mean. Yes, the generosity, too, but especially the . . . title. I wish he'd helped me with some of mine."

"Oh, yours are pretty good—on the whole."

"Not really. Some of the short stories have rather . . . neat names, but the books always gave me difficulty, and I was never able to . . . bring myself to accept the suggestions made by editors and publishers and sometimes even friends."

"Lillian Hellman's play THE LITTLE FOXES has a fine title, and she says Dorothy Parker named the play."

"Dorothy Parker is a . . . great woman," says WSM.

"I like most of your titles well enough," I say, "with the exception of OF HUMAN BONDAGE. That's a dud."

He is surprised. "Oh?" he says. "I think it's . . . good enough."

"Good enough isn't good."

"Perhaps," he says, "you would have . . . preferred the original title—THE ARTISTIC TEMPERAMENT OF STEPHEN CAREY."

"Hardly."

"Strange what fashion is. When the . . . book was written, that first title was thought to be ideal, but when I revised it, I decided to give it a fresh . . . name as well."

We leave title talk and begin to discuss the projected musical version of OF HUMAN BONDAGE. I tell him what I know of Sam and Bella Spewack, who are working on the

177

book. They are old friends and absolutely first-rate writers. He is pleased to have this reassurance, and tells me how much he liked Richard Adler, who has been here to talk to him about it.

We get pretty involved in the conversation, and I cannot help expressing some misgivings about the lyric possibilities of the work. But then I hasten to point out that no one can know in advance what might lend itself to musicalization.

Suddenly I remember Alan Lerner's joke when he heard OF HUMAN BONDAGE was being made into a musical show. Alan volunteered a title, and I tell it to WSM—WORST FOOT FORWARD. WSM looks at me stonily. He does not care for the witticism.

"Now, you must admit that's funny," I say.

"Must I?" he asks.

On to other things.

"Did you really say," I ask, "that intelligent people read practically nothing after the age of thirty?"

"Of course. It's . . . quite true."

"But *you* read all the time!"

"Because I'm . . . not intelligent!"

"I think you are."

"That's because *you're* . . . not intelligent."

I try to get him to go into this more fully. His point is that we read a great deal when we are young and impressionable. Certain authors hit us hard. We grow older, read less; older still, until we read, as he puts it, practically nothing, but the indelible effect of the writers of our youthful reading remains and so we cherish them, remember them as "lit with glamour" and applaud them as they and we grow old together.

The hell of it is that often it is difficult to grab the key

178

of his flow. Sometimes he seems to be jesting when he is at his most serious. At other times he seems to be at his most serious when in reality he is kidding the pants off the public.

1958. Nice.

At Maugham's, with Noël. A discussion of fiction writing. Ruth repeats Thornton's observation that the novel is doomed.

Maugham: "Well, everything is . . . doomed, for that matter, isn't it?"

Afterward he says graciously, "If it is dying, Thornton is doing a . . . good deal to keep it alive, isn't he?"

Finally, his observation that he does not think it doomed at all. He feels it is probably changing, but will always exist in one form or another so long as there is a civilization. Wherever there are people, there are happenings. Whenever there are happenings, they are going to be related, and that will take some form.

All my life, it seems, I have heard that the theatre is dying. Instead, it undergoes mutations and changes, part of it becoming silent film, talking film, television, yet constantly returning to its base of living theatre, or a Punch-and-Judy show.

Later. He sends me a copy of his lecture on THE SHORT STORY with the following passage marked:

But I cannot believe that people will lose their desire to be told stories. It is a desire inherent in the human race. I suggest to you that it may well be satisfied by the radio. It may be that listeners will take the place of readers, and that those who want the

179

entertainment of the short story will be content to hear it over the air. Then the art will have gone full circle. The short story presumably started with the tale told by the hunter home from the hill, sitting round the fire in the cave which was the dwelling of primitive man and, having run its long course, will then return to its origins. The teller of tales, seated before his microphone, will narrate his story to an immense crowd of unseen listeners. But if this happens it is hard to believe that he will have an attentive audience if he tells stories that depend on atmosphere or stories whose meaning is obscure. His stories will have to be direct, gripping, surprising and dramatic. They will have to move swiftly in one unbroken line from the beginning that arouses interest to the end that satisfies the curiosity that has been excited.

June 1958. Nice.

After all these years he pays me a compliment. The first; probably the last.

It was late last night. We had begun to take our leave at about ten, but the evening had developed an interesting rhythm, filled with fortunate matching circumstances of subject. The talk was based upon people we knew and who interested him—among them, George S. Kaufman, Bob Sherwood, Thornton, Alice B. Toklas, and Henri Soulé. Luckily, he had not heard a single one of the anecdotes and reports and accounts we had to offer. So the evening was loaded with surprises. There was a good deal of laughter and salty fast-cracking all around. Ruth was in fine form.

When we started to leave at ten he objected and bade us stay. We were surprised and Ruth said so. She reminded him that usually, at any given hour, if a guest said, "Well . . ." he jumped to his feet, shook the person's hand, thanked him for coming, and disappeared.

WSM denies it, but laughs in a way that shows he knows it is true.

We stay. He feels like talking, and he talks—of his childhood, of his beautiful mother, who died when he was eight, and of his lively, gregarious father, who died two years later; of his early struggles with English, since he had spoken French first. (He was born in Paris. I had forgotten that.) He sketches his three brothers—all his seniors, and all lawyers. Charles ("a saint"), and Henry ("a bore"), who committed suicide at the age of thirty-six, and Frederick ("the great one"), who is Viscount Maugham of Hartfield and Lord Chancellor of England. WSM is awed by his eminent elder brother and I get the feeling that when they meet—infrequently—the Lord Chancellor patronizes his little brother, the scribbler. Ruth gets the same impression.

[*In 1954 Viscount Maugham of Hartfield wrote and published* AT THE END OF THE DAY, *an autobiography. In it he hardly refers to Somerset Maugham, and when he does, it is in passing. I take it that the awe did not go both ways. Understandable. The "bohemian," odd-ball, expatriate, playboy brother could only have been looked upon with a somewhat upturned, crinkled nose by the Lord Chancellor, who had lived a correct, respectable, conservative, step-by-upward-step life as a member of the Establishment.*

Robin Maugham tells George Cukor that WSM once

said to him: "I have met a good many odious men in the course of my seemingly endless life—but never one more odious than your father my brother!"]

It was almost midnight when we left. We stood about in the fragrant courtyard for a while, winding down.

Suddenly WSM kissed Ruth, as he always does. Then he turned to me, offering me that limp hand.

As I took it, he clapped me on the shoulder with his free hand and said, "You most assuredly add to the ... gaiety of nations, old cock!"

I thought it a remark edged with sarcasm, especially in view of the ping-pong quality of the evening. We got into our car and drove away.

We are off the peninsula and well on our way back to the Hotel Negresco in Nice before the full implication of his statement strikes me. For Heaven's sake, he meant it nicely. His compliments are so rare that I failed to recognize this one when it was offered. What I mean, I suppose, are *direct* compliments. He says highly complimentary things about many people when they are not around to hear them. I have heard him praise Sam Behrman at length with great feeling and appreciation.

Once I mentioned Moss Hart and Maugham took off for fifteen minutes telling of Moss's wit and brilliance and warmth and generosity. He goes on, "Above all, Moss Hart is a ... sensitive man. There are not many. He is a rare boy."

[*I repeated this to Moss, who was surprised. "I always feel," he said, "that I am not quite getting over with him. There's a glass wall between us. I wouldn't call him unyielding, but he does hold you at arm's length, doesn't he? Thank you so much for telling me what he said."*]

It seems to be a facet of his complicatedly structured personality. He can say pleasant things about someone to others, but it is difficult for him to do it face to face.

When he came to see Ruth in THE MATCHMAKER at the Haymarket in London, he turned up backstage after the performance with a party of friends, sat on her couch, and chatted pleasantly. All sorts of extravagant things were being said. When the attention turned to him, he said he had enjoyed himself very much indeed, Thornton had written a good play, wasn't it a fine production, and weren't all the others good, too? How glad he was to have been able to see it, and especially here in his beloved Haymarket—the original production of THE CIRCLE played here. Fay Compton in this very dressing room. Memories of Marie Tempest, Henry Ainley, Cyril Maude, Ellen Terry . . . He went on and on.

It was more interesting than satisfactory. I think Ruth was a little let down that he did not have more to say to her about her performance. She had thought it, that night, one of her best. (Ruth says, "You can always tell how much they liked it by how long they stay on the subject.") The party is soon wafted out on clouds of nostalgia.

The next day there arrived for Ruth at Claridge's an enormous floral spill. With it, a letter in Maugham's hand, telling her that he thought her performance in THE MATCHMAKER one of the finest theatrical achievements in his memory.

Why was he not able to convey it to her the night before? It is a form of shyness, I gather, and Maugham is indeed a shy man.

1954. St. Jean–Cap Ferrat.

The visit last night was especially interesting since WSM is just back from Dr. Niehans' clinic in Switzerland. He and Alan have both taken the daring, revolutionary treatment.

WSM says, "I feel strange. I can . . . describe it no other way. Strange. Not myself . . . Not ill, nor especially well, simply—well, strange. I suppose part of it is that we've had no alcohol for weeks, and I have not . . . smoked. It's all part of the cure, you see."

(Cynically, I wonder if it may not be the *principal* part of the cure, or the cure itself, but I say nothing.)

WSM looks unchanged to me. He talks at length about Dr. Niehans and about the rumors that the Pope has taken this treatment, that Chaplin and Adenauer have been taking it. He names many others, and describes what it is like. It sounds like a transfusion of some sort. It seems drastic and dangerous to me, but I withhold comment because what the hell do I know about it? It has been investigated thoroughly by him and by Alan. It must have passed muster since they both went and did it. I gather WSM would like to live on and on. Whatever his denials, I note he goes constantly and regularly to cures in Germany and Italy, watches his diet, exercises, and now this.

He explains, "I don't know that it's . . . worth a damn, and there's always the risk that something as . . . violent as this may . . . kill one. But, at my advanced years, it seems a worthwhile risk, a good . . . gamble. There may be something in it. If so, well and good. If not, well, I haven't . . . gambled *many* years away, have I?"

For him to give up both smoking and drinking, even for this length of time, represents a triumph, because he is so routined, ordered, and set in his ways that it must be a tremendous wrench. But he has done it, and here he is.

[*There may have been something in Dr. Niehans' method after all. WSM was an extremely frail old man that night, yet he lived on and on. Physically. But is it possible the treatment somehow disturbed him mentally or emotionally? Who knows? Certainly I don't. Still it seems that from that time on he became excessively cross and nervous, jumpy, irrational, and unstable. Might this, in turn, have caused him to do those outré things? Adopting Alan legally so as to cut the other relatives out of the will. Fighting the French court which voided the adoption. Selling the pictures. Instituting the lawsuits. Publishing the* SHOW *memoirs. I am probably wrong about all this, but I wonder.*]

As we leave the dining room tonight, I stop to look at an unusual painting which hangs on the wall to the right of the doorway. A few minutes pass and I realize that I am not alone. I become aware of a presence behind me and to my left. I turn and see WSM observing me. He is smoking.

He says, "You don't know . . . a damned thing about pictures, do you?"

"No, I don't. But how would you know that?"

"I could . . . tell from the way you were looking at that one."

"Really?"

"Yes. Just as one knows when . . . Kenneth Clark looks that he knows *all* about pictures."

The subject of my ignorance does not vaguely interest me, so I make pass-the-time conversation.

"Who painted this?" I ask.

"Kenneth Clark didn't ask. He knew at once."

"No doubt."

"It's a . . . Toulouse-Lautrec, actually."

I look at the picture again. It is a figure of a man, nude, wearing only a hat of some sort, kneeling on a stone floor and polishing it. WSM tells me that the picture is called "Le Polisseur." According to the story, the polishing of the stone floor of this building, or church, or whatever it is, was such a dirty job that the men who performed it had to strip naked in order to do it; otherwise they would continually ruin their clothing.

"Don't feel too . . . badly," he says, touching my arm. "Very few people guess it. In fact, it took Kenneth Clark about three minutes, but . . . finally he turned to me and said, 'The only painter whose work I know who could have painted that head and that arm is Toulouse-Lautrec.' "

So, without it being planned, he takes me on a tour of the house, showing me the pictures and talking about them. In all the times I have been here, this has never happened.

Like most owners of fine paintings, he is especially proud of the bargains. He boasts he has never paid more than $15,000 for a picture, but I find this hard to believe. On the other hand, it may be that he bought most of these early on, before the prices became inflated.

Although he owns paintings by Toulouse-Lautrec, Matisse, Sisley, Picasso, Gauguin, Rouault, Utrillo, Renoir, Marie Laurencin and Pissarro, his favorite is a painting by Lépine. Its charm escapes me, but by the time we have reached it, he is tired of the tour and makes no

186

attempt to explain it. He leaves me abruptly and the lesson is ended.

But Alan tells me about that Lépine. He says that it is the last picture Maugham bought. He had seen a Lépine in a gallery, admired it, and for a long time after that kept looking for one. They are rare. One day, by accident, he and Alan were in a gallery on Bond Street when some old canvases were brought in, apparently from someone's attic. WSM watched as they were being unpacked and one of them turned out to be a fine Lépine. He bought it at a good price and the search was over.

No doubt the adventure has as much to do with his appreciation of this canvas as its aesthetic value.

During the course of the tour I asked Maugham if he knows Matisse.

"Yes," he said. "But I met him only recently. A remarkable old . . . gentleman. Everything about him is very nearly dead except his . . . talent, which is livelier than ever. He is absolutely . . . bedridden, you know, but sketches and paints and cuts out colored-paper shapes incessantly. Like most old . . . men, he can be excessively . . . silly at times, especially on the subject of his work. I'm rather like that myself, I expect. This picture of his, called 'The Yellow Chair,' which I own, is so . . . beautiful and means so much to me that once, when I was talking to him, I thanked him for it and told him how much I appreciated what he had done to . . . make my house a far more pleasant . . . place than it would have been without this lovely decoration, and the word made him angry.

" 'Decoration!' he cried. 'Decoration is nothing but a lot of merde!' Imagine Matisse using that word about . . . decoration! Of course, the French use it more easily than we do. Still—and, of all people, Matisse, who is most certainly the supreme . . . decorator of the twentieth century. You do see what I mean, don't you, about old . . . men often talking foolishly about their work?"

"True."

One of his Picassos is an oddity. As WSM describes it, "a double masterpiece." On one side of the canvas is "The Death of Harlequin," which Maugham considers "the most moving painting I have ever seen." On the reverse side of the canvas is another work, called "Woman Seated in a Garden." There are many accounts of how this came to be and all of them, according to Maugham, apocryphal. What does it matter? There they are.

It troubles him that people take on so about the curiosity. I think he would prefer it if the pictures were on separate canvases.

[*Maugham's uneasiness notwithstanding, the nonesuch described above proved to be the star of the show when the collection was auctioned at Sotheby's in the spring of 1962. It went for $244,000, which is said to be the highest auction price ever achieved for a painting by a living artist. The whole collection, some thirty-five paintings, sold for $1,466,864.*]

I ask him if he knows Picasso and he surprises me by replying in the negative. For one thing, Picasso is a sort of neighbor and, for another, is known to be a most gregarious man, constantly traveling about through the area, calling on people, going to galleries, giving dinner parties, and so on. But no, WSM has not met him.

"Our paths never . . . crossed, that's all," he explains. "I would be . . . delighted to receive him here, but the subject has not come up. I rather think he would . . . not turn me down if I asked to go over and see him, but that

188

would mean a trip to Cannes and I . . . don't think I want that. Marie Laurencin came here once. She heard I owned a few of her . . . watercolors and wrote me a letter asking if she could come and see them. I had her over for a meal and . . . found her most amusing. She went through the house looking at all the pictures and in the end said quite gravely that she admired my . . . collection enormously and that there was no doubt in her mind that the best pictures of the lot were my Laurencins. Think of it. A long time after that she told me she wanted to . . . paint my portrait. It made me . . . laugh because I wouldn't have thought myself a fit subject for her style, but I went through with it and sat for her, oh, half a dozen times, and in the end she gave me the result as a . . . gift. I thought it . . . lousy, but I said nothing to her to suggest that. I have it somewhere here, but I don't like to show it."

I press him and with a shrug he takes me into the dressing room adjoining his bedroom. "There it is. Hardly a . . . likeness, but an interesting painting."

Standing before it, we talk about the changes which have come about in the craft of portrait painting. Long ago they were photographic reproductions, but from the time the camera was invented, portrait painting, in order to stay alive, had to become more than a reproduction. It had to become an impression, a comment by the artist upon the sitter, a piece of decoration. Likeness per se became less important.

I say, "Alice Toklas told us the other day that when someone objected to Picasso that his portrait of Gertrude Stein did not look like her, he replied, 'Don't worry, it will.' "

Maugham is amused and says, "Rather like . . . Matisse. Someone once criticized a . . . figure of his because they said it didn't look like a woman and . . . Matisse snapped, 'It's not supposed to be a woman, it's supposed to be a . . . picture.' "

We study the Laurencin and I ask, "Why do you look so startled?"

Maugham replies, "Probably because all the while she was painting me, she was . . . telling me the story of her . . . life." He goes on. "You will . . . notice I'm wearing a robe. She asked me to do so because she said she'd never painted a collar and cravat and didn't want to take the . . . time to learn. When she bestowed the picture upon me, I thought it only fair . . . to give her the robe as a souvenir. I suppose it's a good enough picture, but I'm . . . damned if I wouldn't rather have my robe back." He looks me in the eye and goes on. "I don't much like advice and I try . . . never to give it or to take it, but I should like to advise you . . . never to give anyone anything upon an . . . impulse."

In closing, he says, "It's a good collection because it's a . . . personal one. I've never bought a picture I didn't like, no matter how much I was advised to do so by the . . . kind friends who've helped me. Gerald Kelly and Kenneth Clark and Jean Cocteau and many others, and from time to time I'm sure I've passed up . . . bargains. The pictures are friends and if one is going to live with them, they have to be . . . congenial. So, in the end, this collection, for what it's worth, is my own. I've listened to the expert advice, but I've made my own decisions. A collection reflects or should reflect the personality of the . . . possessor, and that's what mine does. I've heard it's said I don't give a . . . damn about pictures and buy them cheaply to sell them expensively. Nothing could be further . . . from the truth. I've never *sold* a picture! I've traded some, but never . . . sold one. The fact that they've greatly increased in value is . . . no

190

more than a happy accident. I've also been accused of buying them as a tax . . . dodge, but I'm damned if I know what that means or how it could be done. But then people say all sorts of nasty things, especially out of envy or . . . jealousy or just bloody-mindedness. Yes, I suppose the pictures are worth a good deal. How much, I've no idea. I've arranged for their . . . disposition. Some of them will go to Liza as part of her estate and some to various . . . galleries in London, a few to some galleries nearby, and I have . . . surprising plans for several."

He studies me. "You should try to . . . learn more about pictures, but you can't learn from anyone but yourself. It's not a question of value or prestige or . . . reputation, but only one of . . . feeling. You must learn to . . . feel through your eyes. Do you understand?"

March 1951. New York.

A WSM letter to Ruth this morning scribbled swiftly in his hand and difficult to decipher.

The best we can do is as follows:

> Villa Mauresque
> St. Jean–Cap Ferrat
> A.M.
> 9 March, 1951

Sweetheart:

How lovely to think that you are coming to France. You will be too far off to come over to lunch but won't you come for a quiet weekend? I warn you that it is very dull and all I can offer you is a bed and three meals a day.

Do let me know if you are traveling with Garson

or Kanin. It will make quite a difference to me.
My love to you.

Willie

Ruth responds and complains about his scrawl. Shortly there is another communication, this time typed:

Villa Mauresque
St. Jean–Cap Ferrat
A.M.
4 April, 1951

Ruth darling:

I am writing you on the typewriter because I know that you cannot read handwriting. When you are a big girl I trust they will teach you to do that. Some people's letters, St. Paul's for instance, are worth quite a lot of money when they are written in the writer's own hand.

I really don't know what there is that you can bring me unless you would like to bring me half a pound of Dunhill's MY MIXTURE, medium brand, but if that is too much trouble bring me one of Garson's old nylon shirts. I suppose he is now so prosperous he wears a 16 collar as all the tycoons do, and for the matter of fact as I do, though not as a tycoon but only a stagedoor hanger-on of illustrious and blonde actresses.

Love to you.

William S.

March 1943. New York.

We go over today to have tea with Syrie Maugham at her apartment in the Dakota. Her friend Oggie Lynn is with her.

192

Syrie is flushed with excitement about WSM's new book, which is going to be published in a few months.

She has read it—whether in manuscript or galleys is not clear—and pronounces it the finest book he has ever done. It is called THE RAZOR'S EDGE.

Listening to her going on and on about it, observing the pride she takes in his accomplishment, and noting her deep appreciation of his art, it is difficult to remember that she is speaking of her estranged ex-husband with whom, so far as anyone can gather, she never shared a happy day.

I get the feeling that it is not so much the possible material benefits involved as pure literary hero worship.

Apparently she has been heralding the work vociferously all over town and by way of dozens of communications abroad.

"Have you told him?" I asked.

"Of course not," she replies frostily.

1954. London.

Our host, a well-known London bitch, comes on tonight at the mention of Maugham's name:

"But, my dears, you *can't* be *serious!* Sweet? Why, he's the devil incarnate. I tell you he's the antichrist! No, wait, let me tell you. He had this great thing with xx. It went on for *years.* On and on. He was marvelous to him—he's not a bit generous, you know, but he simply *lavished* things on this particular Friend. One of the things he gave him was a beautiful gold-and-lacquer cabinet with a lock, and xx kept all his personal letters and documents in it.

"And then one morning, to Willie's amazement, Friend suddenly announced that he'd got *married*—don't you adore it?—married to this very rich, very old thing.

"Of course Willie was furious—up the wall—and when Friend said he didn't see why it should matter to them, Willie called him every name he could think of, and he could think of plenty.

"Then Willie demanded his letters back. Just *imagine* the old flal having been so idiotic as to have written and written, but Friend told him he could whistle for them.

"Willie tried everything—good Lord, he even tried *me*, and *I* tried—but it was simply no use.

"Then it happened. He's always been a lucky old bastard and his luck held out. Friend simply *died* one night after a bout!

"Willie read the news with his morning tea, got right out of bed, dressed in striped trousers and morning coat and black tie, put on his bowler, and was the very first one there to pay his condolences.

"He sat for an hour talking to the hysterical widow, and finally, as he was about to leave, kissed her and said, 'I gave him this cabinet, you know.'

" 'Yes, I know,' said the widow. 'He loved it so.'

" 'And it was always understood,' said Willie, 'that if anything should happen I was to have it back.'

" 'Oh, do!' she said. '*Do* have it back. I know he would have wanted it so.'

"And Willie—now just *get* this—had a van outside and stepped to the front door, opened it, beckoned the van men in and, before anyone knew what was happening, had whisked the cabinet and his letters and God knows what else out of the place.

"*Everyone* knows the story. Of course, there are variations, but I *swear* that what I've told you is the true version.

"So don't tell *me* about the Old Party. I know him inside out. He's the *wickedest* man in *London!*"

"The second wickedest," says Ruth.

"What?"

"Nothing."

December 1965. Beverly Hills.

Cathleen Nesbitt was making a film at Pinewood, she recalls, on the day WSM came out to do the introduction to TRIO.

They lunched together. Knowing that Maugham was to be there that day, the commissary people had gone to great trouble in order to provide a gourmet feast. Maugham passed it all up disdainfully and asked for a piece of boiled fish, a boiled potato, and a bit of salad.

He explained that he had no faith in the ability of this establishment to provide ambitious food.

Cathleen also suspected that he was nervous about his chore and remembers that his stammer was giving him a great deal of difficulty. She was therefore surprised when he invited her to come over to the sound stage to watch him perform.

She did so. The set was a fine replica of his study. He took his place at the worktable. The director called for a rehearsal. Maugham sailed through it brilliantly and smoothly. The director asked for a few adjustments both in the movement and in the text. Maugham nodded, his make-up was adjusted, silence and lights were ordered, and the take was made. Again he delivered without the slightest hitch.

Even now she cannot understand how he was able to do it. She can hardly connect the stammering wreck at lunch with the charming, graceful, elegant, and assured personality before the cameras.

195

(Frere told us recently that Maugham often used light sedatives and tranquillizers before attempting lectures or television appearances. This might explain the above recollection.)

May 1946. New York.

Larry and Vivien are here. Before their arrival they asked us to make hotel arrangements for them. We chose the St. Regis and it seems to have worked out perfectly. We see a great deal of Vivien, something less of Larry. This is understandable, since Larry has come over with the Old Vic and a heavy repertory. In addition, he has his responsibilities as one of the managing directors. Vivien is simply here with him.

The Old Vic is providing memorable theatre nights, each opening more dazzling than the one which came before. Audiences admire not only the skills and the talents of the players, but respond emotionally to the strength and power with which they have come through the ordeal of war. It does not escape us that London was a battlefield, while New York was not.

Maugham is in New York briefly, too.

THEN AND NOW has just been published, and I am full of excitement about it and its film possibilities, especially for Larry and Vivien.

A crazy quarrel last night with Vivien. It began as a joke, but soon was not a joke. I may not have behaved perfectly, but neither did she. There is no excuse for me, every excuse for her. It must be maddening for her, a young actress at the peak of her powers and popularity, to find herself in the position of a hanger-on who has come along for the ride.

She is in great demand for both plays and films, yet she decided to do nothing except be here with Larry for the length of the Old Vic season. The fact that she has chosen this course does not necessarily remove the tension caused by inactivity.

(I am married to an actress, and I know that the worst times are the times when she is not acting. When she does not have scenes to play in the theatre, she finds it necessary to create them in life.)

We were talking of Maugham's THEN AND NOW. Larry has not had a chance to read it and so all of us were trying to sketch it for him to give him a feeling of the shape of it, more or less. The burden of the telling fell to me.

I said something about the play within the novel called MANDRAGOLA, pronouncing it so.

Vivien threw in a quick correction, "MANDRAGOLA."

Of course, it was silly of me to be irritated. There is no reason why she should not correct me if I am wrong, but the correction came at what I felt to be the wrong moment. I was trying to build the narrative, and it seemed to me petty for her to interrupt in that way. So I simply repeated, the next time the word came up, "MANDRAGOLA."

Again she said, "MANDRAGOLA."

I stopped and said, "What's the difference, for Christ's sake?"

"All the difference in the world," she replied coolly. "You're pronouncing it incorrectly."

"That's how we say it here," I ventured.

"Where?"

"In the United States, where we happen to be," I said.

"Oh, do you?" said Vivien. "Well, in the United States you pronounce it incorrectly."

The others in the room began to see the sparks, and

made jokes and said it seven different ways, including the Italian. It was too late. Vivien and I were joined in edgy conflict.

"There are a good many differences between our speech and yours."

"Yes," she said, "but Mr. Maugham is *our* writer."

"When his books are published in the United States," I argued, "we don't spell it 'l-a-b-o-u-r' or 'f-a-v-o-u-r.' "

"And what's that to do with it, may I ask?" asked Vivien, quite logically.

Flummoxed, I said something like "Oh, the hell with it. *You* tell it."

It all began to go wrong. Soon, bitter things were being said about who was the better educated, who spoke English, who knew more about Maugham and Machiavelli and life and oh, God and oh, hell!

In an hour or so it had cooled off and calmed down and there were hugs and kisses and even some tears. But I wonder if such flare-ups are ever completely forgotten. They are like little fuses blowing, reminding you that they may blow again. They add an unfortunate element of apprehension and tentativeness to a relationship.

I am deeply sorry about the whole damned thing. I said so to Vivien, but I wonder if she really believed me and I wonder if I really meant it.

May 1946. New York.

An unusually rich and rewarding evening with Vivien and WSM. In talking to her the other day, we are astonished to find that she has never met him. Later he confirms this. How can it be? They travel in the same circles. They have scores of mutual friends. Whatever the cause, they have never met and are eager to know each other. We arrange a time convenient to all. It is to be dinner at the Colony. Ruth and I, Vivien and WSM.

We pick up Maugham and together we go to the St. Regis to fetch Vivien. She appears—ravishing, exquisite, invisibly spot-lit. WSM is speechless and cannot take his eyes off her, even in the car. Soon we are seated quietly at a corner table at the Colony. It all begins in high. Vivien falls in love. As for WSM, I have never seen this side of him—the gallant, the courtly gentleman, the man on the make. Every warm instinctive exchange passes between them. Vivien is enormously impressive with her tremendous erudition, her wide reading, her beautiful French, her glorious speech. It is a pleasure to sit there and shut up and listen. He pays her compliments more beautifully than I have ever heard compliments paid. I feel almost an intruder, but nothing could induce me to leave. There are drinks and wines and the food is superb. Once again we all discover the deep delights of conversation, especially of the intimate variety. If this were a party, the things which are happening and the memorable things which are being said could not be. Large parties are for small talk. Even dinner parties are for some sort of social exchange, but not for enriching, nourishing questions and answers, opinions and challenges, and exchanges of feelings and ideas. That is what we are sharing tonight, and all of us are grateful.

Somewhere WSM mentions and Ruth recalls that Alec Woollcott made it a rule never to attend any social function where more than eight people were present. In fact, he carried this rule to perhaps a ridiculous degree. Once, invited to a dinner party at Voisin, he arrived, saw there were ten, and, instead of sitting down, left. He would not break his rule. We discuss this. Maugham and I think he was wrong. Ruth and Vivien defend him, saying that a rule is a rule, a principle a principle. Vivien adds that if a lifeboat is marked for ten passengers, it is wrong to put twelve in.

It seems to me this analogy makes little sense, but, remembering our quarrel the other night, I swallow it.

Maugham is so relaxed tonight, so easy and charming, that his stammer is scarcely noticeable. He makes a few pauses and once or twice the letter "m" does not let go; a bit of trouble with a "w" but, on the whole, he stammers no more than any of us do in the course of passionate or excited conversation.

Dessert is a spendid chocolate soufflé, with a bottle of Lanson, and we are all in the clouds.

Following this, I make my first blunder of the evening, saying, "How about a stinger?"

"Good Lord," said Maugham. "I haven't tasted that dangerous concoction in years."

"I *never* have," said Vivien.

I begin to describe it. Ruth looks worried, as well she might. But I charge ahead, anxious to put a cherry on top of the evening.

George is sent for, stingers are ordered, with specific instruction about which brandy to use. George is entirely disapproving of the idea of mixing his best brandy, but we are insistent. The stingers arrive and are begun and do what they are supposed to do.

Mine must have detached me from the face of the earth, because presently I hear myself saying to WSM, "This beauty and I had one hell of a scrap the other night, and it was all on account of *you*."

"How so?" asks Maugham.

"Well," I explain, "we were talking about THEN AND NOW and I referred to the play as MANDRAGOLA, which is the way we say it in America. At least, it's the way we said it when I was a student at the American Academy and we did the first act of it as an examination play." Maugham's eyebrows are arched. Vivien wants to talk, but I will not let her. "I know it's said differently in England and differently in Italy. But *we* say MANDRAGOLA. So, of course, my friend here put me down pretty sharply—"

Vivien interrupted. "Not sharply enough," she said. "I don't know *why* he insists upon being so stubborn. We all know it's pronounced MANDRAGOLA."

I take over again. "Just a minute, baby. We've got the horse's mouth right here. Mr. Maugham, what *is* the correct pronunciation?"

"Well," said Maugham, "so far as I know, there is no question that the name—" here he took a sip of his stinger before continuing—"is pronounced MMMM-MM-MMMM . . ."

I was horrified. Something about our nervous excitement had communicated itself to him and he was stuck on that "M." In this case it was not possible to switch to another word. Under the table I saw him snap his fingers and punch his palm; above the table his anguished face was still trying to free the word.

"MMMMMM . . ." His face exploded. His jaw went mad, his eyes rolled back in his head, and out roared the word, "MMMAGENAMERINGOLAMEDRANLOLO!"

Ruth closed her eyes. I felt my face flush. People at the surrounding tables looked over at us, and even one or two of the waiters could not help but stare.

"There. What did I tell you?" I heard Vivien say with cool, casual triumph.

201

[*L. P. Hartley has brilliantly observed, "The past is a foreign country. They do things differently there." I am certain he was referring to the past beyond one's own existence. The latter past is less conveniently examined. It is not so much a foreign country as a drama being played out by amateur actors. Or, worse, by professional actors insufficiently rehearsed. It is always a temptation to reach in and rearrange attitudes and actions, to say nothing of words. That is my feeling as I relate the above. How could I have been so childishly stubborn? Clearly, I was wrong and I knew it. What made it necessary for me to assert myself so unattractively? Was there some latent masochism involved? I could not possibly have thought that Maugham was going to support me. I remember vividly that I laughed uncontrollably at Vivien's classic aplomb. We said no more about it, considering the matter closed.*

From what followed, it seemed obvious that Maugham had no awareness of having uttered that horrifying, surrealist sound. I have discussed it since with Alan, and even with a speech expert, both of whom assure me that when such a spasm takes place, the person to whom it has happened has no consciousness of it at all. He hears only the correct sound which he has formed inside his head.

There is some comfort in this.]

September 1953. St. Jean—Cap Ferrat.

We are just back from England, where we put Mom on the *Queen Elizabeth* to return to America. In our week there, we have taken some important steps toward the production of THE MATCHMAKER in London, perhaps in the coming spring or summer.

After this time of frustration and dead ends, it is exciting as hell and we are full of talk and plans.

We go up to Maugham's to dinner. He wants to know all about London. What is playing in the theatre? What do people think of the present government? Who is there? What is being worn? What is being sung at the opera and danced at Sadler's Wells? Where did we eat and what?

I feel sure that all visitors are put through this cross-examination. It is how he keeps in touch.

Finally, he asks about our plans, and Ruth takes off. She tells him the whole, long, complicated history of THE MATCHMAKER from the time Thornton wrote it as THE MERCHANT OF YONKERS. About Tony Guthrie staying with us while putting on CARMEN at the Met and, talking about good unproduced plays one wintry night, he and Ruth agreeing that THE MERCHANT OF YONKERS was worth a revival, and so on. WSM is pleased for Ruth and says he looks forward to seeing her again on the stage. He asks who is going to put it on. We are astonished that the name Tyrone Guthrie does not mean more to him. Ruth begins to tell him and to remind him that Tony was the one who directed THE COUNTRY WIFE at the Old Vic in 1936, which he so admired.

He continues to frown, and says, "It sounds a . . . difficult play. I hope he's a good man."

"Let me talk," I say. "I can assure you that he's as fine a director for the theatre as is now living anywhere. And take my word for it, because this happens to be *one* of the subjects on which I am an expert. Tony Guthrie will do this play surprisingly and brilliantly, and it will be seen for the first time."

Maugham says, "Yes. Well, that interests me . . . greatly. What interests me even . . . more is to know on what *other* subjects you consider yourself an expert."

I reply, glibly and mock-pompously, "Why, of course. I am an expert on Mark Twain, American jazz, Gertrude Stein, nutrition, Zen Buddhism, Benjamin Franklin, films, and fucking."

Maugham: "Is that so? Do tell me all you know about f-f-f-*Franklin!*"

December 1954. London.

Dinner last night at Yvonne and Jamie Hamilton's. About sixteen guests, I should think. Extremely pleasant, although somewhat formal and circumscribed and correct. A thoroughly disciplined evening which went according to plan. Everyone knew his part.

They live in a large, elegant house in St. John's Wood. And Yvonne, being Italian and wonderfully organized, provided a perfect dinner. Maugham and Alan were there. Sir Kenneth and Lady Clark. Mark Bonham-Carter and Joan Drogheda. And a few others whom I did not know.

Jamie is the head of Hamish Hamilton, Ltd., rival publishers to Maugham's people, Heinemann, which meant that the evening had in it a special sort of graciousness, a salute. Maugham was the guest of honor, and carried it off brilliantly.

(There was one moment worth noting. As we were leaving, warm goodnights and thanks were being said. WSM shook hands with Jamie. As Jamie moved away from him, Maugham tugged at Alan's sleeve violently and whispered, "What's *her* name? What's *her* name?"

"Yvonne," said Alan just as she stepped up to Willie.

"Yvonne, my dear," said Willie, "what a perfectly marvelous evening you've given me."

Whereupon he kissed her cheek and sailed out.)

The dinner-table conversation is dominated by Kenneth Clark, and a damned good thing, too. He is an expert and knows what he is talking about. His replies to questions on the subject of art and the administration of the public galleries and museums in London are well worth hearing.

[*When I first came to London during the war, I was attached to the OSS and assigned to SHAEF, the Supreme Headquarters, vaguely in the film division. After some months I was assigned to the job of making, with Carol Reed as the British opposite number, an official report of the invasion, under the direct supervision of the Supreme Commander, General Dwight D. Eisenhower. This brought Carol and me into much contact with the various film organizations, including the Film Division of the MOI (Ministry of Information). The head of the Film Division was Sir Kenneth Clark. For some time British films had been a special province of my interest and I was surprised that I had never heard of Kenneth Clark. I was familiar with the names of underlings and of practically everyone else who was at work in the Film Division, but not with that of the head. Carol told me the following story: In the hectic days when the coalition government was being formed with Churchill at the head, there were frantic all-night meetings to organize the various departments. In the middle of one hard night, around a tired conference table, the constitution of the Ministry of Information was being discussed and appointments considered. Dawn was breaking as they reached a sheet headed "Film Division."*

Winston Churchill said, "What's that?" And someone replied, "Pictures, sir." He thought hard for a moment and said, "Pictures. Well, who knows all about pictures? Ken-

neth Clark, of course." And it seems that because no one at that particular table in that particular room that night wanted to correct the Prime Minister, Kenneth Clark, art expert, historian, and curator, found himself, to his amazement, head of the Film Division of MOI. What gives the story special point is that he made a damned good job of it, too.

The story may be apocryphal, God knows, as are most of the stories of the war. I like it, all the same.]

After dinner the ladies retired. Jamie invited us all to close ranks. The port came on and the cigars and looser talk.

I was not listening too carefully. The presence of Kenneth Clark had started a train of thought about wartime London and the making of THE TRUE GLORY and the feeling of London during the war as contrasted with the feeling of London now. So I do not know how they got around to it, but when my attention returned to the ensuing conversation I was startled to find they were talking about obituaries: the method by which obituaries are prepared at the office of THE TIMES, who writes them, who assigns them, which ones have been especially good, which ones poor, and so on.

Jamie asks me, "Of course, in America you don't have this sort of thing, do you? They just have rewrite men knock them up for the obit page, isn't that so?"

"I'm afraid I don't know," I said hoarsely, because I could not take my attention from WSM, who sat there calmly smoking. When I was able to shift my focus, I looked around to see if I could tell whether anyone else was thinking what I was thinking, which was that it certainly bordered on the tasteless, or at least showed a want of feeling or a lack of judgment, to have introduced this subject in the presence of Maugham, who is, after all, eighty years old.

He did not seem to mind. Jamie told about being asked to write the obituary of a rival publisher. Kenneth Clark knew who had written some of the recent ones. In time, I was able to convey via eye to Jamie that I thought we ought to get off this. He agreed and immediately communicated with the others. There was a long pause. I think everyone at the table was sorry about the lapse, and for a few seconds no one could think of what to say next.

Maugham chirped up, "I've read mine!"

Clark: "Have you? That's most unusual."

Jamie: "How did you happen to get hold of it?"

WSM: "Why, he sent it to me—the editor. He asked me if I'd be . . . good enough to check it for accuracy. I did so. When he called the following day, I said to him, 'Well, I find it . . . accurate enough, but not half . . . *warm* enough.' So he invited me to tidge it up. And I did. I can assure you it's . . . warm enough *now!*"

April 1955. New York.

THE ATLANTIC came out last week with DO RE MI in it and we sent a copy to WSM, among others. This morning a letter from him from the Villa Mauresque:

18 April

Dear Mrs. Kanin,

What a clever husband you have! I have now read his story in THE ATLANTIC which some fan (I hope) sent me, and I read it with pleasure, interest and amusement but clever as the author may be are you sure you are wise to live with a man who uses such language as though it were his native tongue? And my Lord the things he knows! Why speaking as if I were you for a minute not me I would as soon go to bed with a hydrogen bomb as with a man like that. Safety first I say. Excitement is all very well but—well?

This is a letter from a well-wisher, and I hope you will not take it A MISS.

Yours respectfully
W. S. Maugham

June 1958. Nice.

Dinner at Maugham's tonight. Alan and Noël are the only others present.

We got onto the large subject of copyrights.

I report to WSM and to Noël about the work which is being done in the United States by the Authors League and by the Dramatists Guild in an effort to improve the copyright laws. They are both immensely interested. Clearly, Maugham is emotionally involved in the matter. He says that, on the whole, he has always been treated well by the world, by the countries in which he has lived, and by the governments thereof. But on this matter of copyright he feels unjustly used.

Noël teases him. "You've simply lived too long, Willie. It's as simple as that."

"It has not been . . . simple," says WSM. "I have taken great pains."

"And given some too, haven't you?"

"I dare say."

I urge Ruth to tell them her idea for revising the copyright laws. She says she would rather I did it.

"This food is so fine," she says, "I want to concentrate on it."

"All right," I say. "I'll do it." I am about to begin.

Ruth says, "Tell it, don't sell it."

"Ruth's idea," I say, "is this: let copyrights expire after fifty-six years, but at that point instead of going into what is now loosely called the public domain, which means that the work becomes fair game for anyone's usage, let it go into the public domain in the true democratic sense—or public ownership. In other words, after fifty-six years or one hundred years or one hundred and fifty-six years, when it is deemed that the original creator of the work and his estate should no longer derive the benefits from it, have the copyright taken over by the government of the country where the creator was born, lived, and worked. If this were the existing condition, all the copyrights of Emerson, Thoreau, Dickens, Longfellow, Walt Whitman, Herman Melville, Edgar Allan Poe, Shakespeare, Sheridan, Handel, Washington Irving, Bach, Beethoven, Brahms, and so on, would rest in a repository of government, administered by a bureau which would lease the rights in the way that Samuel French or the Shaw estate does it now. Imagine the sums which would be returned. These could be used to establish libraries, theatres, opera houses, schools, academies, or for the printing of books to be inexpensively distributed. The aggregate sums growing year by year would eventually be enough to support the entire cultural life of the nation. Also, the money might be used to find and encourage new talent, to train musicians, painters, actors, playwrights, and so on. A sort of self-sustaining creative-arts foundation or department of government. Doesn't this seem sensible and logical and civilized?"

I make the point that in these days of extended life span,

authors, more and more, outlive their American copyrights. I remind WSM that he has already outlived a good many of his. I tell him about the Mark Twain plan, and he gets all excited.

[*Mark Twain, a fiery fighter for copyright revision in his day, conceived the idea of making his nom de plume a Registered Trade Mark. Thus the name "Mark Twain" is protected forever in the same way as "Coca-Cola" or "Chevrolet." His works may fall into the public domain, but his name, never. That is why we often see, in cheap reprints:* THE ADVENTURES OF TOM SAWYER *by Samuel L. Clemens.*]

There is no way he can make use of it at this point, but he wonders what would have happened had he been able to do so.

I finish the outline of Ruth's proposal. There is such an immediate outcry that I cannot tell for a time who is for it and who is against it. I keep hearing the words "socialistic"; also "government control and interference." I am yelling as loudly as the others.

I ask WSM if he has any serious concern about the financial welfare of his great-great-great-great-grandchildren.

He says, "None whatever. I don't give a tinker's dam about them any more than they give a tinker's dam about me."

I agree that the fifty-six-year limit ought to be knocked out. I cannot imagine how that number was fixed, anyway. In these days of the burgeoning science of geriatrics, more and more people live to be eighty and ninety and one hundred and perhaps even more. If they have written something or created something in their twenties or thirties, does

it not seem reasonable that they should be the ones to derive the benefit from their own creativity later in life?

We begin to discuss the creation of a play or a novel
or a poem or a piece of music in terms of an invention. Is
it not plainly unfair, unjust and inequitable to allow someone to have the protection of a patent in perpetuity, yet
have someone who invents a play or a piece of music run
out of rights at a fixed date?

Very often, created material continues to have value and
people who have had nothing at all to do with it get the
benefit. We do FLEDERMAUS at the Met and there is no
one to claim royalties on behalf of Johann Strauss.

*[Tragic that Felix Frankfurter is gone. This is a subject
I would have liked to have taken up with him.]*

The custom and the rules are clearly anachronistic.
Twenty-eight years plus twenty-eight more. What was the
basis of that law? I wonder. In any case, times change,
geriatrics change, the life span is increased, and we are
still left with odd hangover things like enforced retire-
ments at sixty-five. Think of what WSM has accomplished
since the age of sixty-five. We talk for a time about the
curious problems of the Académie Française, which was
founded upon actuarial tables of the day. It was computed
that there were to be forty members at all times—the forty
immortals—because the rate of replacement would keep it
intact. Every generation or so there would be a new Académie. The rule stayed fixed, but the life span increased.
Men began to live late into their seventies and eighties and
even nineties, and instead of a couple of seats becoming
available every year, which I believe was the original intention, sometimes three, four and five years go by without
death claiming a single Académicien. It has created prob-

lems. Maugham has a good laugh about this.

Now a kind of honors teasing begins. The question of knighthoods comes up. Who gets them and who does not. I ask Noël if it is true he has been offered a knighthood and refused it. He puffs on his cigarette and decides not to answer.

Maugham: "Ask me."

"I do."

Maugham: "I asked that the honor be . . . not given."

Noël, suddenly: "Of course, you crafty old coot. You're holding out for an O.M., aren't you?"

[*Meaning the Order of Merit, which is held by no more than twenty-five subjects at any one time.*]

Plenty of jibing about all this, but I get the impression that Maugham is not terribly interested in formal recognition of this sort. We all point out that Bernard Shaw was never given any official honor of any kind. I remind WSM that his great friend Charlie Chaplin never won an Academy Award, nor did Greta Garbo.

WSM says, "Sobering."

He talks about E. M. Forster (he calls him "Morgan"), who was born in 1879, wrote his principal works shortly after the turn of the century, and now begins to outlive his American copyrights. Just when he needs the income most, when it becomes difficult for him to lecture or to teach and his works could look after him, they go into the public domain for the profit of strangers. We all get highly exercised about this, and I fear that digestion is going to suffer.

"I think it's sort of dashing to outlive your copyrights," I said. "Not many do."

WSM was stony. "You'll feel differently when your . . . times comes."

"I only hope it does."

"At this moment," he says angrily, "tomorrow morning, any publisher in America may . . . print and sell LIZA OF LAMBETH, THE MAKING OF A SAINT, THE HERO, and MRS. CRADDOCK without paying me a penny." ("Paying" and "penny" are fairly spat with vehemence.) "Or my stories ORIENTATIONS, or produce my play A MAN OF HONOUR. What is even more . . . galling is the idea that they may cut my work, emend it, edit, mutilate—change an ending if they like—and I have no recourse whatever. Do you call that . . . *fair?*"

He is furious, fighting us although it is clear that we are all in agreement with him.

[*I can imagine the effect on him of the passing years, each one adding to the use of his works as they fall into the public domain. At present the list includes, in addition to the above:* THE MERRY-GO-ROUND, FLIRTATION, THE BISHOP'S APRON, THE EXPLORER, THE MAGICIAN, THE VENTURE, THE LAND OF THE BLESSED VIRGIN; *and the plays* LADY FREDERICK, JACK STRAW, MRS. DOT, *and* PENELOPE.]

Thank heavens, we leave the problem in the dining room and when we sit in the great, comfortable parlor the subject is closed.

Ruth notices a change in the room. "What happened to your piano?"

"I got . . . rid of it," he explains.

"Why?"

"Because someone came here to . . . dinner one night and . . . *played* the damned thing. It only now occurs to me . . . that what I should have done was throw the . . . *player* out, neck and crop."

. . . Maugham tells a pip of a story:

There was an imposing hostess in London who maintained a famous, formal, carefully planned and arranged salon. Each occasion had a particular subject, and the great lady (damn it, I didn't catch her name; he articulated it sloppily and I did not want to call attention to this by asking him to repeat it) would choose a subject and invite ten or twelve or twenty of the greatest authorities in England on this particular subject to attend. Like all great salons, it was a men-only affair. One woman running it all, and the guests men without women. One night on, say, slum clearance; one night on big-game hunting; another time might find all the experts on Sanskrit present, or J. M. W. Turner, or London theatre history. One night, the one he is telling about, the subject was Lord Byron. Maugham was invited—he is not certain just why. True, he has written about Byron and talked about him, but he does not consider himself an authority by any means.

He says, "Neither, apparently, did she. At these events the . . . guests were seated at the table not according to title or rank or even age, but according to their . . . standing in expertise on the subject of the evening. This put me somewhere . . . below the salt."

He goes on to tell how wonderfully she managed it all, introducing the right questions at the right times. No other subject was considered remotely fit for conversation. He says he heard tremendously impressive talk, extremely erudite spills, and powerful opinions.

The greatest authority, sitting on the hostess' right, did most of the talking; but as the evening wore on she became aware of the fact that the man she had been told was the second greatest authority and therefore had seated at her left had said nothing. He seemed to be enjoying his food

214

and listening with interest, but had contributed not so much as a word.

With the skill of a practiced conversation steerer, she waited for a propitious moment, turned to him and said, "But we haven't heard from you, sir."

He looked up and said, "No, you haven't, and I'm afraid you shan't. You see, I'm not at all *interested* in Byron!"

Naturally, she was astonished, and asked, "Indeed! Why not?"

"Because, Madam," replied the guest on her left, "he was a *bugger!*"

The hostess dropped her fork and splattered her front as she expostulated (as WSM put it), "Oh, dear me. Oh, no. Oh, that couldn't be." In panic, she appealed to the man on her right. "Could it? It isn't true?"

The greatest authority replied grimly, "Yes, Madam, I'm afraid it is quite true. I must answer your question in the decided affirmative."

The hostess, her evening ruined, could only mutter, "Oh, dear. Oh, dear."

Then the man on her left, realizing how he had upset her, touched her arm and said, "But you'll be pleased to know that in later life he redeemed himself—" A faint, hopeful smile flickered on her lips until he added: "—by having a passionate love affair with his sister!"

"That," says WSM, "is the sort of dinner party one can look back upon with . . . pleasure."

June 1958. Nice.

At the end of last evening we invite WSM and Alan and Noël to dinner on Saturday night. WSM accepts for all. We agree upon the time, 8:30, and I suggest La

Réserve in Beaulieu.

"Not at all," says Maugham. "It's . . . far too expensive."

"It's not as expensive as the Villa Mauresque, where we had dinner tonight," I remark.

"That's quite another . . . matter," he says, a bit testily. "I don't propose to see you spend far too much, and that's . . . what you'd do down there."

His feelings seem so strong that I know it would be a mistake to insist. I fear what would happen would be that we would go to La Réserve and that he would hate it.

"All right, then," I say, "why don't you suggest a place?"

"We lunch often in Nice at an excellent little . . . bistro in the market. What's it called, Alan?"

Alan supplies the name.

"That's it," says Maugham. "That will be extremely pleasant, they'll do us well, and you'll stave off going . . . broke for another year or so."

June 1958. Nice.

This afternoon we went to lunch at Maugham's bistro to try it out. It is no good. Aside from the fact that the food is indifferent, the atmosphere is hardly conducive to conversation. We decide to make it La Réserve, after all. We write WSM a note to that effect, a separate one to Alan, another to Noël, and take all three up to the Villa Mauresque and hand them to the butler.

We half expect some further argument on the subject, but when nothing has been heard from the hill by midnight we assume that all is well, and we go forward with plans for the dinner at La Réserve.

June 1958. Nice.

The dinner at La Réserve took place tonight. A whacking success.

We went over in the morning and ordered everything and chose the table. Ruth discussed the flowers. So when we arrived, twenty minutes early, everything was set. We sat in the bar and waited. Promptly at 8:30 our guests arrived.

They joined us in the bar, and drinks were brought immediately without being ordered.

Maugham looked at me and said, "An extremely . . . nice touch."

They make a great fuss over him at La Réserve. The manager stops by to pay his respects and to thank Maugham for honoring his establishment. The waiters and the bartender are all deferential. Maugham looks about the beautifully situated room, sips his drink, and says, "I'm very . . . glad we came here."

. . . WSM teases Alan, saying to us, "Alan likes to come here because he always . . . finds a rich woman in the room to flirt with. I think he rather fancies the idea of . . . marrying one, one day."

Alan takes it good-naturedly and says, "It used to be true, you know. I did have the idea until Willie said to me, 'I advise you not to marry for money. I know you and I know how much you hate hard work.'"

We go in to dinner, which is, as always, a knockout.

WSM talks about this restaurant, which has been here as long as he has been in the vicinity, and he talks of the town of Beaulieu, which has always been a great favorite with the English. They call it "Bewley," he says. Somehow

217

it has faded as its clientele has found other places preferable.

"It is no longer . . . fashionable," he says, "but then . . . neither am I."

He tells us about Cap Ferrat and its history. At one time, he says, virtually the entire peninsula was owned by King Leopold II of Belgium, who believed the spot to be not only healthy but life-giving. This idea was communicated to many others, who began to buy what was left, and as time passed, even Leopold began to sell off some of his holdings. Maugham says he first came here before World War I. It always appealed to him, so when he was in a position to do so he acquired his property. This was in 1928. He bought it, he says, from a retired Catholic bishop who had spent most of his life in Morocco, which is why the house is built in that Moorish style. Apparently it was named Villa Mauresque by the bishop. I had thought Maugham had named it. The fact that his name begins with MAU and the name of the house begins with MAU gave me the notion, I suppose.

He claims he has never noticed this coincidence. He asserts that he loves St. Jean–Cap Ferrat above all other places. It is—has become—his home town.

[*From* The New York Times, *21 December 1965:*

MAUGHAM'S BODY CREMATED;
ASHES GOING TO CANTERBURY

Marseilles, France, Dec. 20—The body of Somerset Maugham was cremated here today. The 91-year-old author's ashes will be flown to Canterbury, England, tomorrow for burial.

The only friends present were his long-time secretary and companion, Alan Searle, the British con-

sul general in Marseilles, Peter Murry, and Mr.
Maugham's financial executor, Gordon Blair.

The town of St. Jean–Cap Ferrat, near which the
writer lived for nearly 40 years, sent flowers. There
were other flowers from friends and admirers.]

. . . I ask him, "How long did it take you to learn to
live?"

"Eighty-four years," he replies.

A good answer.

"Which did you find harder to learn?" I ask. "To write
or to live?"

He thinks and finally says, "I can't answer that. I'm
sorry."

We talk of other things for a time. Then, during a
pause, he says to me, "Let me try to answer that question
of yours in another way. Let me say that I have always enjoyed writing and that I have never enjoyed living."

. . . He says, "I had a neighbor at St. Jean–Cap Ferrat
who was fading away. I could tell you his . . . name, but I
won't. You'll see why in a moment. He was an old . . . man,
my age precisely, and he had a rather young wife and she
was in despair. She found it desperately enervating to sit
by and see him . . . slowly lose his . . . grip on life. All sorts
of . . . doctors came in and each one had a different . . .
diagnosis, but when I called to see him it was clear to me
that the poor beggar was simply . . . suffering old age.
Since it was a . . . malaise I shared with him, I knew all
about it and its symptoms and . . . manifestations. I
strongly recommended that he go to Niehans' clinic, as I
have done. He did . . . not do so at once, but when it seemed
that all else had . . . failed, his young wife took him there.
Believe this or not, as you choose, but in a month's time he
was up and about and quite cured. He sent me a handsome

gift in thanks, but his young wife has . . . never spoken to me since."

. . . When wine has melted away inhibition, I make a literary confession. I tell him of the day our monthly copy of THE CORNHILL arrived and of being pleased to see his name on the cover as one of the contributors. The Maugham piece in that issue was called AUGUSTUS, and since we were in the country and it was a weekend, I sat down and read it immediately. It seemed to me one of the finest things he had ever written, a complete and detailed full-length, richly dimensioned portrait of a type. A whole time and place could be seen and understood by means of the limning of this man—a mirror.

(Thornton says, "A writer's job is to describe human beings. No more, no less.")

Now comes the confession. I took it for granted that Augustus was a fiction, an invented character. Some months later I happened to come upon a two-volume biography of Augustus Hare in FF's study. I realized then, to my chagrin, that he was a real person who had lived a real life. I began to wonder to what extent it was necessary to revise my feeling about Maugham's essay. I read some of the biography and reread the Maugham. Its effect remained unchanged. It hardly mattered. The line between fact and fabrication is small in cases of this sort.

Maugham is kind.

"There's no reason why you should have . . . known about Augustus Hare. He was rather obscure. I'm delighted you thought my . . . work an invention."

I say, "I suppose the great thing about your work is that you're always able to make truth seem like fiction and fiction seem like truth."

Maugham says, "I take that as an exceptional . . . compliment, and I thank you for it."

"Do you get lots of compliments?" asks Ruth.

"Not so many as I should like," he replies. "Let me tell you about one of my . . . favorites. It was during the war, and I was asked, along with many other writers, to make my books available on a royalty-free basis for the . . . forces. I had a letter from a GI in the South Pacific who said, 'You are my favorite writer. I've read three of your books, and I didn't have to . . . look up a single word.'

"Another compliment that . . . stays in my mind is the one paid me by your Gene . . . Tunney. He told me—I can't remember where—probably when I was . . . staying with Billy Phelps. William Lyon Phelps, wasn't it? While I was staying with him in—?"

"Probably New Haven," I suggest.

"Yes, I suppose it was. And Mr. . . . . Tunney came to call one day and surprised me by . . . telling me that when he was in training for his fight with Jack Dempsey the only book he read was OF HUMAN BONDAGE. He won the . . . fight, didn't he?"

"Yes."

"That's what makes it a . . . compliment, don't you see? If he'd lost . . . it wouldn't have been a . . . compliment at all!"

Much talk about the United States. Both he and Noël know it well, and not only New York City. They admire America as a land, as a people, and as a force. I point out that this is only natural since both of them have had enormous success there, as great as, if not greater than, in their native country.

They see the U.S. with different eyes. I find it most moving.

We talk of American writers and writing and philosophers, and begin to wonder about the phrase "New England." Is New England in any way a new England, or is it simply a semantic convenience? There is talk of Emerson and Thoreau and Adams, the notion that they created a philosophy and a style which was peculiarly American and did not relate to England at all, other than by language.

I express my concern about complete acceptance of Thoreau. Living with Ruth, who reads him constantly, and knowing Spencer and Brooks Atkinson, who are Thoreau buffs, I have been led into a fuller study of his works and essays and journals than I might otherwise have undertaken. The more I read his work, the more I realize that he has little of importance to say to the twentieth-century man. He was an interesting nineteenth-century man. Consider the work for which he is most celebrated, WALDEN. He was teaching himself to live alone. That, however, does not seem to be the required or applicable lesson. On the contrary, it seems to me that what we must learn in this century is how to live with others.

Maugham says I am misreading Thoreau, but agrees that learning to live with others is the principal problem of our time.

. . . I tell about FF's cable on the occasion of Thornton's sixtieth birthday. The cable read: "DEAR THORNTON WELCOME TO THE GREAT DECADES LOVE FELIX."

Maugham frowns sharply. "I know that your friend Frankfurter is a . . . man of great intellect and I would not for the world dispute him since I am not a . . . man of great intellect, but I wonder if his message to Thornton is not . . . romantic. For my own part, I've noticed in studying the obituary pages that the sixties are extremely . . . unhealthy. Once those alps have been crossed, the seventies appear often to be a restful plateau, but, oh dear, those sixties! As I entered them, I was convinced that I was . . . for it. I suppose that was why I wrote THE SUMMING UP, in which I set down everything I knew and . . . felt which I thought worth imparting. The damned thing's turned out to be an embarrassing . . . anachronism, but there it is. What can I do?"

As he talks tonight, easily and well, I am aware of something which has not struck me before, which is that Maugham writes as he speaks and speaks as he writes.

(A few minutes ago, with the sound of him still very much in my ear, I picked up a copy of THE VAGRANT MOOD and began to read THE DECLINE AND FALL OF THE DETECTIVE STORY. As I read it with my eyes, I heard him with my ears, a curious experience, and one which has a good deal to say about his style and about what makes him so eminently readable.)

The long dinner ends with the best brandy and the biggest cigars.

When we leave, there is much bowing and smiling in the foyer. A man of letters occupies a position in France quite different from that in other countries. Here he is an aristocrat, a treasure, a mysterious and magical being who exists for the benefit of others.

Even the vestiaire, as she helps Maugham on with his mink-lined coat and gives him his hat, whispers something to him and blushes. He later tells us what it was.

She said to him, "Maître, I am so proud to have been taking care of your hat for thirty years."

In front of the building, in the driveway, stands WSM's imposing new Rolls-Royce. It seems to be a symbol of final affluence. He takes great pleasure and pride in it.

I think we are all glad to see the evening come to a

close. It has been, if anything, a bit too rich, too full, and any more might make it spiritually indigestible. Ruth and I watch the Rolls swing out onto the main highway and up the hill toward the cape.

Then, after thanking the management for the evening, we drive slowly back to the Negresco. We park the car and walk for an hour.

1954. London.

There is a paid advertisement this morning in the Personal Column, traditionally printed on the front page of THE TIMES. It reads as follows:

> Mr. Somerset Maugham thanks the senders of the many hundred letters and telegrams he has received on his birthday. He will acknowledge them in due course, but owing to the writer's cramp from which he suffers, trusts that the recipients of his replies will forgive him if they are typewritten.

There is much to smile about in the above. For one thing, how many men of eighty receive "many hundred letters and telegrams"? How many would feel they had to acknowledge each and every one and, further, to apologize for not writing by hand? Also, there is wry humor in his description of his ailment. After some sixty years of professional authorship, a man is entitled, I suppose, to writer's cramp.

I note, too, that he now publicly drops the "W." from the front of his name.

I know as well as I know anything that this ad will be much laughed about in London. It all seems too old-fashioned and out-of-date for words; and Maugham, a chromo. This is not a time when manners are fashionable, when courtesy is respected, or politeness thought to be anything but a sign of weakness. It is comforting to have Maugham and his ways spilling over into our harsh, disordered time.

October 1962. New York.

We spent some time with Noël last night and it goes without saying that the subject of WSM's show pieces comes up.

Noël is one of the many who take the position that Maugham's behavior is reprehensible and unforgivable. Noël declares that he, for one, wants nothing more to do with WSM. This is a pity—they have been for such a long time close and compatible friends. I try to make out a case for Maugham. I fail.

Noël feels that WSM must have known how his friends would feel about the publication of this scurrilous material but chose to give them up rather than an opportunity for vindictive self-indulgence. He adds that a man who is capable of writing in this way about his former wife and about his daughter is capable of anything and might in the next week or month publish other material detrimental to others around him. Noël, who has firm ideas about behavior, does not believe that people are forced into bad conduct. He believes that there is a certain amount of choice, that vengeful and vicious feelings lie dormant in everyone, and that it is the responsibility of a civilized man to keep these instincts in control.

"The man who wrote that awful slop is not the man who has been my friend for so many years. Some evil spirit

225

has entered his body. He is dangerous, a creature to be feared and shunned."

After we have argued back and forth for some time, Noël appeals to Ruth for her opinion and is amazed when she reveals that she has not read the stuff.

"But how can that be?" he exclaims.

Ruth says that, from what she knows of it, she has no desire to read it.

Noël: "But you must."

Ruth: "Why must I? I don't eat things I know will poison me. Why should I *read* things I know will poison me?"

Noël: "You're an ostrich."

I do not agree. Ruth is not burying her head in the sand, she is simply turning her attention in a preferred direction.

The argument goes on, but, like most arguments, serves only to make each adversary cling more pertinaciously to his own point of view. It ends in a sorry, ill-tempered stalemate.

[*Noël Coward and WSM were, in time, reconciled. When all the facts were made known to him, Coward concluded that Maugham's act was justified, if no less regrettable.*]

16 December 1965. Beverly Hills.

At breakfast this morning we talk of Maugham. What else is there to talk about? Ruth points out that he was her oldest friend. The fact of his death has hit her hard.

I find it odd that in the twenty-fourth year of our marriage she tells me much about him this morning which she has never told me before. I should have thought we knew practically everything about each other after our thousands of hours of exchange. But no. This morning she talks about her first meeting with Maugham, and it is all new to me.

It was the summer of 1928. Alexander Woollcott and Alice Duer Miller and Harpo Marx had taken a house for the summer at Antibes, the Villa Ganelon, and had invited Ruth and Beatrice Kaufman to join them there for a time.

Alec had everything wonderfully organized.

Ruth remembers Harpo once remarking, "Being summoned by Woollcott is like jury duty."

He was a relentless organizer and implementer of ideas. Ruth recalls that they had Mr. and Mrs. Bernard Shaw over to lunch twice; that they met Frank Harris and Lloyd Osbourne; almost saw Edith Wharton, who was living at Hyères; and, of course, a meeting with Maugham was arranged. It was not only that Woollcott was a lion hunter, he was also after copy, I imagine.

Ruth describes the visit to Maugham. Woollcott had written on ahead, saying he would like to call and bring his guests. Maugham wrote back to say that he would be delighted to receive Woollcott and party on such and such an afternoon. They drove over to St. Jean–Cap Ferrat. Ruth says that she took an instant dislike to Maugham, who behaved nicely enough toward Alec, but treated the rest of them in a supercilious, bordering-on-the-rude way. Harpo, of course, being Harpo, returned the attitude in kind.

They had not been there long when Maugham said they were going out to bathe. They all went—all being Alec, Harpo, and Ruth, Maugham, Gerald Haxton, someone called Count Sala, and an unintroduced young man of about nineteen with blond hair and Mediterranean blue eyes. While they were assembled, the mail was brought in and passed around.

The young man opened one of his and exclaimed, "Oh, I *love* to get letters!"

It made Alec and Harpo laugh, and the line became a private joke of theirs for years.

Ruth says she expected an impressive yacht, but found herself aboard a smallish motorboat. They went around the cape into a cove. The men began to change into bathing things.

"Where do I change?" asked Ruth.

"Why, right there," said Maugham. "Where you're standing."

And so she did.

After a swim, they returned to the Villa Mauresque for drinks. Ruth recalls that Harpo, wandering about, came across a copy of a recent issue of VARIETY. Apparently, Maugham was a subscriber. Harpo picked it up and, while the others talked, leafed through it carefully, dropping the pages on the floor as he finished with them. Then he walked away. Maugham stepped over, picked up the pages carefully, sorted them out, reassembled the copy, said, "I'll take care of this," and took it upstairs. He came down a few minutes later. He said nothing more about it, but it was clear that he was displeased.

"Why didn't Bea and Alice go with you?" I asked Ruth.

"Oh," she said, "by that time they were gone."

Alice had gone to visit Pearl White in Egypt. She loved Pearl White, who had written her inviting her to come, pointing out in the letter that she felt she should tell Alice in advance that she was living not only in Egypt but in the palace, and not only in the palace but in sin. Alice went.

19 December 1965. Beverly Hills.

And still we talk of Maugham. Walking this afternoon, Ruth remembers being shown through his house in St. Jean–Cap Ferrat in 1928 and seeing, across the top of the headboard of his bed, a long row of note-books. Thick, she recalls. Perhaps they were those old-fashioned letter files which were in popular office use years ago. In any event, he told her and Woollcott that these were his personal journals, containing all he thought and felt; his opinions of persons, places, and things; and that they were so outspoken in approach, so intimate in style, and so rash in flavor that they could not possibly be pub-lished during his lifetime.

Today, on the obituary page of THE NEW YORK TIMES there is a long story explaining in detail how Maugham's will specifically prohibits publication of any posthumous material.

Could he, then, at the last have had a change of heart about those famous journals?

1954. London.

Korda gave a party for WSM last night in his impressive new flat. He has put a lot into it and, with the help of Alexa [*Lady Korda*], has succeeded brilliantly.

Vivien and Larry are there. Carol and Pempy [*Sir Carol and Lady Reed*]. And a good many Korda nephews. Dur-ing the course of the evening there is discussion of possible film subjects. It begins with a resumption of our discussion of THE ADMIRABLE CRICHTON by J. M. Barrie, about which we have been talking for some months. Larry and

229

Vivien say they will accept my suggestion and recommendation of this material if I will do it with them. My feeling is that I am the wrong man. I think Carol, sitting right there, would be infinitely better for it and, as far as the writing is concerned, it ought to be Noël or Terry or Emlyn or Arthur Macrae or Peter Ustinov. So it has all been floating about. I doubt anything will come of it, even though Korda owns the rights, or claims to own the rights.

Vivien asks Maugham what he thinks of FAR FROM THE MADDING CROWD by Thomas Hardy as a film subject. Maugham gives her an enthusiastically affirmative reaction. There is talk of this. Then someone—I cannot remember who—brings up the subject of THE WINGS OF THE DOVE by Henry James. Maugham takes off and gives one of his devastating screeds on the subject of James.

As it happens, I have been reading a lot of Henry James under Thornton's prodding and am in a position to know that Maugham is dealing from a marked deck.

For no other reason than to add some spice to the evening, I decide to challenge him. Across the table I have the temerity to say, "We all agree that you're one of the finest of writers, but I, for one, consider you a poor critic."

The expected stir is caused.

WSM: "Indeed? I'm generally considered . . . quite a good critic. My services are in great . . . demand."

I: "Yes. But you deal unfairly with your subject. In this case, Henry James. Now, you've decided he's not very good, and why. So you approach every piece of his work with that preconception, and you look for points in it to support your already formulated opinion. You say that his sentences are too long and convoluted. Then your eye scans the page, looking for examples. I'll tell you what it's like. If someone had told the company here before my arrival that it's just been discovered that I'm a sod, I'm sure I'd do something to prove the lie every ten or fifteen minutes. Because all of you would be looking for it. And the most innocent gesture or meaningless joke or well-meant remark would be interpreted in the light of slander."

WSM: "Good Lord! How you ... do go on. It's the *way* of the critic to support his opinion with his ... best ammunition. God knows they do it with me."

I: "Maybe some of them do. But some of them—the better ones—praise you when they like your stuff and pan you when they don't."

WSM (tightly): "I'm a very good ... critic."

Korda, the perfect host, changed the subject.

1954. London.

At Arthur Macrae's last night there is talk of Maugham. Arthur likes him, but does not approve of him. He finds him smug.

"I don't know what you mean by smug, Arthur," I say. "But if I'd accomplished what he's accomplished, I think I might be self-satisfied, too."

"Yes, but would you show it?"

"I don't know."

"All this guff about the discipline of writing and the four hours every morning. What sort of way is that to create?"

"Don't you discipline yourself when you're working?"

"Well, for one thing, dear boy, I don't think of it as work. I think of it as exercising my profession. And I don't try to write anything unless and until I have something to write. When I get an idea for a play, I go off and write it, but I don't feel I must whip myself along a certain route

231

day after day. It seems to me that if you do that, you produce things like UP AT THE VILLA. It would be much better for him and for us if he'd spared us that one."

"Wait a second, Arthur. There are ways and ways. What works for some people doesn't work for others. Think of Goldoni turning up at that theatre and looking for a job as a playwright. They ask him to show a few samples. He does. They say pretty good, but don't fit their company. He comes to see their company that night, goes home, stays up all night and writes a play for their company. They read it and say not bad, but they're devoted to verse plays. He goes home and writes them a verse play. They put him on as their playwright, and he writes them a play every week or so for two years. Now, I'm sure every one of these plays was not of a standard and many of them are unreadable. I'm told by people who know them that some of them are nearly meaningless. But the fact that he was a craftsman practicing his craft, and continued to turn out play after play, meant he did turn up A SERVANT OF TWO MASTERS and THE MISTRESS OF THE INN and a few others which are in the permanent theatre repertory forever."

"Very well," says Arthur. "I suppose there's something to be said for the peg-away method, but the very idea of it is boresome to me. If one wants to work in that way, well and good, but one should have the good sense or judgment to do away with the pot-boiling stuff."

"Ah, yes, but then what's going to keep the pot boiling?"

"No one needs a platinum pot—like Willie's."

I say to Arthur, "Thornton says a writer's best friend is his wastepaper basket and his worst enemy is his couch."

"Hip, hip, hooray for Thornton," says Arthur, "and sour lemons for Willie Maugham."

232

1949. New York.

He tells us the other night that he has undertaken a formidable task.

"And for a formidable fee, I trust," I say.

Maugham puts that sophisticated eye on me and murmurs, "Quite."

He goes on to outline the work. Formidable indeed. He
is to select what he considers to be the ten greatest novels
ever written. He is to edit and abridge these and write an
introduction for each of them.

He begins by saying that of course there is no such thing
as a list of the ten greatest novels, but that he has agreed
to compromise to this extent for the convenience of the
publisher. What he is actually going to do, he says, is
choose ten of the finest novels and prepare them for publication, with biographical essays of the authors.

I look forward to the essays. The art of the essay is
largely lost and Maugham has proved himself to be one of
the most elegant practitioners of this form. I expect much of
his articles on Balzac, Dickens, Henry Fielding, and so on.

On the matter of editing, we have one of our most heated
set-tos.

I maintain that an author's work is or should be invio-
late, that no one should be permitted to cut it or trim it or
change its shape except the author.

Maugham says that authors have often been helped by
objective, intelligent editors, that too often a writer will
fall in love with the sound of his own voice; but his argument does not move me.

I fail to see why the author should not be the final judge
of what should stay in and what should go out, and when

we get into the Maxwell Perkins–Thomas Wolfe case, I insist that, whatever Wolfe may have felt about the enormous cuts, in the end he did approve them, whereas Dostoevski and Jane Austen are not going to be in that position with WSM.

Maugham: "But good heavens, man, when you... read, you skip, don't you?"

"Of course not," I say.

"You must be a... frightfully inexperienced reader," says Maugham. "Most readers skip such parts of a work as do not... particularly interest them. I dare say *all* readers do."

"I don't," I say stubbornly.

Maugham goes on. "But so frequently novels contain occasional... material and comments on events and personalities of their day which mean nothing to a... modern reader."

"Well, then," I argue, "*history* should mean nothing to a modern reader."

WSM stiffens. "That's precisely the... point. A novel is not history. It's a story. I feel that the spirit of the author should be... grateful to any competent literary person who will take the trouble to prepare his text for a... modern reader."

"I'm unconvinced," I say.

Maugham replies, "You're unconvincible."

(I think Thornton would agree with him and not with me. Troubling. Thornton was saying the other day that it is a kindness and a service to Shakespeare to edit, emend, and substitute understandable words for obscure ones. I wonder. Should the writer be adjusted, or the reader?)

There is further argument about my mistrust of abridgments and synopses and digests. Will we get to the point where we have digests of digests, and where college students have little paperback ponies containing the outlines of the outlines of the ten greatest novels? Would it not be better for them to know *one* of these books thoroughly rather than have a smattering of all of them? What's their hurry? Why does everything have to be trimmed down and cut down and pre-digested? It worries me. It does not worry him. I shall be interested to see how it all comes out.

He says he is not going to include REMEMBRANCE OF THINGS PAST by Marcel Proust, although to his mind it is indubitably the greatest novel of the twentieth century.

"And the greatest novel of *any* century?" I ask.

He replies without hesitation, "WAR AND PEACE."

This kicks us off into another tiff, since WAR AND PEACE is not my favorite by any manner of means.

I move in on him further.

"If you could sign as author WAR AND PEACE or REMEMBRANCE OF THINGS PAST, which would you choose?"

Again his reply is immediate.

"PÈRE GORIOT," he says. "Now, surely you admire that."

"I've never read it," I confess.

He looks at me and positively sneers.

"I mean to read it at once," I add quickly.

"Yes," he says scoffingly.

But I do read it at once, or almost at once. I read it the following day, and then I read it again. It knocks me for a loop. I have read it in two different translations, and with those as a base I now propose to try and crawl through it in French.

[*We had many further exchanges about* PÈRE GORIOT *in other times and places. The idea was to analyze it and*

235

to attempt to discover what makes it so surpassing. It was
WSM's point that a novel is made up of the creation of
characters, the construction of the narrative, the style of
the dialogue and prose, and the fluidity of the storytelling.
The accomplished novelist is able to marshal these ele-
ments into proper balance so that the character creation
does not interfere with either the fluidity of telling or the
construction, and so on.

I have read and studied PÈRE GORIOT *often since that*
time, and I consider that of the many debts I owe WSM,
his recommendation of this work is one of the largest.]

November 1954. London.

An odd little Maugham experience. Reading the
Holmes–Laski letters, I came upon a reference to Justice
Maugham, with a footnote which read:

Frederick Herbert Maugham (1866–   ), Baron
Maugham, was judge of the Chancery Division of the
High Court from 1928 to 1934, later becoming a
Lord Justice of Appeal and Lord of Appeal in Or-
dinary and, in 1938, Lord Chancellor. His book, THE
CASE OF JEAN CALAS (1938), was concerned with the
trial of Jean Calas (1698–1762), who was executed
for having murdered his son. The murder was com-
mitted to prevent the son from becoming a Roman
Catholic.

I copy out the reference and the footnote and send it
along to WSM. This evening a note is dropped through the
door. It is on stationery of the Dorchester and is printed
in an intentionally wobbly child's hand. It says:

DEAR UNCLE GAR

THANK YOU VERRY

MUCH FOR YUR

LUVLY

LETTAR

YOR

AFFECSHONET NEVIU

WILLIE

+ + + + + +

At first it makes me laugh. WSM is never more amusing
than when he is being coltish. But then I begin to worry
that I have made a gaffe. I keep studying this scrawl and,
beyond its fun, it seems to contain the edgy sound of him
telling me something. Damned if I know what it is.

November 1954. London.

Maugham speaks with great admiration of
many players he has seen across the years. Johnston
Forbes–Robertson, Charles Hawtrey, Marie Tempest, and
others. But oddly enough, his highest praise is reserved
for a minor character actor named C. V. France.

"He was," says Maugham, "the perfect actor, to . . . my
taste. He did always enough, yet . . . never too much. He
had what so few actors and actresses have—discretion. He
was in my play THE LAND OF PROMISE in 1914. Forty years
ago." (There's that forty again!) "And years . . . later in
FOR SERVICES RENDERED."

"And he created Major Liconda in THE SACRED FLAME,
didn't he?"

"I believe so. Yes. Good heavens—and how in *hell* would
you . . . know a thing like that?"

"Because," I explain, "when I was a student at the American Academy of Dramatic Arts in 1932, we did THE SACRED FLAME—and since I was a diligent student, I researched it completely and looked up all the reviews and so on."

"And what . . . part did you play?" asks WSM.

"Why, Major Liconda, of course."

"Did you say 'of course'?" he asks.

"Yes."

The look on his face is difficult to describe. He seems to be on the verge of laughter or tears or both. He closes his eyes for a moment of recovery.

I say, "I wore a fine white goatee and a pound and a half of greasepaint and tried to think of George Arliss. My friends in the class told me I was great, my rivals said I was unspeakable."

"What did *you* think?" asks WSM.

"I hoped for the best, although I suspected I might have been just a mite miscast. I was nineteen, and the Major is in his sixties; he is British, I am not—it was what we sometimes call 'offbeat casting.' I must say I had a few telling moments—even if the part as a whole eluded me. For instance in the third act, when I said, 'You know what we English are and how uncharitably we regard sexual delinquencies—' "

"Spare me," says WSM.

I am not sure if he means my acting or the reminder of his thirty-year-old dialogue.

He blushes. We laugh.

I tell WSM that Bob Sherwood often speaks of C .V. France, who was in ACROPOLIS when it was done in London in 1933. (Never in New York. Why not? Ask Bob.)

We talk of the dramatist's dependence upon the players.

How the most inspirationally conceived and brilliantly executed role becomes a nonsense in the wrong hands. How no part is "actor-proof," really.

Ruth (who knows best) adds, "But no actor is part-proof, either."

What we hope for in the theatre is the good marriage of part and player.

Ruth recalls exceptions. Laurette Taylor making something memorable out of ordinary ingénue in ALIAS JIMMY VALENTINE.

"Yes," says WSM. "Give me ... players. The best of them—such as C. V. France. I can't imagine what might have happened to THE UNKNOWN without Haidee Wright, or to FOR SERVICES RENDERED without Flora Robson. There were others—Gladys ... Cooper, and Irene Vanbrugh" (he says Irenee) "and Marie Tempest" (he says Maria) "and Fay Compton. Fine girls, all. They made me a ... packet of money."

August 1953. St. Jean–Cap Ferrat.

He tells us about a rough afternoon at Claridge's. The wedding reception. The bride, Liza Maugham Paravicini; the groom, Lord John Hope. The groom's father, Lord Linlithgow. There they all are at Claridge's with their many and distinguished guests. The groom's father toasts the bride, whereupon it is proper form for the bride's father to respond. Maugham does it bravely and well, until he gets to "Linlithgow." Now he is in trouble.

Maugham tells us, "It was not ... easy for me."

I say, "Well, hell, it wouldn't be easy for *anyone*."

A tough break for him. I feel that, despite the jocular

way in which he tells it, he takes it hard. An old embarrassment.

April 1941. Hollywood.

Maugham is here in the United States. I understand that his publisher, Nelson Doubleday, brought him over. I have heard the following account of his arrival: The Doubledays met him at La Guardia. As soon as he had completed the formalities, he asked if he might have a bourbon old-fashioned. They took him to the airport bar, where he ordered his drink carefully, with complete instructions. In time, it was served. He drank it with great relish and thanked the Doubledays. Whereupon he took an ampule of poison out of his vest pocket, put it on the floor, and crushed it under his heel, saying, "I won't need this now, Nelson."

They left the airport and went to the Doubledays' place at Oyster Bay on Long Island.

June 1941. Fort Monmouth.

WSM tells friends that the Doubledays are going to build him a house on their property—Bonny Hall Plantation in Yemassee, South Carolina.

(How come everyone on that level expects the war in Europe to go on for some time? Disquieting. Around here, on the post, the end is expected soon. How?)

In any case, it is good to know that Maugham is safe. There is talk that he is connected with British Intelligence and has a definite assignment in the U.S.A. I wonder how anyone knows. Surely he would not have revealed it. Can it be that the assumption is made only because he was connected with that organization during World War I?

The suggestion of the South Carolina house was apparently made by Ellen Doubleday, and Maugham accepted it at once, gratefully. He has been going over the plans with her and says he is going to furnish it from the plans, using Macy's. He explains that he is more concerned with speed than with aesthetics; further, that he has done one perfect house and does not wish to attempt anything like it here and now. It is to be utilitarian in concept. A temporary abode where he can live and work during this awful time.

No one mentions it, but my guess is that his health is none too good and that he must take care.

He has ordered drapes and rugs and furniture and lamps and seems content with the prospect.

(I wonder how much of this ability he picked up from Syrie? After all, she is an immensely gifted and experienced interior decorator.)

The house is going to be completed in record time—no small achievement in the midst of the growing defense effort. The rich have ways and ways.

The house is, in fact, two houses. A comfortable cottage with accommodations for him, two guests, and staff; and a writing cabin about a hundred yards from the house. A matter of quiet and privacy. His experience has taught him that these things are difficult to achieve in a cottage and he knows, along with the rest of us, that a writer must escape from the sound of the vacuum cleaner if he possibly can.

August 1942. New York.

Maugham tells about his house in South Carolina. He likes it very much. Ruth Gordon, who is present, asks him about staff. He says he told the Doubledays not to be concerned, but to give him one willing person he could train.

November 1942. Washington.

Re WSM in South Carolina. xx has been down to visit him. Apparently, the Doubledays have done extremely well by him. He has, not a servant, but a staff.

A cook, Nora; a housemaid, Mary. A yardman called Sunday, who has a nephew-assistant named Religious. WSM is crazy about that.

xx says the Doubledays were somewhat concerned about conditions at Parker's Ferry (which is what WSM's place is called). Would he and the hands get on? Understand one another? It certainly was a strange intermingling of races and cultures. They hoped that the help would not be too intimidated and that WSM would not expect them to be too pukka. The Doubledays have, after all, read (and published) EAST AND WEST.

About ten days after he arrived, he asked the Doubledays to dinner. They were astounded when on came a superb onion soup, truite au bleu, duck à l'orange, a wondrous salad, and an almond soufflé. They could not imagine who was in the kitchen. Nora, of course, and no one else. WSM had indeed trained her, and shown Mary and Sunday exactly how to serve and clear. Religious was out with Nora, serving happily as her kitchen page. The Doubledays have

242

been describing the event all over the county, but no one wants to believe them.

March 1943. Washington.

Ruth saw Liza over the weekend in New York and they talked about the WSM-Doubleday dinner. Liza is not in the least surprised.

"Oh, yes," she says. "Pa always trains the cooks and maids and gets the house running just right. He knows all about such things. He can't do it himself, but he knows how it should be done and how to get others to do it."

[Years later I got around to asking WSM about all this. I was interested in getting to the bottom of it because, candidly, it seemed something less than a likely story to me—that you move into a cottage in South Carolina and get a couple of people who know about hominy grits and fried chicken and all at once—presto chango!—they turn out a gourmet dinner fit for the most exacting epicure. Come on, now.

I told him what we had heard and asked, "Is it true?"

"Oh, yes," he said easily. "Quite true."

"But how were you able to provide what they called 'a perfect dinner' after ten days with no one but those people who'd never done anything like it before? It's hard to believe."

"Actually," said Maugham, "it's no trouble. No trouble at all. Unless you call trouble having the same meal eight nights running!"

"Well, sir," I comment, "whatever may be said for or against you, you certainly are a practical man."

243

"Is that for me or against me?" he asks wryly.

*"I don't know," I confess. "Some of each, I suppose."
And I repeat Thornton's remark. "'I can take care of
my immortal soul, but who's going to take care of my
laundry?'"*

*Maugham chuckles. "When next you see Thornton,
tell him that a . . . practical Old Party suggests that if he
takes . . . good enough care of his laundry, his soul will
. . . take care of itself." He raises a warning finger and
adds, "But never the other way about!"*

*But at last the secret of the Yemassee dinner is revealed.
A plan and the determination, organization, and patience
required to carry it out. His characteristic, methodical approach. Doing and redoing. Perhaps the first time the
soufflé fell—and the second and the third—but in time it
did not. Apparently he supervised and ate, then commented and corrected. After eight tries they had achieved
it and from that time on could always do it. Like that guy
in the Army who had been taught to make popovers. He
made the best popovers in the world, but that was all he
could do.*

*One thing more. WSM says he has always made it a
point in housekeeping to give his servants the same food
that he has. It makes a difference, I can see, in the long run.*

*Even now, across time, I envisage them in the small
kitchen at Parker's Ferry, Yemassee, South Carolina:
Somerset Maugham, Nora, Mary, Sunday, and Religious
—all eating onion soup and truite au bleu and duck à
l'orange and salad and almond soufflé—criticizing, tasting,
worrying, hoping and, incidentally, growing fatter by the
day.]*

244

December 1959. New York.

I received a note from WSM today from the
Dorchester in London dated December 7, in answer to my
note to him which I sent him with a copy of BLOW UP A
STORM. It reads (in an increasingly unsteady hand):

Dear Uncle Gar,

Thank you very much for sending me your book.
We are just off to France and then to Egypt and I will
take it with me confident that it will be a solace to me
in distress, increase my knowledge of life and reform
my morals.

> Love to the woman Kanin
> Willie

Of course, I do not expect him to read it. Why should
he? His note reminds me of FF's account of Disraeli's
classic acknowledgment: "My dear So-and-so, Thank you
for sending me your new book. I shall lose no time in reading it. Faithfully yours, etc."

November 1954. London.

I have just returned from Amsterdam, where I
spent some time, along with the Hacketts [*Frances Goodrich and Albert Hackett*], researching THE DIARY OF ANNE
FRANK.

I find that Ruth has accepted a dinner invitation from
WSM. It is to be just us, in his suite at the Dorchester.
As we are walking over, I say to Ruth that although I am
brimming over with things to say about Amsterdam and
the people I met there and the things I learned, I want to

stay off the subject entirely tonight. There are a number of reasons for this. First of all, I need time to assimilate and digest the too many impressions. Secondly, I have come to the conclusion that I do not wish to discuss the Anne Frank project with anyone any more. Up to now, I have met with nothing but discouraging reaction. Whenever I say I am going to do this play, almost automatically whoever I have told begins to try to talk me out of it. My confidence, like everyone else's, is not unlimited, and I think it best not to go into the matter any further. Even some of the people in Amsterdam wondered about the wisdom of trying to put the story on the stage, and the few who thought it was possible questioned the taste of it. Ruth understands.

But at the Dorchester the best-laid plans, etc., etc. WSM knows that I have been away and almost immediately begins to question me. What was I doing in Amsterdam? My first attempt to avoid the subject seems so needlessly enigmatic that I decide to tell him and say no more about it. I explain that I have agreed to direct a play by Frances Goodrich and Albert Hackett, based upon THE DIARY OF ANNE FRANK. He does not seem to know much about it, although he has vaguely heard of it. I tell him something of the work.

"But why on earth do you . . . want to do *that?*" he says. "I think it . . . *most* unwise."

"You haven't even read it," I argue.

"Good heavens, you've just . . . told me."

"I want to do it because I want to. I feel that I can. Why shouldn't I?"

"Well," he says, "from my observation, it would appear that in the United States the . . . feeling now is to be as friendly as possible toward the Germans, to re-establish

246

them economically, to . . . turn them into allies. And since you Americans seem to be plunking for good relations with Germany, wouldn't the . . . production of a play of this sort work against that idea? How do you suppose it will be received, in line with the . . . tenor of the day?"

"I can't worry about that," I reply. "All I know is I read it, it impressed me deeply, and I'm very anxious to put it on. Ruth worries about it, too. She thinks it's going to be too harrowing—depressing. I don't agree. To me it seems exalting, a religious experience. It may be that because I don't have a formal religious background or life or discipline, this becomes a substitution for it."

"And do you think it . . . proper to inflict that on the theatregoing public?"

"I don't think of it as *inflicting* anything. Suppose we say no more about it."

"Splendid," he says. "I still think it . . . most unwise."

I am miffed and cannot resist having the last word.

"Forgiving is one thing," I argue, "but forgetting is another. No matter what the future of Germany is to be, I don't see that pretending there was no past is going to help. By that reasoning, your Mr. Churchill and our General Eisenhower are wrong to publish memoirs."

WSM is impressed by this argument, but not very.

[*As it turned out,* THE DIARY OF ANNE FRANK *was a success not only in New York the following year, but internationally later on. For a long time no one in Paris would touch it. Then, when it was produced there, it ran for four years.*

It was selected as the American entry in the International Theatre Festival, which was to take place in Paris. At the last minute all arrangements were canceled. The

247

*mystery was never solved, but the unofficial understanding
was that it had nothing to do with German objections but
rather with diplomatic advice that it was perhaps a bad
time to offend Egypt. (!)*

*Later, when it was performed in Germany, it became
one of the most meaningful of the postwar successes. It
played thousands of performances everywhere in the
country.*

*I note the above here only to point out that Maugham's
political acuity in this instance was less than impressive.
As a matter of fact, it seems never to have been much good.
He was not a political man, and whenever he attempted
analyses of political systems or of sociological patterns,
he stumbled badly.*

*He himself has admitted how inept was his intelligence
work in Russia at the end of World War I. It may be that
this lack was the one important missing quality which
might have improved his work by broadening his choice of
subject and theme. Also by relating it more to the present
time. His gift was for the observation and understanding
of individuals, not types or classes or groups. Who said,
"The more I hate them in the mass, the more I love them
one by one"?]*

November 1954. London.

        After the grand dinner we send him flowers and
enclose a card with our initials.

    The following note from him today from the Dor-
chester:

                             Monday

Dearest Ruth,
    Thank you ever so kindly for the lovely lovely flow-

ers. Of course I know what RG and the heart means, but who is GK? G for George of course and I immediately thought of George Sand and George Eliot. But the K beats me. Surely not Kukor? Of course I knew that I couldn't expect you to be faithful to me any more than the Queen of Sheba was faithful to King Solomon or Helen of Troy to Menelaus; you made that quite plain to me at the beginning, but I thought it understood that before you take on a new lover you should let me find out if he belongs to the right clubs. After all I have my self-respect to consider.

Yours more in sorrow than in anger,

Willie

June 1958. The Hotel Negresco, Nice.

I am not sure exactly what the hell we are doing here. We were to have come down last New Year's Eve, but at the last minute Ruth fell ill. She ate some bum mussels at Prunier's, and as a result we were unable to travel. Since that time we have talked of going down to St. Tropez, but did not make it. Now, with the assorted horrors at home and Joel's [*my nephew, Joel Kanin, 1945– 1958*] continuing illness, we both know, although we do not often speak of it, that we shall have to return soon.

Ruth is constantly drawn to the South of France. She wants to see Maugham and the place again. And so, suddenly, we are here. We decided upon Nice because it is within easy reach of Maugham's on the one hand and the Clairs' on the other. Also, as an added piece of distraction, there is a great gala the night after tomorrow in Monte Carlo. A preview, of all things, of a movie produced by my friend Frank Ross, which stars Frank Sinatra and

249

Tony Curtis and Natalie Wood. It is being shown at Monte Carlo under the auspices of the United Nations Children's Fund, for some reason, and under the sponsorship of Prince Rainier and Princess Grace. We have been invited. I do not know whether or not we shall get there, but we are glad to be in Nice, a favorite city.

Maugham taught it to us, showing us the Old City and the new; the market; the flower market; where Chekhov lived; the Matisse museum; the old film studios; and the promenade which the English gave to Nice as a gift of gratitude for hospitality.

This afternoon we are walking down the Promenade des Anglais and are about to cross the street to walk into the Old City when a small car swerves and stops short a few feet from us. I want to yell at the driver, but am delayed in trying to get the proper French expletive formed. When I am ready, I see that the driver is Noël. He parks, hops out, and we have a chat. He is on his way to Maugham's, where he is a weekend guest. They are going to the gala at Monte Carlo, and he is delighted when he hears that we are coming up there to dinner tomorrow night. He urges us to do the Monte Carlo thing, too. He seems in fine shape, says he has been staying with Edward Molyneux at Biot and working his head off. We have a drink on the terrace of the Hotel Ruhl, and he drives off.

June 1958. The Hotel Negresco, Nice.

Monte Carlo. In the crush last night Art Buchwald makes his way over to Maugham. I introduce them. Buchwald says, "Could I come over to see you sometime tomorrow, Mr. Maugham?"

Maugham looks at him and answers, "Why, yes. If you think it would be . . . worth your while."

The great ballroom of the Sporting Club is decorated as though it were the exterior of a French village. This has something to do with the picture around which the occasion is built—called KINGS GO FORTH. Frank S. is here with a considerable entourage, and there are glad-to-see-yous all around. Many familiar faces. The picture is shown. The UN representative who makes the address of thanks turns out to be Jim Reed, whom we met on one of the crossings.

The great banquet. The arrangements are somewhat catch-as-catch-can. We are rescued by Leonard [Lyons], who takes us to his table, where he also has Maugham and Alan and Noël. So this part of the evening is saved.

At one point the royal party enters. Everyone in the room stands. In a corner of the room, at one of the worst tables, I see two people who do not stand. I wonder if they are revolutionaries about to throw a bomb. When we are seated again I mention it to Maugham.

He looks about, puts on his glasses, turns back, and says, "They didn't rise because they . . . don't have to. They are the . . . King and Queen of Yugoslavia."

An entertainment is presented. Noël is the compère. He does it beautifully in French and in English. Frank gets on and breaks it up. On his way back to his table he stops. Noël introduces him to Maugham.

Frank says, "Hiya, baby!"

Maugham replies, "Very well, indeed. But hardly a . . . baby."

I have never seen Maugham in circumstances as strange as these. There are too many people, too much noise, the band is blaring, the food is indifferent, the organization sloppy. But he takes it all in good part and sees to it that he has a good time. He has a positive gift for enjoying himself. He stays as long as he wants to, then takes his leave, making certain to stop at the main table in the middle of the room on his way out to pay his respects to the Prince and Princess. He does it elegantly, with particular style.

1951. New York.

We saw WSM on television tonight, introducing THE SOMERSET MAUGHAM THEATER. He sat on a windowseat in his house at St. Jean–Cap Ferrat, charmingly attired, and did what was required of him with great charm. What fascinates me is to see with what efficiency he manages to remain a part of the changing order. When he was writing these stories which are now being dramatized for this series, surely he had no idea they might ever be used in this way. In fact, the notion of television was as remote as the idea of a picnic on the moon. I remember first hearing the invention described and having doubts as to whether or not it would come about practically in my lifetime. In 1939, in England, the RKO people took me along to watch a television demonstration. I was greatly impressed with the result of the transmission. Later we went to a theatre where the image was flashed on a large screen. The effect was less good, but still impressive.

The very idea of this use of Maugham's material is a rebirth in the strictest sense of the word. Here he is, introducing a dramatization of one of his stories. He seems to take pride in it and does it with dignity and personal modesty which are not in the least cloying.

November 1954. London.

Word comes today, via cable from Ted Weeks in Boston, that he wants to publish DO RE MI in THE ATLANTIC. I can hardly believe it. It would not have occurred to me even to submit it to him.

He was on one of his scouting trips and, when he got to Texas, was spending some time with Tom Lea, whom I have never met but who is a friend of Bob Parrish's. Weeks saw a manuscript lying on Lea's table. Since he knows me, he asked if he could read it. Lea apparently recommended it, and that is how it all came about.

Coincidentally, we are to go up and see WSM later in the day. I can hardly wait to tell him. I know how pleased he will be.

Later. We had not been with Maugham long when I told him I had an interesting announcement.

"I've written a long story," I tell him, "called DO RE MI. Actually I wrote it in St. Moritz when we were up there with Thornton last year. Nothing has been happening about it—all pretty discouraging—and a few hours ago I heard from Ted Weeks that he's going to publish it in THE ATLANTIC. How about that?"

Maugham says, "THE ATLANTIC. They don't . . . pay very much, do they?"

End of excitement.

In an effort to impress upon him how pleased I am to appear in these pages at *any* price, I point out that I have written screenplays in such and such a length of time, getting such and such a price. In two or three seconds he has figured out exactly how much I earned per day and per hour.

October 1965. New York.

Reading Maugham today (STRICTLY PER-
SONAL), I come upon something which points up a contradiction. Not that the great old man is not allowed a
contradiction or two. As Walt Whitman said, "Do I contradict myself? Very well, then, I contradict myself. I
contain multitudes." So, God knows, does WSM. But this
has to do with something he has harped on across the years.
I refer to his fixed schedule of work. He has told us and
others that his unvarying schedule, except when he is
traveling, is to rise at eight, breakfast, be at his desk by
nine, and work until one.

At various times when we have stayed with him, this
would seem to have been the case. We never saw him until
lunchtime, and as we walked about the house and grounds,
it was clear he was up in his study. There have been times
in New York and in London when it has been necessary to
phone him in the morning. He has never been available.

Here in STRICTLY PERSONAL, however, he writes about
the summer of 1939 at St. Jean–Cap Ferrat: "The life we
led was simple, and we did pretty much the same thing
every day. I am an early riser and have my breakfast at
eight, but the rest of the party sauntered downstairs at all
hours in their pyjamas and dressing gowns. When at last
everyone was ready we drove to Villefranche, where the
yacht was moored, and went round to a little bay on the
other side of Cap Ferrat, where we bathed and lay in the
sun till we were as hungry as wolves. We had brought
some food with us, but Pino, the Italian sailor, cooked us
a great dish of macaroni to take the edge off our appetite.
We drank the light red wine called Vin Rosé which I got

by the barrel from a place away back in the hills. Then we dawdled and slept till we could bathe again and after tea went back to the house to play tennis. We dined on the terrace among the orange trees, and when the moon was full over the sea strewing her brilliance on the calm water in a great highway of white light, the scene was so lovely it took your breath away. When there was a pause in the light chatter and in the laughter, you heard the vociferous croaking of hundreds of little green frogs in the lily ponds down in the garden. After dinner Liza and Vincent and their friends took the car and drove in to Monte Carlo to dance."

Well, where were the work hours in this routine? One may explain that this was a holiday time, but was it? He was at home and, ostensibly, following the schedule he has made famous. I wonder about this today.

July 1953. St. Jean–Cap Ferrat.

I ask him today, "How many short stories have you written? Do you know?"

WSM: "Of course I know. I know exactly. One hundred and four, mainly immoral." He adds cheerily, "And I shall . . . never write another." After a moment's reflection: "It's been said that I've written only for money. I assure you that this is . . . not true. Had financial gain been a primary motivation, I should have stopped early on. Twelve months after LIZA OF LAMBETH had been . . . published, my royalties amounted to about . . . twenty pounds, or what then would have been about a hundred dollars. Hardly a . . . munificent sum, would you say—or one likely to encourage?"

1951. St. Jean–Cap Ferrat.

There is talk today of Jonathan Swift and of Daniel Defoe. WSM greatly admires the plainness of Swift. It is the quality to which he has long aspired in his own work. He talks of others: George Meredith and Jeremy Taylor, who represent another world—flowery, ornate. Nothing wrong with it, but he does not feel it belongs to this century.

I remember having read somewhere about Defoe describing his idea of perfect writing: that which would be understood in the meaning which the author intended by a conglomerate group of two hundred people representing a complete cross-section of the time—young and old, rich and poor, educated and not—adding, "The insane and moronic excluded."

Maugham says, "Yes, I accept that. But I should . . . like to *include* the insane and moronic."

1942. New York.

We have dinner with WSM at the Ritz tonight, where he is living. Afterward, since we have been talking a good deal about movies, I suggest we go along to see the highly praised IN WHICH WE SERVE, which is playing at the Capitol.

WSM declines, saying, "I have a special relationship with the clock these days, you know. Round about . . . ten I find it wise to let the day go."

"What will you do?" asks Ruth.

"Oh, don't trouble yourselves about me. I'm happy as a

grig. I shall make myself . . . quite comfortable in my bed upstairs and settle down to what we used to . . . call at home 'a good read.' "

"What are you reading?" I ask.

"A French novel," he replies. "The title of it escapes me. I find I read . . . French now almost exclusively. I miss France, don't you know, and it's a way of . . . going back there easily and conveniently, at least in my . . . mind."

October 1965. New York.

A letter from Alan today, sad and despairing. WSM is having it hard, a bad ending. He is not often conscious, but when he is, he is in misery. His sorry existence seems to drag on and on. He will not, cannot, recover; will not, cannot, die. He weeps a great deal. Is this, then, the hell he did not believe in?

February 1966. New York.

Now that he is dead, his so-called friends and acquaintances and strangers-become-friends and critics and commentators feel more free in discussing him. He has become fair game for his posterity, which knows he will not talk back. Nasty cracks are more frequent and even some of the obituaries were less than kind.

He once said, "I have observed that death, as a rule, solves more problems than it creates."

Certainly this is true about *his* death. One can sense a collective, silent sigh of relief heaved by many interested parties.

A number of pieces have appeared in newspapers and

magazines (prematurely, I think) attempting to place him in literary history. Like every other eminent writer who ever lived, he will have fluctuating fortune. There will be times when he will be in fashion or out. He will be neglected and rediscovered; but his true measure, for the time being at least, is no more than a matter of opinion.

1954. London.

His looks are changing, and so is his height. I am aware of this, since I am short myself and most men I meet are taller than I am. WSM is one of the few who are shorter. He keeps himself always extremely erect, in almost a military bearing.

He is small, but perfectly proportioned; always impeccably groomed and dressed and shod. His mustache is not at all careless, but wonderfully arranged to suit the contours of his face. He has sharp, bright, piercing, expressive eyes.

Tonight, for the first time, I am aware of his age. It has never occurred to me before, but it is time to face it. He is an old man. He moves now with greater care, sits and stands with difficulty. What used to seem like straight posture now seems stiff. His movements are deliberate and precise, and every act seems to be a problem—lighting a cigarette, opening a door, shaking hands.

Diminutive as he always seemed, tonight he seems more so. What can it be? Is he, literally, shrinking? I am certain that he weighs less than ever before and that he is somehow changing shape as well.

(On his last birthday, he is reported to have said in this connection, "I believe that if one is small, as I am, there is a possibility that Death may overlook one.")

1954. London.

Alan reports that he often says, "Every night when I go to bed, I pray that I will not wake."

In the case of WSM, as with so many of us, what we say and what we think or feel are not always the same, are not always even related. It seems to me that a man who cares so little for his existence would hardly take the trouble Maugham takes to preserve his health and to promote his longevity. Those endless trips to the cures, those journeys to Abano for the mud baths, the regular program of exercise and rest. Surely all this is designed not only for well-being but for longevity. Why does he say such things?

1963. New York.

I hear a story today that has to do with WSM. Bennett [*Cerf*] tells me that a few months ago xx came to him, said that he was going abroad and wanted letters of introduction to a few literary folk.

"I'm getting others to VIP's in their respective fields," he explained, "but I thought you'd know the literary bunch. John Osborne and Somerset Maugham and Angus Wilson. People like that."

Bennett said he hated the idea, but since he is indebted to xx for a number of things, he did arrange the letters.

He reports that last week he ran into xx, who thanked him profusely for having provided the letter to Maugham. It did indeed work. He was asked to lunch at the Villa Mauresque and went up there and spent an afternoon. He talks on and on about how impressed he was with Somerset

259

Maugham, and ends by saying, "He really is marvelous—
a great listener!"

1954. London.

Maugham: "I owe a great deal to Eddie Marsh.
An extraordinary creature. A scholar. He's gone over the
... page proofs of many of my works and saved me from
embarrassing error. He *'diabolizes'* the work of his ...
friends. He may have invented that word. By it, he means
to say that he finds fault and carps and is as ... disagreeable as possible. He picks on one, and nags, and simply
will not take ... less than perfection. Of course, he is far
from ... perfect himself. His punctuation is pixieish, in
my opinion. But he is a remarkable ... man, and I am
deeply in his ... debt."

June 1960. Provincetown, Massachusetts.

We are here on one of our invaluable talk-trips
with Thornton. His generosity is boundless, as is his un-
selfishness.

Our meetings began four days ago in West Harwich
at the Belmont. All went well until a convention of postmasters arrived and we were asked for our rooms. Thornton wanted more than anything to stay and mingle with
the postmasters, but the management had other ideas.

We decided to move up the Cape to Provincetown, and
our conference continues.

This afternoon, while Thornton was taking his post-
lunch nap, Ruth suggested we drive over to Wellfleet. She

has not been there in years and wants to case it in connection with some work she is doing. We drive over, park the car. The local church is having a rummage sale. We attend, buy some old books (Volume II of Mark Twain's Letters, fifteen cents) and step out onto Main Street.

Ruth says, "Edmund Wilson lives here in the summer."

As she says this, a portly man comes out of the supermarket and walks by us, laden with grocery bags. He proceeds to his car at the curb.

"And there he is," I add.

We hail him, stop and talk for a few minutes. He compounds the coincidence by telling me that he has just this morning read a review of my book in THE SUNDAY TIMES, which has just arrived from London. (He says no more than this, and I hesitate to question him further.) Learning that Thornton is with us, he insists that we come over later in the afternoon for a drink or the following day for tea. We choose the following day, subject to Thornton's availability, and part.

June 1960. Provincetown, Mass.

We are just back from the afternoon at Wilson's. It did not work out well.

Earlier, Thornton gave us a lunchtime lecture on the subject of Edmund Wilson, known to him as "Bunny." He made it clear that Wilson is without doubt the outstanding literary critic now living, that we were to mind our manners and hold our tongues, be seen but not heard, and take it easy. I was perfectly prepared to do this in any case. We drove over.

Wilson is delighted to see Thornton. We greet Mrs.

Wilson, whom we have not seen for some time, and meet his children (whom we have never met) —a boy of eighteen or so, a little girl of twelve. There is also a willowy female student-secretary. A curious out-of-this-time-and-place atmosphere, but we sit around and Wilson talks fascinatingly. The main subject is Scott Fitzgerald, about whom he is now writing. He digs Thornton deeply on the subject. In some way—I cannot remember how, since my mind kept wandering—the subject of Somerset Maugham comes up, and I am shocked to hear Wilson take off on him in a violent way. He avers, didactically, that Maugham is second-rate, a fraud, overrated, and interested only in money. We listen to this for a while, and when it is impossible to remain silent I make it clear to Wilson that I have no intention of engaging in a literary discussion with him.

"For one thing," I tell him, "I don't have the equipment. And you have not only a right but a duty and a responsibility to make your opinion clear. But Mr. Maugham is my friend, and I find it hard to sit by and hear him attacked on a personal level. Now, I know him and he's certainly not a fraud in the sense you indicate. He's a man who's devoted his life and his best efforts to his work. And, in any case, why don't we get off the subject?"

Wilson goes on to say that a man and his writing are inextricably intertwined and cannot be separated.

"True," I say, "and I'm fond not only of Maugham but of what he writes. And so are many others."

This serves only to intensify the attack. After a while Ruth finds a convenient moment to leave politely. She had said earlier she wanted to call on Elizabeth Freeman, a childhood friend from Wollaston, whose sister Katherine married Chester Nimitz. Ruth takes off, leaving me to the fray. It would have seemed clumsy for both of us to go. Fortunately, Wilson grabs Wilder and takes him into his study to get some further Scott Fitzgerald dope. I am left to chat about Wellfleet and the weather with the kids. The little girl takes me out to show me her new horse. The young man seems preoccupied. Presently we are sitting silently and I have an opportunity to think about what has been happening in the past hour.

To begin with, it is clear that Wilson is not all that knowledgeable on the subject of Maugham's work. His outburst was based upon his contempt for Maugham's book THEN AND NOW. He did not seem to be familiar with the short stories, out of which surely a dozen, at least, are in the top rank. He seemed to know next to nothing about Maugham's plays, although THE CIRCLE and OUR BETTERS are certainly considered by theatre people to be first-class examples of their kind. He did not wish to discuss OF HUMAN BONDAGE, CAKES AND ALE, or THE MOON AND SIXPENCE. He wanted to stay on the subject of THEN AND NOW.

This led us into a discussion of the standards by which to judge any artist. Should he be judged by his best work or his worst? Should it be computed into a sort of artistic average? Or should the judgment be on the complete body of the work? More particularly, should not an artist be judged by what he has attempted as much as by what he has achieved? No one made any commitment on these questions, but the noise went on, and I began to gather that there is something personal in all this. There frequently is, as there is with Maugham and Henry James.

I wonder what it is. Can it be that Wilson is jealous of his position as a critic and resents Maugham entering his sphere of activity, as he sometimes does?

For my part, I wish that Maugham did not do this. Perhaps no creative artist should ever move over into the critical area. It does not seem to be his business.

It seems to me that anyone living a creative life has work to do. A critic has work to do, as well. Where they cross, they cross. But to mix the two does not seem to be healthy for members of either group. Certainly Wilson's attempts at playwriting have been less than effective. His novels and stories are not what he will be remembered for, any more than Maugham will have a reputation as a critic or commentator on the literary scene.

This is only a guess, but it may be a beginning of understanding. The fact that Maugham often pretends to be a critic, the fact that he has written both fiction and drama successfully, might understandably rankle Wilson. He is furious about Maugham's criticism of Henry James and remembers with irritation that WSM even said some less than enthusiastic things about James Joyce. He thinks it tasteless of Maugham to criticize William Butler Yeats. He makes fun of Maugham's work on AN INTRODUCTION TO MODERN ENGLISH AND AMERICAN LITERATURE and says that the choices for inclusion were childish. (Imagine putting in Katherine Brush and Michael Arlen!) More and more I sense that Wilson looks upon Maugham as a competitor in his field, and, what is more, one who has no right to be there.

Still, he is pretty damned hard on WSM.

To sum up, I think it fair to say that Maugham is a distinguished writer, that Wilson is a supereminent critic and one who simply cannot see anything of value in Maugham's work. This happens.

Shaw deviled Henry Irving for a lifetime, and there have

been many cases where work which later lived was not found acceptable by important critics of its day.

For my own part, I feel that Shakespeare should not be judged on the basis of CYMBELINE nor Maugham on the basis of THEN AND NOW.

June 1960. Provincetown, Mass.

At dinner I try to review with Thornton the drama of our afternoon, but he wishes to remain neutral. He wants to think it through, he says.

He goes on to explain—in the abstract—certain critical attitudes. He says that in a large body of critics the notion persists that if something sells or is commercially successful, it is suspect. To put it another way, if the author profits by it in a material sense, there must be something wrong with it. He traces this to the old idea of writing being a gentleman's avocation, a giving of one's self and spirit and intellect for the instruction or entertainment or edification of others. If one gave of self or spirit for money, it was related somehow to prostitution. According to this concept, Maugham, having sold over three hundred million copies, is in real trouble.

Wilson, I point out, seemed to attack Maugham on certain prearranged standards. For instance, he got onto the subject of Maugham's rhythm and said that his writing had no rhythm. I have been back to it since that remark and the criticism seems to me to be unwarranted. Not that it proves anything, but Maugham is, if anything, supremely readable. Far more so than, say, Wilson, who is difficult—but what does that matter?

Careful. It is no good saying in answer to a critic, "Well, you can't do it any better yourself."

He does not need to, should not have to. My point in bringing up the question of rhythm is that it is largely a matter of ear, and Wilson's work would indicate that his is less sensitive to rhythms than is Maugham's, which might explain why he cannot sense the rhythm in Maugham.

1946. Beverly Hills.

George tells us that WSM gave a dinner last night: formal, elegant, and planned to the last rose petal. There were a good many celebrities there, and some people considered important, but Maugham, at the head of the table, had on his right Miss Ethel Barrymore and on his left Miss Billie Burke.

I wish I could have seen that.

Maugham has often told the story of Ethel and THE CONSTANT WIFE. How he came over for rehearsals, how she had difficulty with her lines, and how on the first night out of town she blew them completely, improvised badly, said things from other plays, said third-act lines in the first act, but somehow got through it. He went back to see her afterward in a fury.

As he walked into her dressing room, she said, "Oh, darling, I've ruined your beautiful play, but it'll run a year."

Maugham then says, "She had and it did!"

It is one of his few set-piece stories. I have heard him tell it seven or eight times, and always word for word the same.

[*In 1949, on that broadcast celebrating Ethel's seven-tieth birthday, Maugham, in his part of it, said quite plainly that during rehearsals he had fallen madly in love with her.*]

April 1965. Beverly Hills.

Dinner with George tonight. The evening is marred by the news we have all read in the late papers. Maugham has collapsed and has been taken to the British-American Hospital in Nice.

That is what it says, but, having been there, I know that the hospital is not exactly in Nice but between Cap Ferrat and Nice.

I was told it is a perfectly adequate little provincial hospital, but when a man is ninety-one years old and has had tuberculosis twice, a good deal of surgery, and other illnesses, one would hope that the medical attention he receives would be on a somewhat higher plane.

We talk about this and, knowing Alan, are convinced that, had it been possible to move Maugham immediately to London or to Paris or to Lausanne, he would have done so. It looks bad, we agree, and he has probably been taken to the local hospital to provide final comfort.

There is the conventional view that, after all, ninety-one is pretty damned good, especially when you consider that he has been remarkably active almost up until the last. Five years ago, at eighty-six, he made a trip to the Far East and went to Singapore and Tokyo and Hong Kong—made, in fact, a full tour of Asia. So, all things considered, he has had a full, long life.

We decide to put through a call to Alan to see what is happening, but, what with time differences and other complications, the call is never completed.

Afterward it occurs to me that, with this report, all the news agencies and magazines and radio and television people would be phoning through to the hospital and to his home to get minute-to-minute information. That is probably why we were not able to get our call through.

April 1965. Beverly Hills.

Further news about WSM. It is all bad and does not seem hopeful in the least. According to the evening papers, he is in a coma. We try again, unsuccessfully, to phone.

April 1965. Beverly Hills.

Today we cannot find anything about Maugham in any of the newspapers. I call New York. There was apparently nothing reported there, either. What can be happening?

April 1965. Beverly Hills.

A little squib today. Maugham is still in the hospital. Alan is reported as saying he is very ill. No mention of any family coming down.

April 1965. Beverly Hills.

The damnedest thing. Maugham has walked
out of the hospital! There was a photograph in the paper
this morning which caught my eye. I recognized Maugham
and, just beyond him, Alan. I took it, of course, to be a
photograph of him entering the hospital and was startled
to see him walking in. When I read the story, however, I
learned that the photograph was one of him walking out,
not in.

Ruth bursts into tears. I get on the phone to tell George,
who has not heard this news.

We are all thrilled.

What excites especially is the spectacle of human en-
durance and power and indestructibility. It is moving
enough when we hear of people coming through ordeals at
sea, in the desert, caught in a cave, but what gives this account special significance is the plain, unbelievable but
accurate fact that Somerset Maugham, ninety-one years
old, has walked out of the hospital and gone home.

We send a cable.

1954. London.

Talking today of physical writing problems,
WSM reveals he has never in his life so much as touched
what he calls "a typewriting machine," nor has he ever
dictated a single sentence of his work. No wonder his right
hand is the hand of a laborer—callused and bumpy.
"Writer's cramp" has a jocular sound, but not when it is
called "mogigraphia" and requires orthopedic attention. I

269

do not suppose it is possible to compute the number of words he has written in longhand. About fifty million by my rough reckoning.

A doctor in Nice has constructed a sort of brace for his right hand. It looks like a doll's corset. He wears it and uses a weighted, balanced fountain pen to relieve the discomfort of the later hours at his desk. (Come to think of it, until recently practically all his letters were handwritten, too.)

December 1954. London.

The other night at dinner we all talk of movement plans. WSM surprises us by telling us he is returning to St. Jean–Cap Ferrat on Christmas Day.

Ruth asks, "Do you mean you're going to travel on that day?"

Maugham: "Of course. Why not?"

Ruth: "Well, I thought it being a holiday and you full of family here, you might be spending Christmas Day in England."

"Oh, no," says Maugham. "We have found it wise to ... travel on holidays. One has so much more room. There's never a crowd. It's easy to get the accommodations one wants. And the ... service is excellent. We do this often and sometimes it's rather like ... traveling in a private car. Or like royalty."

This leads us to talk of doing things at off-times. Thornton's scheme of going to resorts out of season. We tell about going with him to St. Moritz in early November and having the hotel and facilities pretty much to ourselves. Thornton's love of Florida in summer.

In connection with this, Ruth amuses WSM with the story of Elsie Mendl in New York, who saw every movie without any difficulty simply by getting up in the morning and having breakfast and going right to the movie house. Whereas other people had to queue up or be turned away, she saw every film as it was released by going to the Paramount or the Rivoli or the Capitol at 10:00 A.M. and sometimes 9:00 A.M.

There is more talk about Christmas Day, and Maugham asks us what we are going to do.

It is not clear, since the routine here is strange to us. As it happens, Christmas falls on a Saturday. Ruth does not play, but has two performances on Monday, Boxing Day. We had been asked to a number of Christmas celebrations, but it is all Ruth can do to handle those eight performances a week. So Sunday is officially and religiously a day of rest. We have been discussing the idea of doing something on Saturday, Christmas Day, and using Sunday as her day of rest as usual.

Maugham says, "Why don't you . . . come along with us?"

I see the light brighten in Ruth's eyes. The thought of even one whiff of Parisian air is enough to excite her. It takes us only a minute to agree. I wonder if he means it. We ask him again the following day, and he says, "Of course I meant it. We'll have a splendid Christmas . . . dinner on the Golden Arrow."

It is arranged and planned. WSM is quite right. There is no difficulty at all in getting accommodations, a private compartment on the Golden Arrow, a stateroom on the Channel boat, rooms at the Hotel Raphael, and so on. Everyone seems to be delighted to have us.

271

Christmas Day, 1954. Paris.

It has been quite a day. Early up and plans for the crazy trip. It is hardly more than a long train ride from London to Dover, a voyage across the English Channel on the Channel boat, a trip from Calais to Paris by train, spend the night in Paris, and return almost at once. There was some talk of taking the night ferry back on Sunday, since Ruth is not due at the theatre until Monday afternoon, but she begins to worry about delays or weather or cancellations and says she would feel a fool to be stuck somewhere. To play it safe, we decide to travel to Paris on Saturday and back to London on Sunday. A crazy trip indeed. But, as it turns out, worth it.

We turn up at the station. We see WSM and Alan, tremendously well organized. Alan is carrying many newspapers, WSM is jaunty but morningy, and, without going into the matter at all, we stay in our compartment and they stay in theirs until we reach Dover. When we have settled in on the Channel boat, Alan comes by and asks us to join them in their cabin. We do so.

You might think they had been living in it for a week. Everything is perfectly laid out and arranged. We have sherry and a biscuit.

We have just been round to the purser's office to get our passports stamped—a formality of which Maugham is hardly aware since, in his case, they come over and take care of it. Ruth is still clutching her passport case. Maugham admires it. Ruth shows it to him.

"Look," she says gaily. "American money, French money, English money, and there's even some Italian money." (I suppose she is carrying about $25 of each.)

Maugham glances at it, turns to Alan and says, "Show them ours."

Alan is surprised.

Alan: "Really?"

Maugham: "Yes, do as I say."

Alan picks up one of the attaché cases, unlocks it, and opens it. I damn near fall out because there, neatly stacked and packed, are huge piles of American currency. I see nothing but $100 bills in fat stacks.

"Holy God!" I exclaim.

Ruth says practically, "Is it safe to carry that much around?"

Maugham: "Certainly not. It's most . . . dangerous. There's over a hundred thousand dollars there. It might easily be lost or stolen. The train might be . . . derailed, or the Channel boat might sink."

I ask the logical, dumb question, "Why do you do it, then?"

"Because," says Maugham, "I was once trapped in the . . . fall of France without sufficient currency in my possession, and vowed at that time that, should I . . . come through, I would never again permit myself to be caught in a similar situation. Experience has . . . taught me that American currency is usually the best coin. Had I had some at that time, I might have saved myself and my friends a good deal of . . . difficulty and discomfort."

He reaches out and touches the money with his fingertips, reassuringly. Alan closes the attaché case, locks it again, and puts it with the others.

For the rest of the trip I am pretty nervous about it and keep glancing around to see if it is still there.

All his luggage is clearly marked in oversized letters— W. SOMERSET MAUGHAM. Every bag, every case has it painted on. We tease him about this.

He, unperturbed, explains, "I have it fixed in that way to assure myself of . . . swift attention and good service. It has done me well in many parts of the world. If you don't believe me, I suggest you observe . . . carefully what happens when we . . . disembark. If you're wise, you'll stay close and put your things with ours."

How right he is. The bags are scarcely dropped onto the Calais dock when a swarm of porters, saluting and doffing their hats and bowing and shaking hands, swarm about, giving him special attention.

On the Golden Arrow, which has now become La Flèche d'Or, we put away our things and assemble in the Wagon Restaurant.

There, a long Christmas dinner with vintage recollections on the part of WSM about his numberless trips back and forth over this route: as a child, as a student, as a professional writer, and as an intelligence agent. He has been traveling it for more than seventy years.

"Never," he says, "without interest and . . . fascination."

We reach Paris and say goodbye. They stay on the Train Bleu car, which is continuing to the Côte d'Azur. There are embraces and kisses and holiday gifts, greetings.

They wave from the platform of the train. Will we ever see him again?

We go to the Raphael to spend the night.

January 1949. Beverly Hills.

WSM is in San Francisco with the Alansons. George says that in 1924 they made a date to meet in San Francisco twenty-five years later. Maugham has remembered it and respected it.

274

He once told us about a man in San Francisco to whom he had given a sum of money which he had earned doing some film work.

He had said to the man, "You're clever about money, they say. Take care of this for me."

Maugham said that he made a stipulation that the man was never to ask him about it or tell him about it, and the man never did so. Many years went by (he said how many, but I have forgotten) and curiosity got the better of him.

He was in California, phoned the man, and said, "I am curious to know what happened to that money I left with you."

And the man said, "It has multiplied by ten. Do you want it?"

Maugham reports that he was speechless.

I wonder if this is Bertram Alanson.

July 1951. St. Tropez.

René [*Clair*] talks to me this morning about a newly formulated plan. A four-part film: French, Italian, British, American. Three reels (or so) each. He has agreed, in principle, to do the French one. De Sica will do the Italian. Will I do the American, and whom do I think of for the British? I immediately suggest Carol Reed—but about myself, I tell him at once, I have misgivings. For one thing, I have not directed a film for some time. For another, I am not sure I want to. Further, if I do, shouldn't I do a proper full-length one? Finally, I think it pretty fast company and I would hate to be the weak link. Holy smoke —René Clair! Vittorio De Sica! René is insistent and even mentions three of my short stories which he thinks would adapt well. One in particular, THE DOG ACT, which appears in the current VOGUE.

"What is the unifying theme?" I ask.

René shrugs. "You know. The best. Men and women. How."

He says De Sica has a great yarn for his. Tells it. He is right.

[*The story was one by Cesare Zavattini which De Sica made years later with Sophia Loren and Marcello Mastroianni as part of* YESTERDAY, TODAY AND TOMORROW.]

René himself is in his habitual quandary—"I have thirty ideas, but I have not *one*."

Carol could certainly find a short story or an original. I promise to think about it.

Two days later Ruth and I are on our way to St. Jean–Cap Ferrat and I am telling her about René's plan and she says, "Maybe Willie would have something for him."

"I shouldn't think so. You know how René is about France for the French. Maugham might have the Carol Reed one, though."

"Maybe both."

"No. They wouldn't want two Maughams, I shouldn't think."

"I'd take four."

"You're a fan."

"Ask him."

July 1951. Villa Mauresque.

At lunch today I tell WSM about the planned four-part film. He is, after all, an expert, having been connected with three such ventures: TRIO, QUARTET, and

276

ENCORE. I tell him, briefly, De Sica's story. He thinks it is fine.

I tell him mine, not only briefly, but badly. I do not know why, but I got scared.

He says it is good, but not as good as De Sica's.

I ask him if he has anything that might suit René's needs.

"Yes," he says at once. "I have."

It is as though he had expected to be asked. I dare say he began to go through his stuff in his head as soon as the subject came up.

"Do you mean something specific?"

"Quite specific."

"Great!"

"Why not read it before pronouncing a ... literary opinion?"

"I meant great that you have something," I explain, flustered.

Talk turns to other matters: the long-ago purchase of the Cap Ferrat peninsula by the King of Belgium for £40,000—and its subsequent development.

Cures at Abano, Montecatini, and Bad Gastein.

New England food and his love for Boston baked beans.

The placement of the sexual force. The French, he says, have it mainly in their speech. They love to talk about it. Americans have it in their hearts—all sentiment and romantic notions. The Russians, in their arms and legs and torsos—those back-breaking hugs! The Germans have it in their heads, he claims, for the purpose of intellectualizing, philosophizing, and analysis. Now, the Italians—ah, the Italians. Theirs is located in the sexual organs; they are the lovers on earth. We might all learn from them.

"What about the British?" I ask.

277

"They don't . . . have it at all," he says. "Not anywhere."

Lunch ends on this curtain line. We leave the table.

"Wait out there," says Maugham, pointing to the terrace. To Alan he says, "I want an envelope for a book."

They both disappear. Alan into his office, WSM scampering up the stairs in a quick, businesslike way.

They return in about five minutes. WSM with a book into which he has put a marker. He puts the book into the envelope which Alan has handed him and gives it to me.

"This is the story for your friend René Clair."

I am struck by the swift, efficient, no-nonsense, professional approach. I admire it. I had forgotten about René and the movie—but WSM had not. (I recall he has been bitchily referred to as "The Grand Old Businessman of British Letters.")

After a few sips of his coffee (*very* strong), he says, "It is a great favorite of mine. I hope your friend will . . . share my enthusiasm."

"I'll bet on it."

"I wouldn't in your place. The French are a jealous people—it comes of pride, I suppose, and he may not take . . . kindly to an Englishman's creation of French characters."

"René is a consummate professional," I assure him. "All he cares about is a good story and a spellbinding way to tell it."

"Perhaps if you told it to him? Your words might not offend him so much as mine. I'm being practical, not at all . . . modest."

"Let's stick to *your* words," I suggest.

"The story," says WSM, "is called APPEARANCE AND REALITY. I pinched the title from a great philosophical work I admire, by Francis Bradley. I could not, to save my . . . soul, think of a better. In any case, the two works are not likely to be . . . confused. Read it at your leisure."

He finishes his coffee, rises, and says, "See you at . . . tea, unless you want a swim beforehand."

With that, he is gone. Alan suggests a drive into Nice to see the Old City. I am tempted, but I cannot wait to get to the story. I wonder if it is one I know.

Ruth goes into town with Alan. I go at once to my room and begin to read.

The first reading is a gulp and its effect is that of a double brandy taken in a single swallow. I am enthralled. My heart is thumping. I feel like going to his room, waking him, and telling him I think it one of the most nearly perfect creations I have ever known. I consider going in to Nice to find Ruth and tell her. Shall I phone René, the lucky sonofabitch? What a story! René is all set. It lays out cinematically like a dream. I begin to cast it: Pierre Brasseur? Louis Jouvet? Suzanne Flon? For René, Gérard Philipe might be willing to play the young man. Martine Carol? Daniele Delorme! Hold it. That's René's business. I go out and walk around the garden, half hoping to run into someone to tell it to. I return to my room, drink a bottle of Vichy, and sit down to read it again—slowly this time. Calmly. I almost make it, but halfway through I am on my feet reading aloud and acting the parts. When I finish, I sit down and begin to sketch a screenplay. Would René let me work with him on it?

Ruth returns. I tell her about my adventure, jumping up and down. She sits down to read. I leave her. When I return, she is in tears—often her reaction to something superlative.

We talk of the luck of the game, of the gossamer thread of fate. Our coming here at the moment when René is looking for a short story. We go up to the pool. WSM is there and I tell him. He is pleased and says—rubbing a thumb and forefinger together—that he hopes my commission will not be too high.

(I resent the tease, but try not to show it. What's the matter with me? The excitement of the afternoon has made me nervy, I suppose. Also, I have come to recognize by instinct a certain brand of British anti-Semitism—it is not vicious, but patronizing; not hateful, only comic; not ugly, merely superior. I am wrong to bristle this time and I know it. Just as I was wrong to quarrel so bitterly with Larry and Vivien the night I saw their production of THE SCHOOL FOR SCANDAL and objected to the portrait of Moses, the Jew. That superlative, angelic Larry who kept reminding me that Richard Brinsley Sheridan had written the play, not he—and how the hell would *I* have done it, or played it, for that matter? And I, wounded and truculent, ruining the rest of the evening. Did I ever apologize to him? I suppose not.)

[*Malcolm Muggeridge has written: "The upper-class English are not, like their American equivalents, overtly anti-Semitic, but they create a milieu in which Jews seem outlandish, and therefore feel alien and ill at ease. The worst thing we do to well-off Jews in England is to make them as stupid, snobbish, and Philistine as the well-off natives. This is our version of Dachau. It took a Disraeli to break into the English upper classes on his own terms and triumph over them. Beerbohm was by no means a Disraeli, and desperately wanted to substitute Burke's Landed Gentry for the family Talmud. The English upper classes do not persecute Jews; they ruin them. A Mailer or a Bellow over here, at any rate in Beerbohm's time, would be sporting a guard's tie, and like Siegfried Sassoon, wearing himself out riding to hounds. Behind Beerbohm's façade of a Yellow Book aesthete there lurked a frightened Rabbi."*

(It strikes me that even Muggeridge's tone has within it something of the attitude he is apparently criticizing.)

The atmosphere is almost impossible to describe. The equivalent in the United States would be the benign, kindly, patronizing, avuncular attitude of certain enlightened upper-middle-class Southerners toward Negroes.

I remember an afternoon in Paris—Carol Reed and I running our rough cut of THE TRUE GLORY *for General Eisenhower. We sit in a large projection room above the theatre in the Champs-Elysées, Carol on the General's right, I on his left. We had shown him parts of the film before. This time we had been asked to include shots of Negro soldiers whenever we could. We had done so. Every time one of these clips came on, the General chuckled or smiled or laughed. Not in an unkindly way, not in ridicule—but only because Negroes in uniform manning guns and using rifles seemed comically incongruous to the Texas-born, Regular Army-bred Supreme Commander.*

The British attitude toward Jews is much like this. (Shylock was written as a comic character and played strictly for laughs for a couple of hundred years. When Shakespeare wrote the part, he had never so much as seen a Jew.) The English do not hate Jews, they tolerate them. Who wants to be tolerated?

Still, I see now that I was wrong to take offense at WSM's innocent jest.]

I try out on WSM a few of my ideas for the film treatment of his story. He is delighted. He adds a couple of masterly camera notions of his own. The hour at the pool, full of sparkling creativity, is the best sort of enjoyment.

After tea, I discuss with Ruth the question of phoning René. She is against it. These phones are funny, she reminds me, and so is René's English.

July 1951. St. Tropez.

Driving home today, we talk of whether it would be better if I did tell René the story, after all. He might misread it from the page. We weigh the pros and cons of both methods and finally decide to let him read the delicious Maugham work on his own. To hell with salesmanship. Further, the telling by WSM is masterful and can only be damaged, not improved upon.

Later. We have been to dinner with René and Bronja at L'Escale on the port. We tell about our visit, about the house, the pictures. René chides us about it. I begin to worry a bit. What has he got against Maugham?

Dinner over, I make the important announcement. René stops kidding. He is in earnest and richly excited by the prospect of a Maugham story even though it is about French characters. I remind him that Maugham has lived in France more than he has lived in England, that he is a matchless observer of the human race, and that this film is meant to be international in concept, execution, and appeal. I have to restrain myself as the selling part takes over.

I give René the book containing the story, but beg him not to read it until morning, when he is fresh and receptive.

"Yes," says René. "You say that, but you wish I shall read it tonight."

"No."

"Else why do you give it to me now and not in the morning?"

He has me there.

René says, "Let's all to the house and you read it out."

Ruth signals no and says, "It's late."

René: "It's a short story!"

We float out on the laugh and soon sit, back at the Clairs' house, cups of fresh tisane before us, and I read.

(Reading aloud is an integral part of the French literary life. When René is writing, he reads every scene to Bronja as soon as it is finished.

That writer across the street from the Hotel Raphael—each morning I see him hunched over his enormous desk. Every afternoon I see him reading aloud from manuscript pages to an impassive young man. I have invented a whole series of characterizations for this pair. I have no idea who they are. And Sainte-Beuve—handing a piece of his writing to his secretary and saying, "Read it to me like an enemy.")

APPEARANCE AND REALITY is told as though written in French—"By blue!" exclaims one of the characters—and deals with a middle-aged Senator who takes as a mistress a pert young mannequin named Lisette. The Senator is brilliantly drawn as a member of the haute bourgeoisie, and the story of his liaison with the lovely Lisette is touchingly related. All goes well until he discovers himself betrayed. There is the obligatory scene of confrontation, followed by the surprising denouement: Lisette and the Senator discuss the unfortunate situation. It transpires that what he objects to most is her amorality. He cannot forgive that she, an unmarried girl, should have behaved in this way. She taunts him, saying, "I suppose if he were my husband and you were my lover, you would think it perfectly natural." The Senator says, "Why, of course!"—

283

and goes on to explain with French logic why that would be a classic situation which he could understand. As it is, she is simply a girl of loose morals—she has no intention of marrying this young man nor has he of marrying her. Lisette tells him he is wrong. The young man would marry her like a shot if she had any money. The room brightens as the Senator begins to see a solution. He settles a dowry on her. She marries the young man, a commercial traveler, and the situation is saved. The girl and the young man are married, with the Senator and Lisette's employer standing up with the couple. At the end, the Senator reflects that he has improved his situation by making it more fitting to his station—he is about to become a Minister of the government. His mistress will be not just a little mannequin in a dressmaker's shop, but a respectable married woman.

I try not to act it too hard, or sell. I try to read it as though I were the author. It does not take me long to sense that I am not connecting. What is called "flop-sweat" begins to form on my face, but I press on. The room gets sullen and more sullen. I finish.

"Yes," says René. "Let me think. We speak in the morning, yes?"

"You bet."

Bronja says, "You read it very well."

"Thank you."

René just looks at her.

On the way home I say I am a fool for having been sucked into reading, and Ruth agrees. I do not want her to agree, but she does.

"And I guess the way I read it didn't help, either, did it?"

"I shouldn't think so," says Ruth.

Troubled sleep.

July 1951. St. Tropez.

When René had not called by noon today, I knew something was amiss—but how amiss I could never have guessed. I am to learn it is not just that he does not feel the story is suited to his purpose, but that he hates the story. What is more, he is offended by it and is a bit off me for exposing him to it.

I phoned him directly after lunch and asked if he wanted to meet for a cup of coffee at Senequier's on the port.

"Yes. Of course," he said.

If he was going to be annoyed or upset or angry, I preferred to provide the discipline of a public place.

We meet, order coffee, and sit for a moment.

"You're crazy," he announces.

"Funny, that's what my wife says."

"You call that a story?"

"Yes."

"In one way remarkable. This person living so long a time in France and does not know even the smallest piece."

"René, I'm sorry. I meant well. Forget it."

"I wish I could. It is as if you have fed me a bad oyster and you say to me 'Forget it.'"

"That bad, huh?"

And he begins. He castigates Maugham and his story, adding a good many irrelevancies. I let him go on and do not interrupt, because I see that he has been upset.

I half listen, reflecting upon my foolishness. Why can't I mind my own goddam business? See how my desire to make things come out even—or is it to have a finger in the pie?—has led me into this uncomfortable, untenable position?

Being a go-between is a bum job. I suppose I should have been less confident with WSM and less enthusiastic with René. Too late. The damage is done. There is a chasm of misunderstanding between them and I am neither large enough nor skillful enough to make the bridge. I see now that my clumsiness probably damaged a deal which might have been consummated.

At last René comes to the end of his tirade.

"Cher maître," I say, "why is it your English gets better when you get mad?"

"Because I was mad every minute *learning* it."

"You don't really think I'm crazy, do you?"

"Everybody is. You know what's the main matter with Maugham?"

"What?"

"He doesn't like me."

"I think he does."

"No. I can always tell. Oh, to hell. He's a nice man."

"Sure."

"But I don't want the story."

"Okay."

At any rate, it is all over and I am left with the awkward chore of telling WSM that his work has been rejected. I consider a few euphemistic approaches, but know he is far too sharp in these matters to be fooled and, in any case, I owe him the dignity of truth, even if it is to be unpleasant.

Shall I be brave and phone, or cowardly and write? It takes me only a moment to decide. I write. The letter is awful. I try again. No better. Reluctantly, I phone. Thank God, he is not at home. I leave careful word that I have phoned, rush to the post office and send a wire: "DEAR BOY TRIED PHONING NO LUCK TO SAY READ STORY TO RENE WHO LOVES IT OF COURSE BUT FEELS IT UNSUITABLE FOR

PRESENT PURPOSES STOP THERE MUST BE SOMETHING
WRONG WITH PRESENT PURPOSES STOP LETTER FOLLOWS
STOP LOVE BOTH TO BOTH. GAR"

August 1951.

A letter from WSM this morning, some of
which is pertinent to the René Clair matter.

> Villa Mauresque
> St. Jean–Cap Ferrat,
> A.M.
> 2nd August, 1951

Gracious and God-Like Garson,

You know it is quite absurd for you and my beloved Ruth to write me bread-and-butter letters because you are both such wonderful value for the
money that it is I that ought to have written you a
bread-and-butter letter thanking you for your visit. In
fact I am rather surprised not to have received a bill
for entertainment provided by Gordon and Kanin at
the Villa Mauresque between 15th and 17th July.

Thank you for having read my story to Rene Claire.
To tell you the truth I never really thought he would
find it to his liking. The rejection has not robbed me
of more than a fortnight's sleep.

> My love to you both,
> Willie

I read between the lines of the last paragraph and find
harsh words. No one, not even WSM, likes to be turned
down. And one never gets used to it. (I wonder if "Claire"
is deliberately misspelled?) Small comfort to know that,
having written his short story RAIN (then called MISS

THOMPSON) he had great difficulty placing it—and he a world-famous dramatist and novelist. The editors of one magazine after another, he relates, rejected it. It was finally sold to SMART SET for $200.

I regret this whole damned affair. Good intentions—we all know what road is paved with them, don't we? His disclaimer notwithstanding, I contributed to a needless shock.

That sainted Fanny Brice said it once, memorably, in these words precisely: "The older you grow, kid, it's harder to brush off them knocks!"

[I recall that the next time we met face to face, WSM sensed my remembered embarrassment and conversed easily on the subject at once.

"I still think he should have done that story," I said.

"I suppose he didn't . . . get it."

"I suppose not."

"Yes. You see, the French find it . . . difficult to understand the French."

When my wife read the above account in these notes she remembered that the first meeting of Maugham and Clair had been unfortunate.

It was 1942. Beverly Hills. The Clairs were living on Bedford Drive. Maugham had rented a house in Beverly Glen. Ruth was making EDGE OF DARKNESS at Warner Brothers and living at the Beverly Hills Hotel. The Clairs were her family, so to speak, and she saw them constantly. Contiguously, her friendship with Maugham deepened. Having accepted his hospitality a number of times, she wished to reciprocate and, rather than risk a wrong restaurant meal, she asked the Clairs if she could give a dinner for Maugham at their house. They agreed, happily. Bronja

288

*and Ruth began the arrangements. Gerald was consulted
as to WSM's food preferences and Bronja (one of the
world's great cuisinières) supervised the preparations.*

*On the night, Maugham and Gerald arrived punctually
and were greeted warmly. Matchless martinis were served
with never-seen-before canapés (based upon caviar,
smoked salmon, pâté de foie gras), yet Ruth knew almost
at once she was in trouble.*

*Perfect host and gracious guest shook hands, smiled,
and bowed.*

"We are honored," said René, pronouncing the "h."

"Enchanté," said Maugham.

It was clear they loathed each other on sight.

*Built upon a quicksand base of disaffection, no structure
could be sustained. Each remark took on a second, often a
third meaning. Tempers were being controlled. Subjects
were introduced and dropped as they seemed too hot to
handle. The strain was becoming intolerable.*

*At 10:45 precisely (just as at a Washington social-dip-
lomatic function) Maugham rose, thanked René, kissed
Bronja's hand and Ruth's cheek, and left.*

*René said a few René things and all agreed the evening
had been a nervous disaster.*

*It took Ruth the weekend to recover. She continued to
see the Clairs regularly and WSM often, but it was like
moving back and forth from one world to another.*

*Maugham never asked the Clairs to his house, although
Ruth claims to have dropped several heavy hints.*

*The Clairs, on the other hand, could hardly wait to be
asked so that they could refuse.*

*What had happened? It is easy to understand now,
with the advantage of perspective.*

Two men had been rudely displaced, torn from their

friends and homes and possessions and fortunes and activities. Both were unhappy, frustrated, and unfulfilled.

When such is the case, we seek to place the blame. Where? On fate, on the war, on circumstance? Too abstract. On Hitler? Unrealistic. What we need is a group of people, a set of persons, to make it personal. The armament makers and profiteers had been used up by World War I.

This was the moment when France blamed England and England blamed France—which means that the French blamed the English and the English blamed the French; that a Frenchman blamed an Englishman and that WSM blamed René Clair.

In that time and place, WSM was England to René, and René was France in the eyes of WSM. (In point of fact, neither of them typified nationality. Both were men of the world. But this was 1942, and it was hard to think.)

Beyond this, there were other complicating factors: neither man involved in the war and each loath to explain why not; neither man able to adjust to the ways of Southern California; both bitter and angry and sad. Each found that night a convenient and easy target for the release of tension.

Ruth thinks this carried over for ten years. So do I.

The French had asked, "Where are the British troops?" They were there, all right, but security made it necessary to keep the number and location secret.

German propaganda was doing all it could to cause bad blood among the Allies of the Entente Cordiale.

It is said that the widely circulated cynicism "The British will fight to the last Frenchman" was created by a German propagandist.

The seeds of evil bear the damnedest fruit. From Berlin

to Beverly Hills and beyond, in time, it was compounded and cheated Clair and Maugham and the audience out of something notable.

Looking back upon this unfortunate involvement, I wonder anew at what went wrong. This morning I reread APPEARANCE AND REALITY, *the story in question. As I come to the end of it, I whack myself in the head, good and hard, with my fist. How could I have been so dense, so thick, as not to have seen that it would offend René? Not alone the story, but the fact that it was written by an Englishman. If the story were signed by Guy de Maupassant, all might have turned out otherwise. It would be the same story, but it would be different. Is this difficult to understand? Not for me. I can listen with amusement to Jewish stories if they are told by Lou Holtz or Jack Benny or Phil Silvers, but I have always found them objectionable when told by Gentiles, especially those who attempt Yiddish accents. Maugham was attempting some French accents in this story, and although from my point of view he brought it off very well, I can see now how deeply it must have offended René. Live and learn.*]

October 1965. New York.

Good old Eric Ambler has put out a dazzling book. It is a collection of spy stories, seven of them, with an introduction written by himself. The stories are by John Buchan, Somerset Maugham, Compton Mackenzie, Graham Greene, Eric Ambler, Ian Fleming, Michael Gilbert.

In his introduction Eric quotes a TIMES LITERARY SUPPLEMENT review of a reprint of Maugham's ASHENDEN, and says that in this review the point was made that Am-

bler's early books were "strongly influenced by the ASHEN-
DEN ethos."

Eric goes on to say, "They were indeed. The break-
through was entirely Mr. Maugham's. If the reviewer was
only expressing his regret that there has been no body of
work in the field of the same quality written since ASHEN-
DEN, then I am with him. I hope that is really what he
meant to convey. There is, after all, a lot of Simenon, and
a satisfactory quantity of W. R. Burnett, but only one
ASHENDEN."

Eric further refers to it as: "the first fictional work on
the subject by a writer of stature with first-hand knowledge
of what he is writing about."

Screens the world over these days, both large and small,
are filled with spy stories, intelligence adventures, and the
like. The material appears to have become a staple. Works
in this genre by Graham Greene, John Le Carré, William
Haggard, and others are enjoying an unparalleled vogue.
Is it not interesting to note that Maugham's ASHENDEN is,
for this subject, one of the original forms, one of the deep-
est sources?

Very likely a good many people working in the field
have no knowledge of this, and may even be unaware of
the existence of the ASHENDEN stories. Yet what they are
doing from day to day is probably a copy of a copy of an
imitation of an imitation of an influence.

18 December 1953. London.

Supper at Durham Cottage with Larry and Vivien. Maugham there and Clemence Dane. Maugham
leaves first, and we all fall to talking about him.

292

Ruth tells how he is often on us about our extravagant ways, and quotes him as saying, " 'If you're not careful, you'll end in penury, like poor Eddie Knoblock.' "

Clemence Dane gave a hoot of disagreement.

"What of it?" she cried. "Poverty is an experience, in the same way that affluence is. Good Lord, why spend your life thinking and worrying about money and finances for the future?"

She went on about this for some time. Most relaxing it was, too, and as she spoke, it seemed right and just and wise. On reflection, I wonder. Perhaps it is wrong to go on about it too much. I am certain that I have. At the same time, organization in these matters is important. The economic side must be arranged so that it does not become necessary to expend too much time and energy and effort doing things simply to make a living and for no other reason.

22 July 1962. Washington.

Visiting FF, he says, "Thank God for Dean Acheson, who comes in every day and brings me a little gossip and tells me some dirt."

"Speaking of dirt," says Ruth, "have you seen the new Somerset Maugham articles?"

FF says he has not and wants to know all about them. We tell him. He wonders why Maugham did it.

I tell him my theory: that Maugham has been keeping that celebrated notebook, getting things off his chest. He had intended it to be published—at least parts of it—after his death. Now, close to the end, he has changed his mind and decided that, instead of holding it back, he wants the pleasure of seeing some of it in print while he is still alive. After all, he is now unassailable. What does he care? What can anybody do to him? He is simply going to have things his own damned way. This is one last little bitchy pleasure.

I repeat the comment which has been made that it is a wildly faggoty thing to have done. FF does not see that this has anything to do with it at all.

He believes that it is a case of a man expressing himself in the purest possible way. He says he would like to see these pieces, and I promise to send them.

(There is no denying that they are exceptionally well written, in Maugham's best vein, probably because he is not writing superficially, but from the innards, with great feeling and meaning and even purpose, although in this case the purpose is less than commendable, since it is to smear, besmirch, and scandalize.)

1954. London.

I say to WSM, "I think we all talk too much and do not enough. That seems to me to be one of the troubles with the times. There's too much talk. Most of it's hot air and, communication being so easy, the telephone being so at hand, we just go on talking, talking, talking."

"I don't agree with you at all," he says. "People for the most part . . . prattle very pleasantly, but act foolishly; so it seems to me it would be . . . better if they did less and . . . talked even more."

Very well. He is being Maugham—cynical, biting, epigrammatic—but I hold to my own opinion.

1958. Nice.

I tell WSM tonight something I have recently read—Turgenev saying toward the end of his life, "I am left with but a single pleasure: writing the last line."

"Oh, how true," says Maugham. "How very true. I feel that—have felt that for some time, but have not ... cared to reveal it. Now I shall. I align myself with ... Turgenev. I've always admired him."

11 December 1965. Beverly Hills.

Dinner with Kate and Spencer. George comes in and says there is a report on the radio news about WSM. He has been taken to the hospital in Nice and is, says George, "in some kind of a coma, I think they said."

Disquieting, this.

Last April he beat it. Will he, can he again? Does he want to?

Later. The eleven-o'clock news on TV has no further details, but the story has the look and sound of a premature obituary.

The unhappy word has made Ruth restive and we go for a walk in the gardens of the hotel. She remembers walking these same paths with him in 1945, discussing the problems of Liza. She recalls him taking her often to the Hollywood Bowl, which he admired. One night Gerald Haxton brought her home. They went to the bar—we stop and look in—and Gerald insisted upon telling her the story of his life.

295

We return to our rooms in time for the midnight news. Nothing more.

Four A.M. Sleep will not come. I am thinking of the end of Maugham, of the death of a friend. It was here, in February, that the news about Felix came to us.

Age is not fashionable in our country, in our time. I wonder if we do not cheat ourselves in consigning the aging and the aged to limbo.

Many of them have an important part to play, a vital balance to strike.

I miss FF. And Mr. Lee. And John Golden. Lloyd Lewis. George Kaufman. Bob Sherwood. Kurt Weill. Ned Sheldon. Ethel and Fanny and Cole.

Now WSM is fading from being. Damn.

11 December 1965. Beverly Hills.

There is one word in the news dispatches from St. Jean–Cap Ferrat which has been gnawing at me all day—the word "fall." It is reported that Maugham had a bad fall on December 10. We wonder how such a thing could have happened. He has been ill and under care and supervision. Was he allowed to walk about? Did he fall out of bed? What sort of fall? What broke it? His elbow, his knee, his head? Was the fall caused by the stroke or was it the other way about?

12 December 1965. Beverly Hills.

We keep buying all the newspapers. There are AP dispatches, Reuter's, UPI, and others. It seems strange that no further mention of the fall is made in any of the medical bulletins. Am I making too much of this? He is a very old man really and his time appears to have run out. Accept the fact.

14 December 1965. Beverly Hills.

THE NEW YORK TIMES carries a short item today. WSM is recovering. Can it be? After a stroke at ninety-one? Has he sufficient power to come out of the coma and back into life? It is hard to believe, yet his physician is directly quoted as saying, "He is responding to our treatment."

"We are creatures of habit," WSM often said.

His body, after ninety-one years, is finding it difficult to break its habit of living.

Across the six thousand miles and more—we cheer him on.

It strikes me today that WSM pursued his profession for sixty-nine years. Is this not the longest writing career ever?

December 1954. London.

Maugham came to dinner with us last night here at the hotel. Alan, too. We have dinner in, only because the date was made some time ago and when we saw him the other night he said something about being terribly tired of eating in restaurants. Since we no longer have the house, we could only suggest dinner in the dining room at Claridge's, usually quiet. He turns this down brusquely.

Ruth asks, "Would you want to have it up in our apartment? We do that often."

He jumps at this idea and says, "I should enjoy that.

I haven't . . . done it in years."

(He is greatly entertained by the account of how we come to be living at Claridge's. Why did we give up the charming house in Charles Street? And the other one in Hanover Terrace? We explain that our tax consultants have told us that, according to the Office of Inland Revenue, if we rent a house, we may not deduct the expense of keeping it even though Ruth is clearly here for professional purposes; but that if we live in a hotel, the expenses may de deducted. Since Ruth is playing here for an unusually low salary, it was necessary for us to take advantage of this condition. Maugham is especially amused by it because anything irrational about the system of taxation tickles him.)

He arrives and is impressed by the apartment.

"How clever of you to . . . bring your own furniture," he says.

He can hardly believe it when we tell him we have done no such thing, that it all belongs to the hotel. He wants to know how much we pay. He wants to see all the rooms, to examine the closets. He inquires about the service. He looks out the windows and under the beds. He certainly knows about the mechanics of living, this guy.

We return to the sitting room.

Before we sit down he says, "I have an explanation to . . . make, and an apology. I'm afraid I was rather rude in the way in which I . . . declined your invitation to dine in the restaurant downstairs. You could not have known why I never go there. It has unpleasant—no, uncomfortable—memories for me. It is where I always took Liza to lunch when she was a child. Usually once a year—you can imagine what an ordeal it was for me—and must have been for her, poor . . . darling. I wonder if she ever goes there now? At any rate, I looked in before coming up. The ghosts have . . . departed and we can go down if you like."

"Too late," I explain. "It's all ordered here."

"I prefer it," says WSM as he sits and accepts the martini I have made for him.

He becomes especially playful. We sit down to table and when the first course is served, smoked salmon, there is a large sprig of parsley on it. He picks it up at once and sticks it into his lapel buttonhole as a boutonnière.

I ask him what he has been doing, and he tells me. It is an exhausting schedule. He takes full advantage of London while he is here. He sees virtually everything in the theatre. He goes to concerts. He walks. He visits museums and sees the exhibitions at the private galleries.

(In connection with this, he tells us confidentially of where there is a bargain to be acquired. A small, obscure gallery, a fine painting. The dealer in need of money at the moment. He advises us strongly to buy the picture.

I point out to him that it is something we do not do, because we do not feel we know enough about it.

"You may . . . take my word," he says.

"We're very grateful to you, but, honestly, you'd better tell someone else."

"But I have chosen you. I want you to have it. I assure you that I am doing you a very good . . . turn indeed. You may resell it almost at once for . . . double the price."

"But that's not our business. Or even our activity."

"You're very . . . foolish," he says, and never mentions it again.)

In a pause, he looks about. "Oscar Wilde knew this hotel," he says, "and so did Pinero. I have had adventures here. Who has not? I heard the abdication speech downstairs. In a corner of the . . . public lounge. We had to

299

borrow a portable radio from one of the . . . porters. And there we all were, huddled about. Eddie Marsh, Graham Greene, Osbert Sitwell, and I. There was nothing to say. We could only listen. It was . . . degrading, somehow."

This trip is more active than others because it is filled with various affairs and occasions and events having to do with his eightieth birthday. There is an exhibit of Maugham manuscripts and first editions and photographs and letters at the London Times Book Shop, where, in addition, two of his portraits are being shown—one by Sir Gerald Kelly, the other by Graham Sutherland. There has been the dinner at the Garrick Club and a Maugham season on the BBC. He has been invested by Queen Elizabeth with the Order of the Companions of Honour. All this is a considerable amount of activity for a very old man, but he carries on in the most efficient, organized way, and, what is more, I get the impression he enjoys it.

We talk of age and the span of life. I ask why it is so few are able to end well. Achievements fall farther and farther into the past. Has he observed that the longer you live, the fewer friends you seem to have and the more, shall I say, enemies? Well, no, not necessarily enemies, but people who have offended you or whom you have offended in one way or another. Colleagues who are doing better than you are, or not as well, either condition creating an awkward situation. The longer you live, the more possibilities you have for error, for irritation, for friction, for giving and taking offense.

He agrees absolutely and adds, "Yes, that is all as . . . sad and unfortunate as it is true. But what is even worse is the . . . burden of memory."

I think that was his phrase. I am not certain what he meant by it.

"If you live long enough," he says, "you can become known. And if you live too long, you may become unknown again."

This strikes me hard and worth noting. I get up and go out into my room to jot it down because I want to get the words right.

[*I think of this long after when, in New York, I am directing* FUNNY GIRL. *In the course of staging one of the scenes I give the following instructions to one of the chorus girls: "In this bit, you're a plain girl. Get your make-up off, put on some glasses, and loosen your hair, maybe. And be sure Irene* [Irene Sharaff, designer] *gives you something to wear that doesn't quite fit. But here's the point. You're a plain girl and the audience should see that you are, but you think you look like—well, Garbo."*

"What's that?" asked the girl.

"What's what?" I said, astonished.

"What you said." She frowned. " 'Garbo'? I don't know what that means."

I try once more. "Greta Garbo," I enunciate clearly as I wonder if she is putting me on.

She looks at me and shakes her head.

"Take ten," I said and walked out into the auditorium to recover. Here is a girl in the theatre who has never heard of Greta Garbo.

In a sense I can see how this might happen. There has not been a Garbo film in twenty-four years. True, the old ones are revived constantly, but you would have to be interested in order to go. There have been some on television, but not everyone watches television, and it would be possible even if you do to have missed Garbo's films. Further, consider the circles in which this girl has traveled: from

Wisconsin to Chicago, dancing school in New York, auditions, and so on. What the hell. She never heard of Greta Garbo. So what. But I must say it gave me a turn. And it reminded me of this conversation with Maugham.]

"What is most difficult about the . . . passage of time," says WSM, "is to stay in the fashion. It is extremely difficult to do so, since the constant repetition of a way of . . . dress or a way of speech or of life is comfortable. And we don't any of us much like to change. But fashion waxes and wanes. I can recall when CAKES AND ALE was considered a shocking book from the . . . moral point of view, so much so that there was some question as to whether or not it . . . would be . . . published. Compare it with some of the things that are being printed nowadays. And that was only about twenty-five years ago, no more. I suppose one . . . digests and becomes accustomed to a certain idea or a certain word, and when that has been used a good many times, it loses its power to shock, and so it is necessary to take the . . . next step and the next and the next. I wrote a line in THE CONSTANT WIFE that caused a stir. I thought it . . . perfectly innocent and telling—but real, don't you know? It comes in the third act, at the point where a young woman and her . . . mother are discussing a man.

"The daughter asks: 'How does one know if one's in love?'

"The mother replies: 'My dear, I only know one test. Could you use his . . . toothbrush?'

" 'No,' says the daughter.

"And the mother says, 'Then you're . . . not in love with him.'

"Many said I'd . . . gone too far. I received outraged

302

letters. I was, for a time, notorious as that vulgar, taste-less, anything-for-effect, cheap-jack ... dramatist. Compare that little sally with what they hear now, what?"

I say, "I suppose there's a limit somewhere, isn't there?"

"I shouldn't think so," he replies. "The mind of ... man is so fertile that it will continue to provide new shocks and embarrassments for itself. I suppose it's always quite easy to shock if what you have in mind is the ... desire to shock."

He looks off into the distance, smiles a faint, one-sided smile, and murmurs a word which is not immediately coherent.

"What was that?" I ask.

He looks at me and says, "Belly."

"Belly?"

"What an adventure! That single word very nearly caused the cancellation of the ... publication of my first novel, LIZA OF LAMBETH, and—who knows?—a cancellation at that point in my life might have discouraged me sufficiently to ... cause me to continue in medicine. In which case, you might now be calling upon me in my ... capacity as a physician, if at all."

"Tell me about 'belly,' " I prompt.

"So far as I know, the word had never been used in ... polite British fiction. At least, not in the way I used it. And the publishers, T. Fisher Unwin, were rather conservative. Some of the directors were dead set against printing my sort of ... novel at all. Others were for it. In time a compromise was reached. They would bring it out, but in an infinitesimal edition. I can't remember precisely, but surely it was no ... more than a few hundred copies. Collectors tell me that these are virtually unobtainable. At the last moment I was ordered to excise the word 'belly,' although the . . . manuscript was already in proof —so that when the book appeared it was not there."

"What word did you substitute?"

"I don't remember. But about thirty years later when Unwin . . . brought out a new edition, I had the enormous satisfaction in striking the substitute, whatever it was, and writing—I recall, in an extra-large hand—the word 'belly'! I found it greatly . . . satisfying to have outlived the silliness of that censorship."

We talk further about the passage of time and the complications it engenders. He gets onto the subject of his old friend Max Beerbohm.

"Max, you know, solved the . . . problem of adjusting to the present by stepping out of it. What he did was to leave London, leave England, and move to Rapallo, where he continues to live as though he were still living at the . . . turn of the century. He dresses in the same way, reads pretty much what he read then, writes practically nothing, nor does he draw. He has . . . frozen himself, as it were, in time. But what's most astonishing is that without lifting a finger he becomes more and more famous, more celebrated and highly thought of. Someone said that his reputation grows with every . . . book he doesn't write. Whereas I keep working like a . . . bloody fool and am constantly told that it's not as good as my last."

In connection with this remark, Ruth tells the story of René Clair's father and mother. His mother, each Sunday, making a certain dish. What was it? I must find out. Something to do with mushrooms, I think. The poor woman would work for two days, knocking herself out. Then it would be served. René's father would taste it, think, taste it again, and nod with conservative approval, saying. "Good. It's good—but *not* as good as last time!"

René relates that this went on for twenty-five or thirty years.

WSM is charmed by the story.

"It's very . . . French, that," he says, "especially the relationship between the father and the . . . mother."

I suggest that perhaps the wisest thing to do is to drop dead as soon as you have had a great success, so that for years to come people will say, "Oh, what he would have accomplished had he lived!"

Maugham laughs, rather to himself, and has that look of someone wondering whether or not to embark upon a story. We remain silent until he decides. He tells it.

"I wrote LIZA OF LAMBETH in 1897, and though it was not a sensation, it was . . . something of a success. One of the . . . most important critics of the day, Edmund . . . Gosse—I don't suppose you've ever heard of him?"

"Of course I have."

"Don't say 'of course.' He's largely forgotten now. At any rate, he . . . liked it and wrote quite a good review. I never knew him well, but I used to run into him once in a while, and for the next forty years every time we . . . met, he would look at me in a patronizing way and say, 'Oh, yes, Maugham. LIZA OF LAMBETH. *Such* a good book. How clever of you . . . never to have written anything else!'"

It has all been jolly and improvisational and fanciful, and we have been laughing, but all at once he is serious.

"No," he says, "no matter what its . . . miseries, life should be grasped."

I tell him, "Ruth sometimes says, 'It pays to stay alive.'"

He looks at her lovingly for a long time and says, "Ruth is . . . right."

INDEX

310

GARSON KANIN

A Man to Remember was the prophetic title of the first film directed by Garson Kanin. For more than three decades Mr. Kanin has been very much on the scene—as playwright, screenwriter, novelist, short-story writer, essayist, opera librettist, stage and film director, Broadway producer, and as the spouse of the eminent actress and playwright Ruth Gordon.

Garson Kanin emerged in his early twenties as a leader of his generation on Broadway, first as an actor, then as a director, later as the playwright of the world-famous comedy *Born Yesterday*. *The Diary of Anne Frank*, which he directed, won the Pulitzer Prize. As a onetime jazz musician (saxophone), Mr. Kanin took special pleasure in directing two musicals: *Funny Girl* and *Do Re Mi*. His bright new libretto and direction of *Fledermaus* have added luster to the repertoire of the Metropolitan Opera.

When he was the youngest director in Hollywood, Garson Kanin proved a challenging force with such memorable films as *Bachelor Mother*, *My Favorite Wife*, *They Knew What They Wanted* and *Tom, Dick, and Harry*. As Captain Kanin of the Army of the U.S. during the war years, he made top-secret films for the O.S.S. With Carol Reed he co-directed General Eisenhower's classic film report on the victory in Europe, *The True Glory*, winning the Academy Award.

As an author, Garson Kanin is versatile and unpredictable, with numerous screenplays and dramatic works to his credit, with several novels in print, with a long list of television credits, and with some two-score short stories published in *The Atlantic Monthly*, *The Saturday Evening Post*, *Vogue*, *McCall's*, and *Esquire*.